Poly-Olbion by Michael Drayton

PART II (of II) - The Nineteenth Song to The Thirtieth Song (1622)

Michael Drayton was born in 1563 at Hartshill, near Nuneaton, Warwickshire, England. The facts of his early life remain unknown.

Drayton first published, in 1590, a volume of spiritual poems; The Harmony of the Church. Ironically the Archbishop of Canterbury seized almost the entire edition and had it destroyed.

In 1593 he published Idea: The Shepherd's Garland, 9 pastorals celebrating his own love-sorrows under the poetic name of Rowland. This was later expanded to a 64 sonnet cycle.

With the publication of The Legend of Piers Gaveston, Matilda and Mortimeriados, later enlarged and re-published, in 1603, under the title of The Barons' Wars. His career began to gather interest and attention.

In 1596, The Legend of Robert, Duke of Normandy, another historical poem was published, followed in 1597 by England's Heroical Epistles, a series of historical studies, in imitation of those of Ovid. Written in the heroic couplet, they contain some of his finest writing.

Like other poets of his era, Drayton wrote for the theatre; but unlike Shakespeare, Jonson, or Samuel Daniel, he invested little of his art in the genre. Between 1597 and 1602, Drayton was a member of the stable of playwrights who worked for Philip Henslowe. Henslowe's Diary links Drayton's name with 23 plays from that period, and, for all but one unfinished work, in collaboration with others such as Thomas Dekker, Anthony Munday, and Henry Chettle. Only one play has survived; Part 1 of Sir John Oldcastle, which Drayton wrote with Munday, Robert Wilson, and Richard Hathwaye but little of Drayton can be seen in its pages.

By this time, as a poet, Drayton was well received and admired at the Court of Elizabeth 1st. If he hoped to continue that admiration with the accession of James 1st he thought wrong. In 1603, he addressed a poem of compliment to James I, but it was ridiculed, and his services rudely rejected.

In 1605 Drayton reprinted his most important works; the historical poems and the Idea. Also published was a fantastic satire called The Man in the Moon and, for the for the first time the famous Ballad of Agincourt.

Since 1598 he had worked on Poly-Olbion, a work to celebrate all the points of topographical or antiquarian interest in Great Britain. Eighteen books in total, the first were published in 1614 and the last in 1622.

In 1627 he published another of his miscellaneous volumes. In it Drayton printed The Battle of Agincourt (an historical poem but not to be confused with his ballad on the same subject), The Miseries of Queen Margaret, and the acclaimed Nimphidia, the Court of Faery, as well as several other important pieces.

Drayton last published in 1630 with The Muses' Elizium.

Michael Drayton died in London on December 23rd, 1631. He was buried in Westminster Abbey, in Poets' Corner. A monument was placed there with memorial lines attributed to Ben Jonson.

Index of Contents

The Nineteenth Song
The Twentieth Song
The One and Twentieth Song
The Two and Twentieth Song
The Three and Twentieth Song
The Foure and Twentieth Song
The Five and Twentieth Song
The Sixe and Twentieth Song
The Seaven and Twentieth Song
The Eight and Twentieth Song
The Nine and Twentieth Song
The Thirtieth Song
Michael Drayton – A Short Biography by Cyril Brett
A Chronology of Michael Drayton's Life and Works
Michael Drayton – A Concise Bibliography. The Major Works

THE NINETEENTH SONG

THE ARGUMENT

The Muse, now over Thames makes forth,
Upon her Progresse to the North,
From Cauney with a full carrere,
Shee up against the streame doth beare;
Where Waltham Forrests pride exprest,
Shee poynts directly to the East,
And shewes how all those Rivers straine
Through Essex, to the German mayne;
When Stoure, with Orwels ayd prefers,
Our Brittish brave Sea-voyagers;
Halfe Suffolke in with them shee takes,
Where of this Song an end shee makes.

Beare bravely up my Muse, the way thou went'st before,
And crosse the kingly Thames to the Essexian shore,
Stem up his tyde-full streame, upon that side to rise,
Which, though her lower scite doth make her seeme but meane,
Of him as dearly lov'd as Shepey is or Greane,

And him as dearly lov'd; for when he would depart,
With Hercules to fight, she tooke it so to heart,
That falling low and flat, her blubberd face to hide,
By Thames shee welneere is surrounded every tyde:
And since of worldly State, she never taketh keepe,
But onely gives her selfe, to tend, and milke her sheepe.
But Muse, from her so low, divert thy high-set song
To London-wards, and bring from Lea with thee along
The Forrests, and the Floods, and most exactly show,
How these in order stand, how those directly flow:
For in that happy soyle, doth pleasure ever wonne,
Through Forrests, where cleere Rills in wild Meanders runne;
Where daintie Summer Bowers, and Arborets are made,
Cut out of Busshy thicks, for coolenesse of the shade.
Fooles gaze at painted Courts, to th'countrey let me goe,
To climbe the easie hill, then walke, the valley lowe;
No gold-embossed Roofes, to me are like the woods;
No Bed like to the grasse, nor liquor like the floods:
A Citie's but a sinke, gay houses gawdy graves,
The Muses have free leave, to starve or live in caves:
But Waltham Forrest still in prosperous estate,
As standing to this day (so strangely fortunate)
Above her neighbour Nymphs, and holds her head aloft;
A turfe beyond them all, so sleeke and wondrous soft,
Upon her setting side, by goodly London grac'd,
Upon the North by Lea, her South by Thames embrac'd.
Upon her rising point, shee chaunced to espie,
A daintie Forrest-Nymph of her societie.
Faire Hatfield, which in height all other did surmount,
And of the Dryades held in very high account;
Yet in respect of her stood farre out of the way,
Who doubting of her selfe, by others late decay,
Her sisters glory view'd with an astonish'd eye,
Whom Waltham wisely thus reprooveth by and by.
Deare Sister rest content, nor our declining rue,
What thing is in this world (that we can say) is new;
The Ridge and Furrow shewes, that once the crooked Plow,
Turn'd up the grassy turfe, where Okes are rooted now:
And at this houre we see, the Share and Coulter teare
The full corne-bearing gleabe, where sometimes forrests were;
And those but Caitifes are, which most doe seeke our spoyle,
Who having sold our woods, doe lastly sell our soyle;
Tis vertue to give place to these ungodly times,
When as the fostred ill proceeds from others crimes;
Gainst Lunatiks, and fooles, what wise folke spend their force;
For folly headlong falls, when it hath had the course:
And when God gives men up, to wayes abhor'd and vile,
Of understanding hee deprives them quite, the while

They into errour runne, confounded in their sinne,
As simple Fowles in lyme, or in the Fowlers gynne.
And for those prettie Birds, that wont in us to sing,
They shall at last forbeare to welcome in the Spring,
When wanting where to pearch, they sit upon the ground,
And curse them in their Notes, who first did woods confound.
Deare Sister Hatfield, then hold up thy drooping head,
We feele no such decay, nor is all succour fled:
For Essex is our dower, which greatly doth abound,
With every simple good, that in the Ile is found:
And though we goe to wracke in this so generall waste,
This hope to us remaines, we yet may be the last.
When Hatfield taking heart, where late she sadly stood,
Sends little Roding foorth, her best-beloved Flood;
Which from her Christall Fount, as to enlarge her fame,
To many a Village lends, her cleere and noble name,
Which as she wandreth on, through Waltham holds her way,
With goodly Oken wreaths, which makes her wondrous gay;
But making at the last into the watry Marsh,
Where though the blady grasse unwholesome be and harsh,
Those wreaths away she casts, which bounteous Waltham gave,
With Bulrush, Flags, and Reed, to make her wondrous brave,
And her selves strength divides, to sundry lesser streames,
So wantoning shee falls into her Soveraigne Thames.
From whose vast Beechy bankes a rumor straight resounds,
Which quickly ran it selfe through the Essexian grounds,
That Crouch amongst the rest, a Rivers name should seeke,
As scorning any more the nickname of a Creeke,
Well furnisht with a Streame, that from the fill to fall,
Wants nothing that a Flood should be adorn'd withall.
On Benge's Batfull side, and at her going out,
With Walnot, Foulnesse faire, neere watred round about.
Two Iles for greater state to stay her up that stand,
Thrust farre into the Sea, yet fixed to the land;
As Nature in that sort them purposely had plac'd,
That shee by Sea and Land, should every way be grac'd.
Some Sea-Nymphs and besides, her part (there were) that tooke,
As angry that their Crouch should not be cald a Brooke;
And bad her to complaine to Neptune of her wrong.
But whilst these grievous stirres thus hapned them among,
Choice Chelmer comes along, a Nymph most neatly cleere,
Which welneere through the midst doth cut the wealthy Sheere,
By Dunmow gliding downe to Chelmsford hold her chase,
To which she gives the name, which as she doth imbrace
Cleere Can comes tripping in, and doth with Chelmer close:
With whose supply (though small as yet) she greater growes.
She for old Maldon makes, where in her passing by,
Shee to remembrance calls that Roman Colony,

And all those ominous signes her fall that did foregoe,
As that which most expres'd their fatall overthrow;
Crown'd Victory reverst, fell downe whereas shee stood,
And the vast greenish Sea, discoloured like to blood.
Shreeks heard like peoples cries, that see their deaths at hand;
The pourtratures of men imprinted in the sand.
When Chelmer scarce arrives in her most wished Bay,
But Blakwater comes in, through many a crooked way,
Which Pant was call'd of yore; but that, by Time exild,
Shee Froshwell after hight, then Blakwater instil'd,
But few, such titles have the British Floods among.
When Northey neere at hand, and th'Ile of Ousey rung
With shouts the Sea-Nymphs gave, for joy of their arrive,
As either of those Iles in curtesie doe strive,
To Tethis Darlings, which should greatest honor doe;
And what the former did, the latter adds thereto.
But Colne, which frankly lends faire Colechester her name,
(On all the Essexian shore, the Towne of greatest fame)
Perceiving how they still in Courtship did contend,
Quoth she, wherefore the time thus idly doe you spend?
What is there nothing here, that you esteeme of worth,
That our big-bellied Sea, or our rich land brings forth?
Thinke you our Oysters here, unworthy of your praise?
Pure Walfleet, which doe still the daintiest pallats please:
As excellent as those, which are esteemed most.
The Cizic shels, or those on the Lucrinian coast;
Or Cheese, which our fat soyle to every quarter sends;
Whose tacke the hungry Clowne, and Plow-man so commends.
If you esteeme not these, as things above the ground,
Looke under, where the Urnes of ancient times are found:
The Roman Emp'rours Coynes, oft dig'd out of the dust,
And warlike Weapons, now consum'd with cankring rust:
The huge and massy Bones, of mighty fearefull men,
To tell the worlds full strength, what creatures lived then;
When in her height of youth, the lustie fruitfull earth
Brought foorth her big-limb'd brood, even Gyants in their birth.
Thus spoke shee, when from Sea they suddenly doe heare
A strong and horrid noyse, which struck the land with feare:
For with their crooked Trumps, his Tritons, Neptune sent,
To warne the wanton Nymphs, that they incontinent
Should straight repaire to Stour, in Orwells pleasant Road;
For it had been divulg'd the Ocean all abroad,
That Orwell and this Stour, by meeting in one Bay,
Two, that each others good, intended every way,
Prepar'd to sing a Song, that should precisely show,
That Medway for her life, their skill could not out-goe:
For Stour, a daintie flood, that duly doth divide
Faire Suffolke from this Shire, upon her other side;

By Clare first comming in, to Sudbury doth show,
The even course she keepes; when farre she doth not flow,
But Breton a bright Nymph, fresh succour to her brings:
Yet is she not so proud of her superfluous Springs,
But Orwell comming in from Ipswitch thinkes that shee,
Should stand for it with Stour, and lastly they agree,
That since the Britans hence their first Discoveries made,
And that into the East they first were taught to trade.
Besides, of all the Roads, and Havens of the East,
This Harbor where they meet, is reckoned for the best.
Our Voyages by Sea, and brave discoveries knowne,
Their argument they make, and thus they sing their owne;
In Severns late tun'd lay, that Empresse of the West,
In which great Arthurs actes are to the life exprest:
His Conquests to the North, who Norway did invade,
Who Groneland, Iseland next, then Lapland lastly made
His awfull Empires bounds, the Britans acts among,
This God-like Heroes deeds exactly have beene sung:
His valiant people then, who to those Countries brought,
Which many an age since that, our great'st discoveries thought.
This worthiest then of ours, our Argonauts shall lead.
Next Malgo, who againe that Conquerors steps to tread,
Succeeding him in Raigne, in conquests so no lesse,
Plow'd up the frozen Sea, and with as faire successe,
By that great Conquerors claime, first Orkney overran;
Proud Denmarke then subdu'd, and spacious Norway wan,
Ceasd Iseland for his owne, and Goteland to each shore,
Where Arthurs full-saild Fleet had ever toucht before.
And when the Britans Raigne came after to decline,
And to the Cambrian hils their fate did them confine,
The Saxon swaying all, in Alfreds powerfull raigne,
Our English Octer put a Fleet to Sea againe,
Of th'uge Norwegian Hilles, and newes did hither bring,
Whose tops are hardly wrought in twelve dayes travailing.
But leaving Norway then a Sterboard, forward kept,
And with our English Sayles that mightie Ocean swept,
Where those sterne people wonne, whom hope of gaine doth call,
In Hulkes with grapling hooks, to hunt the dreadfull Whall;
And great Duina downe from her first springing place,
Doth roule her swelling waves in churlish Neptunes face.
Then Woolstan after him discovering Dansig found,
Where Wixels mighty mouth is powrd into the Sound,
And towing up his streame, first taught the English Oares,
The usefull way of Trade to those most gainefull shores.
And when the Norman Stem here strong and potent grew,
And their successefull sonnes, did glorious acts pursue,
One Nicholas nam'd of Lyn, where first he breath'd the ayre,
Though Oxford taught him Art, and well may hold him deare:

Ith'Mathematicks learnd, (although a Fryer profest)
To see those Northerne Climes, with great desire possest,
Himselfe he thither ship'd, and skilfull in the Globe,
Tooke every severall height with his true Astrolobe;
The Whirlpooles of the seas, and came to understand,
From the foure Card'nall winds, foure indraughts that command;
Int'any of whose falls, if th'wandring Barque doth light,
It hurried is away with such tempestuous flight,
Into that swallowing gulfe, which seemes as it would draw
The very earth it selfe into th'infernall maw.
Foure such Immeasur'd Pooles, Phylosophers agree,
Ith foure parts of the world undoubtedly to bee;
From which they have supposd, Nature the winds doth raise,
And from them to proceed the flowing of the Seas.
And when our Civill warres began at last to cease,
And these late calmer times of Olive-bearing Peace,
Gave leasure to great Minds, farre Regions to descry;
That brave adventrous Knight, our Sir Hugh Willoughby,
Ship'd for the Northren Seas, mongst those congealed Piles,
Fashioned by lasting Frosts, like Mountaines, and like Iles,
(In all her fearefulst shapes saw Horror, whose great mind,
In lesser bounds then these, that could not be confin'd,
Adventured on those parts, where Winter still doth keepe;
When most the Icy cold had chaind up all the Deepe)
In Bleake Arzina's Road his death neere Lapland tooke,
Where Kegor from her scite, on those grim Seas doth looke.
Two others follow then, eternall fame that wonne,
Our Chancellor, and with him, compare we Jenkinson:
For Russia both imbarqu'd, the first ariving there,
Entring Duina's mouth, up her proud streame did steere
To Volgad, to behold her pompe, the Russian State,
Moscovia measuring then; the other with like Fate,
Both those vast Realmes survay'd, then into Bactria past,
To Boghors bulwarkt walls, then to the liquid wast,
Where Oxus roleth downe twixt his farre distant shores,
And o're the Caspian Maine, with strong untyred Oares,
Adventured to view rich Persias wealth and pride,
Whose true report thereof, the English since have tride.
With Fitch, our Eldred next, deserv'dly placed is;
Both travailing to see, the Syrian Tripolis.
The first of which (in this whose noble spirit was showne)
To view those parts, to us that were the most unknowne,
On thence to Ormus set, Goa, Cambaya, then,
To vast Zelabdim, thence to Echubar, agen
Crost Ganges mighty streame, and his large bankes did view,
To Baccola went on, to Bengola, Pegu;
And for Mallaccan then, Zeiten, and Cochin cast,
Measuring with many a step, the great East-Indian wast.

The other from that place, the first before had gone,
Determining to see the broad-wald Babylon,
Crost Euphrates, and row'd against his mightie streame;
Licia, and Gaza saw, with great Hierusalem,
And our deare Saviours seat, blest Bethlem did behold,
And Jourdan, of whose waves, much is in Scriptures told.
Then Macham, who (through love to long adventures led)
Mederas wealthy Iles, the first discovered,
Who having stolne a mayd, to whom he was affi'd,
Yet her rich parents still her marriage rites deni'd,
Put with her foorth to Sea, where many a danger past,
Upon an Ile of those, at length by tempest cast;
And putting in, to give his tender Love some ease,
Which very ill had brook'd, the rough and boystrous Seas;
And lingring for her health, within the quiet Bay,
The Mariners most false, fled with the Ship away,
When as it was not long, but shee gave up her breath;
When he whose teares in vaine bewayld her timelesse death:
That their deserved Rites her Funerall could not have,
A homely Altar built upon her honoured grave.
When with his folke but few, not passing two or three,
There making them a Boat, but rudely of one Tree,
Put foorth againe to Sea, where after many a flaw,
Such as before themselves, scarce Mortall ever saw;
Nor miserable men could possibly sustaine,
Now swallowed with the waves, and then spu'd up againe;
At length were on the coast of Sun-burnt Affrick throwne:
T'amaze that further world, and to amuse our owne.
Then Windham who new wayes, for us and ours to trie,
For great Morrocco made, discovering Barbarie.
Lock, Towerson, Fenner next, vast Guiney forth that sought,
And of her Ivory, home in great abundance brought.
The East-Indian Voy'ger then, the valiant Lancaster,
To Buona Esperance, Comara, Zanziber,
To Nicuba, as hee to Gomerpolo went,
Till his strong Bottome strucke Molluccos Continent;
And sayling to Brazeel another time he tooke
Olynda's chiefest Towne, and Harbour Farnambuke,
And with their precious Wood, Sugar, and Cotton fraught,
It by his safe returne, into his Countrie brought.
Then Forbosher, whose fame flew all the Ocean o'r,
Who to the Northwest sought, huge China's wealthy shore,
When nearer to the North, that wandring Sea-man set,
Where hee in our hotst Mon'ths of June and July met
With Snow, Frost, Haile, & Sleet, and found sterne Winter strong,
With mighty Iles of Ice, and Mountaines huge and long.
Where as it comes and goes, the great eternall Light,
Makes halfe the yeare still day, and halfe continuall night.

Then for those Bounds unknown, he bravely set againe,
As he a Sea-god were, familiar with the Maine.
The Noble Fenton next, and Jackman we preferre,
Both Voyagers, that were with famous Forbosher.
And Davies, three times forth that for the Northwest made;
Still striving by that course, t'inrich the English Trade:
And as he well deserv'd to his eternall fame.
There by a mightie Sea, Imortaliz'd his Name.
With noble Gilbert next, comes Hoard who tooke in hand
To cleere the course scarse knowne into the New-found Land,
And view'd the plenteous Seas, and fishfull Havens, where
Our neighbouring Nations since have stor'd them every yeare.
Then Globe-engirdling Drake, the Navall Palme that wonne,
Who strove in his long Course to emulate the Sunne:
Of whom the Spaniard us'd a Prophecie to tell,
That from the British Isles should rise a Dragon fell,
That with his armed wings, should strike th'Iberian Maine,
And bring in after time much horror upon Spaine.
This more then man (or what) this Demie-god at Sea,
Leaving behind his backe, the great America,
Upon the surging Maine his wel-stretch't Tacklings flewd,
To fortie three Degrees of North'ly Latitude;
Unto that Land before to th'Christian world unknowne,
Which in his Countries right he nam'd New Albion;
And in the Westerne Inde, spight of the power of Spaine,
Hee Saint Iago tooke, Domingo, Cartagene:
And leaving of his prowesse, a marke in every Bay,
Saint Augustins surpriz'd, in Terra Florida.
Then those that foorth for Sea, Industrious Rawleigh wrought,
And them with every thing, fit for discovery fraught;
That Amadas, (whose Name doth scarsely English sound)
With Barlow, who the first Virginia throughly found.
As Greenvile, whom he got to undertake that Sea,
Three sundry times from hence, who touch'd Virginia.
(In his so rare a choyce, it well approov'd his wit;
That with so brave a Spirit, his turne so well could fit.
O Greenvile, thy great Name, for ever be renown'd,
And borne by Neptune still, about this mightie Round;
Whose Navall Conflict wanne thy Nation so much fame,
And in th'Iberians bred feare of the English name.
Nor should Fame speake her low'dst, Of Lane, shee could not lie,
Who in Virginia left, with th'English Colony,
Himselfe so bravely bare, amongst our people there,
That him they onely lov'd, when others they did feare.
And from those Barbarous, brute, and wild Virginians wan
Such reverence, as in him there had been more then man.
Then he which favoured still, such high attempts as these,
Rawleigh, whose reading made him skil'd in all the Seas,

Imbarqu'd his worthy selfe, and his adventurous crue,
And with a prosperous Sayle to those faire Countries flew,
Where Orenoque, as he, on in his course doth roule,
Seemes as his greatnes meant, grim Neptune to controule;
Like to a puisant King, whose Realmes extend so farre,
That many a potent Prince his Tributaries are.
So are his Branches Seas, and in the rich Guiana,
A Flood as proud as he, the broad-brim'd Orellana:
And on the spacious firme Manoas mightie seat,
The land (by Natures power) with wonders most repleat.
So Leigh, Cape Briton saw, and Rameas Iles againe;
As Tompson undertooke the Voyage to New-Spaine:
And Hawkins not behind, the best of these before,
Who hoysing sayle, to seeke the most remotest shore,
Upon that new nam'd Spaine, and Guinny sought his prize,
As one whose mighty mind small things could not suffice,
The sonne of his brave Syre, who with his furrowing Keele,
Long ere that time had touch'd the goodly rich Brazeel.
Couragious Candish then, a second Neptune here,
Whose fame fild every mouth, and tooke up every eare.
What man could in his time discourse of any Seas,
But of brave Candish talk'd, and of his voyages;
Who through the South Seas past, about this earthly Ball,
And saw those Starres, to them that onely rise and fall,
And with his silken sayles, stayn'd with the richest Ore,
Dar'd any one to passe where he had been before.
Count Cumberland, so hence to seeke th'Asores sent,
And to the Westerne-Inde, to Porta Ricco went,
And with the English power it bravely did surprize.
Sir Robert Dudley then, by sea that sought to rise,
Hoyst Sayles with happy winds to th'Iles of Trinidado:
Paria then he past, the Ilands of Granado;
As those of Sancta Cruz, and Porta Ricco: then
Amongst the famous ranke of our Sea-searching men,
Is Preston sent to Sea, with Summers foorth to finde,
Adventures in the parts upon the Westerne-Inde;
Port Santo who surpriz'd, and Coches, with the Fort
Of Coro, and the Towne, when in submissive sort,
Cumana ransome crav'd, Saint James of Leon sack'd;
Jamica went not free, but as the rest they wrack'd.
Then Sherley, (since whose name such high renowne hath won)
That Voyage undertooke, as they before had done:
He Saint Iago saw, Domingo, Margarita,
By Terra firma sayl'd to th'Ilands of Jamica,
Up Rio Dolce row'd, and with a prosperous hand,
Returning to his home, touch'd at the New-found-land,
Where at Jamicas Iles, couragious Parker met
With Sherley, and along up Rio Dolce set,

Where bidding him adue, on his owne course he ran,
And tooke Campeches Towne, the chief'st of Jucatan.
A Freegate, and from thence did home to Britan bring,
With most strange Tribute fraught, due to that Indian King,
At mightie Neptunes beck, thus ended they their Song,
When as from Harwich all to Loving-land along,
Great claps and shouts were heard resounding to the shore,
Wherewith th'Essexian Nymphs applaud their loved Stour,
From the Suffolcean side yet those which Stour preferre
Their princely Orwell praise, as much as th'other her:
For though cleare Briton be rich Suffolkes from her spring,
Which Stour upon her way to Harwich downe doth bring,
Yet Deben of her selfe a stout and stedfast friend,
Her succour to that Sea, neere Orwels Road doth send.
When Waveney to the North, rich Suffolks onely meere,
As Stour upon the North, from Essex parts this Sheere;
Lest Stour and Orwell thus might steale her Nymphes away,
In Neptunes name commands, that here their force should stay:
For that her selfe and Yar in honor of the Deepe,
Were purposed a Feast in Loving-land to keepe.

THE TWENTIETH SONG

THE ARGUMENT

The Muse that part of Suffolke sings,
That lyes to Norfolke, and then brings
The bright Norfolcean Nymphes, to ghest
To Loving-land, to Neptunes Feast;
To Ouze the lesse then downe shee takes,
Where shee a Flight at River makes:
And thence to Marsh-land shee descends,
With whose free praise this Song shee ends.

From Suffolke rose a sound, through the Norfolcean shore
That ran it selfe, the like had not bin heard before:
For he that doth of Sea the powerful Trident weld,
His Tritons made proclaime, a Nymphall to be held
In honor of himselfe, in Loving-land, where he
The most selected Nymphes appointed had to be.
Those Seamayds that about his secret walkes doe dwell,
Which tend his mightie heards of Whales, and Fishes fell,
As of the Rivers those, amongst the Meadowes ranke,
That play in every Foar'd, and sport on every banke,
Were summon'd to be there, in paine of Neptunes hate:
For he would have his Feast, observ'd with god-like state,

When those Suffolcean Floods, that sided not with Stoure,
Their streames but of themselves into the Ocean powre,
As Or, through all the coast a Flood of wondrous fame,
Whose honored fall begets a Haven of her name.
And Blyth a daintie Brooke, their speedy course doe cast,
For Neptune with the rest, to Loving-land to hast:
When Waveney in her way, on this Septentriall side,
That these two Easterne Shires doth equally divide,
From Laphamford leads on, her streame into the East,
By Bungey, then along by Beckles, when possest
Of Loving-land, 'bout which her limber Armes she throwes,
With Neptune taking hands, betwixt them who inclose,
And her an Iland make, fam'd for her scite so farre.
But leave her Muse awhile, and let us on with Yar,
Which Gariena some, some Hier, some Yar doe name;
Who rising from her spring not farre from Walsingham,
Through the Norfolcean fields seemes wantonly to play,
To Norwich comes at length, towards Yarmouth on her way,
Where Wentsum from the South, and Bariden doe beare
Up with her, by whose wealth she much is honored there,
To intertaine her Yar, that in her state doth stand,
With Townes of high'st account, the fourth of all the land:
That hospitable place to the Industrious Dutch,
Whose skill in making Stuffes, and workmanship is such,
(For refuge hither come) as they our ayd deserve,
By labour sore that live, whilst oft the English starve;
On Roots, and Pulse that feed, on Beefe and Mutton spare,
So frugally they live, not gluttons as we are.
But from my former Theame, since thus I have digrest,
Ile borrow more of Time, untill my Nymphs be drest:
And since these Foods fall out so fitly in my way,
A little while to them I will convert my Lay.
The Colewort, Colifloure, and Cabidge in their season,
The Rouncefall, great Beanes, and early ripening Peason;
The Onion, Scallion, Leeke, which Housewives highly rate;
Their kinsman Garlicke then, the poore mans Mithridate;
The savory Parsnip next, and Carret pleasing food;
The Skirret (which some say) in Sallats stirres the blood;
The Turnip, tasting well to Clownes in Winter weather.
Thus in our verse we put, Roots, Hearbs, and Fruits together.
The great moyst Pumpion then, that on the ground doth lie,
A purer of his kind, the sweet Muske-million by;
Which dainty pallats now, because they would not want,
Have kindly learnt to set, as yearely to transplant:
The Radish somewhat hote, yet urine doth provoke;
The Cucumber as cold, the heating Artichoke;
The Citrons, which our soyle not easly doth affourd;
The Rampion rare as that, the hardly gotten Gourd.

But in these triviall things, Muse, wander not too long,
But now to nimble Yar, turne we our active Song,
Which in her winding course, from Norwich to the Mayne,
By many a stately seat lasciviously doth straine,
To Yarmouth till she come, her onely christned Towne,
Whose fishing through the Realme, doth her so much renowne,
Where those that with their nets still haunt the boundles lake,
Her such a sumptuous feast of salted Herrings make,
As they had rob'd the Sea of all his former store,
And past that very howre, it could produce no more.
Her owne selves Harbour here, when Yar doth hardly win,
But kindly she againe, saluted is by Thrin,
A faire Norfolcean Nymph, which gratifies her fall.
Now are the Tritons heard, to Loving-land to call,
Which Neptunes great commaunds, before them bravely beare,
Commanding all the Nymphs of high account that were,
Which in fat Holland lurke amongst the queachy plashes,
Or play them on the sands, upon the fomy washes,
As all the watry brood, which haunt the German deepes,
Upon whose briny Curles, the dewy morning weepes,
To Loving-land to come, and in their best attires,
That meeting to observe, as now the time requires.
When Erix, Neptunes sonne by Venus, to the shore
To see them safely brought, their Herault came before,
And for a Mace he held in his huge hand, the horne
Of that so-much-esteem'd, sea-honoring Unicorne.
Next Proto wondrous swift, led all the rest the way,
Then she which makes the calmes, the mild Cymodice,
With god-like Dorida, and Galatea faire,
With daintie Nets of pearle, cast o'r their braided haire:
Analiis which the Sea doth salt, and seasoned keepe;
And Batheas, most supreame and soveraigne in the deepe,
Brings Cyane, to the waves which that greene colour gives;
Then Atmis, which in Fogs and mistie vapours lives:
Phrinax, the Billowes rough, and surges that bestrides,
And Rothion, that by her on the wilde waters rides;
With Icthias, that of Frye the keeping doth retaine,
As Pholoë, most that rules the Monsters of the Maine:
Which brought to beare them out, if any need should fall,
The Dolphin, Sea-horse, Gramp, the Wherlpoole, and the Whall.
An hundred more besides, I readily could name,
With these as Neptune wil'd, to Loving-land that came.
These Nymphs trick'd up in tyers, the Sea-gods to delight:
Of Currall of each kind, the blacke, the red, the white;
With many sundry shels, the Scallop large, and faire;
The Cockle small and round; the Periwinkle spare,
The Oyster, wherein oft the pearle is found to breed,
The Mussell, which retaines that daintie Orient seed:

In Chaines and Bracelets made, with linkes of sundry twists,
Some worne about their wasts, their necks, some on the wrists.
Great store of Amber there, and Jeat they did not misse;
Their lips they sweetned had with costly Ambergris.
Scarcely the Neriad's thus arrived from the Seas,
But from the fresher streames the brighter Niades,
To Loving-land make haste with all the speed they may,
For feare their fellow-Nymphes should for their comming stay.
Glico the running Streames in sweetnesse still that keepes,
And Clymene which rules, when they surround their deepes.
Spio, in hollow bankes, the waters that doth hide:
With Opis that doth beare them backward with the Tyde.
Semaia that for sights doth keepe the water cleare:
Zanthe their yellow sands, that maketh to appeare,
Then Drymo for the Okes that shaddow every banke,
Phylodice, the boughs for Garlands fresh and ranke.
Which the cleare Naiades make them Anadems withall,
When they are cald to daunse in Neptunes mightie hall.
Then Ligea, which maintaines the Birds harmonious layes,
Which sing on Rivers banks amongst the slender sprayes,
With Rhodia, which for them doth nurse the Roseat sets,
Ioida, which preserves the azure Violets.
Anthea, of the flowers, that hath the generall charge,
And Syrinx of the Reeds, that grow upon the Marge.
Some of these lovely Nymphes wore on their flaxen haire
Fine Chaplets made of Flaggs, that fully flowred were:
With Water-cans againe, some wantonly them dight,
Whose larger leafe and flower, gave wonderfull delight
To those that wistly view'd their Beauties: some againe,
That soveraigne places held amongst the watry traine,
Of Cat-tayles made them Crownes, which from the Sedge doth grow,
Which neatly woven were, and some to grace the show,
Of Lady-smocks most white, doe rob each neighbouring Mead,
Wherewith their looser locks most curiously they breyd.
Now thus together com'n, they friendly doe devise,
Some of light toyes, and some of matters grave and wise.
But to breake off their speech, her reed when Syrinx sounds,
Some cast themselves in Rings, and fell to Hornepipe rounds:
They ceasing, as againe to others turnes it falls,
They lustie Galiards tread, some others Jiggs, and Braules.
This done, upon the banke together being set,
Proceeding in the cause, for which they thus were met,
In mightie Neptunes praise, these Sea-borne Virgins sing:
Let earth, and ayre, say they with the high praises ring,
Of Saturne by his Ops, the most renowned Sonne,
From all the gods but Jove, the Diadem that wonne,
Whose ofspring wise and strong, deare Nymphes let us relate,
On mountaines of vast waves, know he that sits in state,

And with his Trident rules, the universall streame,
To be the onely syre of mightie Polypheme.
On fayre Thoosa got old Phorcus loved child,
Who in a fained shape that god of Sea beguild.
Three thousand princely sonnes, and lovely Nymphs as we,
Were to great Neptune borne, of which we sparing be:
Some by his goodly Queene, some in his Lemmans bed;
Chryasor grim begot, on sterne Medusas head.
Swart Brontes, for his owne so mightie Neptune takes,
One of the Cyclops strong, Joves Thunder-bolts that makes.
Great Neptune, Nelius got, (if you for wisedome seeke)
Who was old Nestors syre, the grav'st and wisest Greeke.
Or from this King of waves, of such thou lov'st to heare,
Of famous Nations first, that mightie Founders were;
Then Cadmus, who the plot of ancient Thebes contriv'd,
From Neptune God of Sea, his Pedigree deriv'd,
By Agenor his old Syer, who rul'd Phenicia long:
So Inachus, the chiefe of Argives great and strong
Claim'd kinred of this King, and by some beautious Neece,
So did Pelasgus too, who peopled ancient Greece.
A world of mightie Kings and Princes I could name,
From our god Neptune sprung; let this suffice, his fame
Incompasseth the world; those Starres which never rise,
Above the lower South, are never from his eyes:
As those againe to him doe every day appeare,
Continually that keepe the Northerne Hemisphere;
Who like a mightie King, doth cast his Watched robe,
Farre wider then the land, quite round about the Globe.
Where is there one to him that may compared be,
That both the Poles at once continually doth see;
And Gyant-like with heaven as often maketh warres;
The Ilands (in his power) as numberlesse as Starres,
He washeth at his will, and with his mightie hands,
He makes the even shores, oft mountainous with Sands:
Whose creatures, which observe his wide Emperiall seat,
Like his immeasured selfe, are infinite and great.
Thus ended they their Song, and off th'assembly brake,
When quickly towards the west, the Muse her way doth take;
Whereas the swelling soyle, as from one banke doth bring
This Waveney sung before, and Ouse the lesse, whose spring
Towards Ouse the greater poynts, and downe by Thetford glides,
Where shee cleere Thet receives, her glory that divides,
With her new-named Towne, as wondrous glad that shee,
For frequency of late, so much esteemd should be:
Where since these confluent Floods, so fit for Hauking lye,
And store of Fowle intice skil'd Falkoners there to flye.
Now of a flight at Brooke shall my description be:
What subject can be found, that lies not faire to me.

Of simple Shepheards now, my Muse exactly sings,
And then of courtly Loves, and the affaires of Kings.
Then in a Buskind straine, the warlike speare and shield,
And instantly againe of the disports of Field;
What can this Ile produce, that lyes from my report,
Industrious Muse, proceed then to thy Hawking sport.
When making for the Brooke, the Falkoner doth espie
On River, Plash, or Mere, where store of Fowle doth lye:
Whence forced over land, by skilfull Falconers trade:
A faire convenient flight, may easily be made.
He whistleth off his Hawkes, whose nimble pineons streight,
Doe worke themselves by turnes, into a stately height:
And if that after check, the one or both doe goe,
Sometimes he them the Lure, sometimes doth water show;
The trembling Fowle that heare the Jigging Hawk-bels ring,
And find it is too late, to trust then to their wing,
Lye flat upon the flood, whilst the high-mounted Hawks,
Then being lords alone, in their etheriall walkes,
Aloft so bravely stirre, their bells so thicke that shake;
Which when the Falkoner sees, that scarce one plane they make:
The gallant'st Birds saith he, that ever flew on wing,
And sweares there is a Flight, were worthy of a King.
Then making to the Flood, to force the Fowles to rise,
The fierce and eager Hawkes, downe thrilling from the Skies,
Make sundry Canceleers e'r they the Fowle can reach,
Which then to save their lives, their wings doe lively stretch.
But when the whizzing Bels the silent ayre doe cleave,
And that their greatest speed, them vainly doe deceive;
And the sharpe cruell Hawkes, they at their backs doe view,
Themselves for very feare they instantly ineawe.
The Hawkes get up againe into their former place;
And ranging here and there, in that their ayery race:
Still as the fearefull Fowle attempt to scape away,
With many a stouping brave, them in againe they lay.
But when the Falkoners take their Hawking-poles in hand,
And crossing of the Brooke, doe put it over land:
The Hawke gives it a souse, that makes it to rebound,
Well neere the height of man, sometime above the ground;
Oft takes a leg, or wing, oft takes away the head,
And oft from necke to tayle, the backe in two doth shread.
With many a Wo ho ho, and jocond Lure againe,
When he his quarry makes upon the grassy plaine.
But to my Floods againe: when as this Ouze the lesse
Hath taken in cleere Thet, with farre more free accesse
To Ouze the great shee goes, her Queene that commeth crown'd,
As such a River fits, so many miles renown'd;
And poynting to the North, her Christall front she dashes
Against the swelling sands of the surrounded Washes;

And Neptune in her Armes, so amply doth imbrace,
As she would rob his Queene, faire Thetis of her place.
Which when rich Marsh-land sees, least she should loose her state,
With that faire River thus, shee gently doth debate.
Disdaine me not, deare Flood, in thy excessive pride,
There's scarcely any soyle that sitteth by thy side,
Whose Turfe so batfull is, or beares so deepe a swath;
Nor is there any Marsh in all Great Britaine, hath
So many goodly seats, or that can truely show
Such Rarities as I: so that all Marshes owe
Much honor to my name, for that exceeding grace,
Which they receive by me, so soveraigne in my place.
Though Rumney, as some say, for finenesse of her grasse,
And for her daintie scite, all other doth surpasse:
Yet are those Seas but poore, and Rivers that confine
Her greatnesse but meane Rills, be they compar'd with mine.
Nor hardly doth shee tyth th'aboundant Fowle and Fish,
Which Nature gives to me, as I my selfe can wish.
As Amphitrite oft, calls me her sweet and faire,
And sends the Northrene winds to curle my braided haire,
And makes the Washes stand, to watch and ward me still,
Lest that rough god of Sea, on me should worke his will.
Old Wisbitch to my grace, my circuit sits within,
And neere my banks I have the neighbourhood of Lyn.
Both Townes of strength and state, my profits still that vent:
No Marsh hath more of Sea, none more of continent.
Thus Marsh-land ends her speech, as one that throughly knew,
What was her proper praise, and what was Ouzes due.
With that the zealous Muse, in her Poetique rage,
To Walsingham would needs have gone a Pilgrimage,
To view those farthest shores, whence little Niger flowes
Into the Northrene Maine, and see the gleabe where growes
That Saffron, (which men say) this land hath not the like,
All Europe that excels: but here she sayle doth strike.
For that Apollo pluckt her easly by the eare;
And told her in that part of Norfolke, if there were
Ought worthy of respect, it was not in her way,
When for the greater Ouze, her wing she doth display.

THE ONE AND TWENTIETH SONG

THE ARGUMENT

Now from New-market comes the Muse,
Whose spacious Heath, shee wistly viewes,
Those Ancient Ditches and surveyes,

Which our first Saxons here did raise:
To Gogmagog then turnes her tale,
And shewes you Ring-tailes pleasant vale.
And to doe Cambridge all her Rites,
The Muses to her Towne invites.
And lastly, Elies praise shee sings,
An end which to this Canto brings.

By this our little rest, thus having gotten breath,
And fairely in our way, upon Newmarket-Heath:
That great and ancient Ditch, which us expected long,
Inspired by the Muse, at her arrivall song:
O Time, what earthly thing with thee it selfe can trust,
When thou in thine owne course, art to thy selfe unjust!
Dost thou contract with death, and to oblivion give
Thy glories, after them, yet shamefully dar'st live?
O Time, hadst thou preserv'd, what labouring man hath done,
Thou long before this day, mightst to thy selfe have wonne
A Deitie with the gods, and in thy Temple plac'd,
But sacriligious thou, hast all great workes defac'd;
For though the things themselves have suffered by thy theft,
Yet with their Ruines, thou, to ages mightst have left,
Those Monuments who rear'd, and not have suffred thus
Posteritie so much, t'abuse both thee and us.
I, by th'East Angles first, who from this Heath arose,
The long'st and largest Ditch, to check their Mercian foes;
Because my depth, and breadth, so strangely doth exceed,
Mens low and wretched thoughts, they constantly decreed,
That by the Devils helpe, I needs must raised be,
Wherefore the Devils-Ditch they basely named me:
When ages long before, I bare Saint Edmonds name,
Because up to my side, (some have supposed) came
The Liberties bequeath'd to his more sacred Shrine.
Therefore my fellow Dykes, ye ancient friends of mine,
That out of earth were raisd, by men whose minds were great,
It is no marvaile, though Oblivion doe you threat.
First, Flemditch next my selfe, that art of greatest strength,
That doest extend thy course full seaven large mile in length:
And thou the Fivemile cald, yet not lesse deare to me;
With Brenditch, that againe is shortest of the three,
Can you suppose your selves at all to be respected,
When you may see my truth's bely'd, and so neglected:
Therefore deare Heath, live still in prosperous estate,
And let thy wel-fleec'd Flocks, from morne to evening late,
(By carefull Shepheards kept) rejoyce thee with their praise;
And let the merry Larke, with her delicious layes,
Give comfort to thy plaines, and let me onely lye,
(Though of the world contemn'd) yet gracious in thine eye.

Thus said, these ancient Dykes neglected in their ground,
Through the sad aged earth, sent out a hollow sound,
To gratulate her speech; when as we met againe,
With one whose constant heart, with cruell love was slaine:
Old Gogmagog, a Hill of long and great renowne,
Which neere to Cambridge set, o'rlookes that learned Towne.
Of Balshams pleasant hilles, that by the name was knowne,
But with the monstrous times, he rude and barbarous growne,
A Gyant was become; for man hee cared not,
And so the fearefull name of Gogmagog had got:
Who long had borne good will to most delicious Grant:
But doubting lest some god his greatnesse might supplant.
For as that daintie Flood by Cambridge keepes her course,
He found the Muses left their old Beotian source,
Resorting to her banks, and every little space,
He saw bright Phœbus gaze upon her Christall face,
And through th'exhaled Fogs, with anger looked red,
To leave his loved Nymph, when he went downe to bed.
Wherefore this Hill with love, being fouly overgone:
And one day as he found the lovely Nymph alone,
Thus wooes her; Sweeting mine, if thou mine owne wilt be,
C'have many a pretty gaud, I keepe in store for thee.
A nest of broad-fac'd Owles, and goodly Urchins too;
Nay Nymph take heed of me, when I begin to wooe:
And better yet then this, a Bulchin twa yeares old,
A curld-pate Calfe it is, and oft could have beene sold:
And yet beside all this, c'have goodly Beare-whelps twa,
Full daintie for my Joy, when shee's dispos'd to play,
And twentie Sowes of Lead, to make our wedding Ring;
Bezides, at Sturbridge Fayre, chill buy thee many a thing:
Chill zmouch thee every morne, before the Sunne can rise,
And looke my manly face, in thy sweet glaring eyes.
Thus said, he smug'd his Beard, and stroked up his hayre,
As one that for her love he thought had offered fayre:
Which to the Muses, Grant did presently report,
Wherewith they many a yeare shall make them wondrous sport.
When Ringdale in her selfe, a most delicious Dale,
Who having heard too long the barbarous Mountaines tale,
Thus thinketh in her selfe, Shall I be silenc'd, when
Rude Hills, and Ditches, digg'd by discontented men,
Are ayded by the Muse; their Mind's at large to speake:
Besides my sister Vales supposing me but weake,
Judge meanly of my state, when she no longer stayd,
But in her owne behalfe, thus to the other said.
What though betwixt two Sheeres, I be by Fortune throwne,
That neither of them both can challenge me her owne,
Yet am I not the lesse, nor lesse my Fame shall be:
Your Figures are but base, when they are set by me;

For Nature in your shapes, notoriously did erre,
But skillfull was in me, cast pure Orbiculer.
Nor can I be compar'd so like to any thing,
By him that would expresse my shape, as to a Ring:
For Nature bent to sport, and various in her trade,
Of all the British Vales, of me a circle made:
For in my very midst, there is a swelling ground,
About which Ceres Nymphs dance many a wanton Round.
The frisking Fairy there, as on the light ayre borne,
Oft runne at Barley-breake upon the eares of Corne;
And catching drops of dew in their lascivious chases,
Doe cast the liquid pearle in one anothers faces.
What they in largenesse have, that beare themselves so hie,
In my most perfect forme, and delicacie, I,
For greatnesse of my graine, and finenesse of my grasse;
This Ile scarce hath a Vale, that Ringdale doth surpasse.
When more she would have said, but suddenly there sprung,
A confident report, that through the Countrey rung,
That Cam her daintiest Flood, long since entituled Grant,
Whose fountaine Ashwell crown'd, with many a upright plant.
In sallying on for Ouze, determin'd by the way,
To intertaine her friends the Muses with a Lay.
Wherefore to shew her selfe er'e she to Cambridge came,
Most worthy of that Towne to which she gives the name,
Takes in her second head, from Linton comming in,
By Shelford having slid, which straightway she doth win:
Then which, a purer Streame, a delicater Brooke,
Bright Phœbus in his course, doth scarcely overlooke.
Thus furnishing her bankes; as sweetly she doth glide
Towards Cambridge, with rich Meads layd forth on either side;
And with the Muses oft, did by the way converse:
Wherefore it her behooves, that something she reherse,
The Sisters that concern'd, who whispered in her eare,
Such things as onely shee, and they themselves should heare,
A wondrous learned Flood; and she that had been long,
(Though silent, in her selfe, yet) vexed at the wrong
Done to Apollo's Priests, with heavenly fire infused,
Oft by the worthlesse world, unworthily abused:
With whom, in their behalfe, hap ill, or happen well,
Shee meant to have a bout, even in despight of Hell,
When humbly lowting low, her due obedience done,
Thus like a Satyre shee, deliberatly begun.
My Invective, thus quoth she, I onely ayme at you,
(Of what degree soe'r) ye wretched worldly crue,
In all your brainlesse talke, that still direct your drifts
Against the Muses sonnes, and their most sacred gifts,
That hate a Poets name, your vilenesse to advance,
For ever be you damn'd in your dull ignorance.

Slave, he whom thou dost thinke, so meane and poore to be,
Is more then halfe divine, when he is set by thee.
Nay more, I will avow, and justifie him then,
He is a god, compar'd with ordinary men.
His brave and noble heart, here in a heaven doth dwell,
Above those worldly cares, that sinks such sots to hell:
A caitife if there be more viler then thy selfe,
If he through basenesse light upon this worldly pelfe,
The Chimney-sweepe, or he that in the dead of night,
Doth emptie lothsome vaults, may purchase all your right;
When not the greatest King, should he his treasure raine,
The Muses sacred gifts, can possibly obtaine;
No, were he Monarch of the universall earth,
Except that gift from heaven, be breath'd into his birth.
How transitory be those heaps of rotting mud,
Which onely to obtaine, yee make your chiefest good?
Perhaps to your fond sonnes, your ill-got goods yee leave,
You scarcely buried are, but they your hopes deceive.
Have I not knowne a wretch, the purchase of whose ground,
Was valued to be sould, at threescore thousand pound;
That in a little time, in a poore threed-bare coat,
Hath walk'd from place to place, to beg a silly groat?
When nothing hath of yours, or your base broods been left,
Except poore widdowes cries, to memorize your theft.
That curse the Serpent got in Paradise for hire,
Descend upon you all, from him your devillish Sire,
Groveling upon the earth, to creepe upon your breast,
And licke the lothsome dust, like that abhorred beast.
But leave these hatefull heards, and let me now declare,
In th'Helliconian Fount, who rightly christned are:
Not such as basely sooth the Humour of the Time,
And slubberingly patch up some slight and shallow Rime,
Upon Pernassus top, that strive to be instal'd,
Yet never to that place were by the Muses call'd.
Nor yet our Mimick Apes, out of their bragging pride,
That faine would seeme to be, what nature them denide;
Whose Verses hobling runne, as with disjoynted bones,
And make a viler noyse, then carts upon the stones;
And these forsooth must be, the Muses onely heires,
When they but Bastards are, and foundlings none of theirs,
Inforcing things in Verse for Poesie unfit,
Mere filthy stuffe, that breakes out of the sores of wit:
What Poet reckes the praise upon such Anticks heap'd,
Or envies that their lines, in Cabinets are kept?
Though some fantasticke foole promove their ragged Rymes,
And doe transcribe them o'r a hundred severall times,
And some fond women winnes, to thinke them wondrous rare,
When they lewd beggery trash, nay very gibbrish are.

Give me those Lines (whose touch the skilfull eare to please)
That gliding flow in state, like swelling Euphrates,
In which things naturall be, and not in falsely wrong:
The Sounds are fine and smooth, the Sense is full and strong,
Not bumbasted with words, vaine ticklish eares to feed;
But such as may content the perfect man to read.
What is of Paynters said, is of true Poets rife,
That he which doth expresse things neerest to the life,
Doth touch the very poynt, nor needs he adde thereto:
For that the utmost is, that Art doth strive to doe.
Had Orpheus, whose sweet Harpe (so musically strung)
Intised Trees, and Rocks, to follow him along:
Th'moralitie of which, is that his knowledge drew
The stony, blockish rout, that nought but rudenesse knew,
T'imbrace a civill life, by his inticing Layes.
Had he compos'd his lines, like many of these dayes,
Which to be understood, doe take in it disdaine:
Nay, Oedipus may fayle, to know what they would meane.
If Orpheus had so play'd, not to be understood,
Well might those men have thought the Harper had been wood;
Who might have sit him downe, the trees and rockes among,
And been a veryer blocke, then those to whom he sung.
O noble Cambridge then, my most beloved Towne,
In glory flourish still, to heighten thy renowne:
In womans perfect shape, still be thy Embleme right,
Whose one hand holds a Cup, the other beares a Light.
Phocis bedew'd with drops, that from Pernassus fall,
Let Cirrha seeke to her, nor be you least of all,
Yee faire Beotian Thebes, and Thespia still to pay
My Cambridge all her Rites: Cirrhea send this way.
O let the thrice-three Maids, their dewes upon thee raine,
From Aganippa's fount, and hoofe-plow'd Hyppocrene.
Mount Pindus, thou that art the Muses sacred place
In Thessaly; and thou, O Pimpla, that in Thrace
They chose for their owne hill, then thou Pernassus hye,
Upon whose by-clift top, the sacred company
About Apollo sit; and thou O Flood, with these
Pure Hellicon, belov'd of the Pierides.
With Tempe, let thy walks, and shades, be brought to her,
And all your glorious gifts upon my Towne conferre.
This said, the lovely Grant glides eas'ly on along,
To meet the mighty Ouze, which with her watry throng,
The Cantabrigian fields had entred, taking in
Th'in-Iled Elies earth, which strongly she doth win
From Grants soft-neighbouring grounds, when as the fruitfull Ile,
Much wondring at her selfe, thought surely all this while,
That by her silence shee had suffred too much wrong.
Wherefore in her selfe praise, loe thus the Iland sung.

Of all the Marshland Iles, I Ely am the Queene:
For Winter each where sad, in me lookes fresh and greene.
The Horse, or other beast, o'rway'd with his owne masse,
Lies wallowing in my Fennes, hid over head in grasse:
And in the place where growes ranke Fodder for my Neat;
The Turffe which beares the Hay, is wondrous needfull Peat:
My full and batning earth, needs not the Plowmans paines;
The Rils which runne in me, are like the branched vaines
In humane Bodies seene; those Ditches cut by hand,
From the surrounding Meres, to winne the measured land,
To those choyce waters, I most fitly may compare,
Wherewith nice women use to blanch their Beauties rare.
Hath there a man beene borne in me, that never knew
Of Watersey the Leame, or th'other cal'd the New.
The Frithdike neer'st my midst, and of another sort,
Who ever fish'd, or fowl'd, that cannot make report
Of sundry Meres at hand, upon my Westerne way,
As Ramsey mere, and Ug, with the great Whittelsey:
Of the aboundant store of Fish and Fowle there bred,
Which whilst of Europes Iles Great Britaine is the Head.
No Meres shall truely tell, in them, then at one draught,
More store of either kinds hath with the Net been caught:
Which though some pettie Iles doe challenge them to be
Their owne, yet must those Iles likwise acknowledge me
Their soveraigne. Nor yet let that Islet Ramsey shame,
Although to Ramsey-Mere shee onely gives the name;
Nor Huntingdon, to me though she extend her grounds,
Twit me that I at all usurpe upon her Bounds.
Those Meres may well be proud, that I will take them in,
Which otherwise perhaps forgotten might have bin.
Besides my towred Phane, and my rich Citied seat,
With Villages, and Dorpes, to make me most compleat.
Thus broke she off her speech, when as the Muse awhile,
Desirous to repose, and rest her with the Ile,
Here consumates her Song, and doth fresh courage take,
With warre in the next Booke, the Muses to awake.

THE TWO AND TWENTIETH SONG

THE ARGUMENT

The Muse, Ouze from her Fountaine brings
Along by Buckingham, and sings:
The Earth that turneth wood to stone,
And t'holy Wells of Harlweston:
Then shewes wherefore the Fates doe grant,

That shee the Civill warres should chant:
By Huntingdon shee Waybridge meetes,
And thence the German Ocean greetes.

Invention as before, thy high-pitcht pinions rouze,
Exactly to set downe how the far-wandring Ouze,
Through the Bedfordian fields deliciously doth strain,
As holding on her course, by Huntingdon againe,
How bravely shee her selfe betwixt her Bankes doth beare,
E'r Ely shee in-Ile, a Goddesse honored there;
From Brackley breaking forth, through soiles most heavenly sweet,
By Buckingham makes on, and crossing Watling-Street,
Shee with her lesser Ouze, at Newport next doth twin,
Which from proud Chiltern neere, comes eas'ly ambling in.
The Brooke which on her banke doth boast that earth alone:
(Which noted) of this Ile, converteth wood to stone.
That little Aspleyes earth we anciently instile,
Mongst sundry other things, A wonder of the Ile:
Of which the lesser Ouze oft boasteth in her way,
As shee her selfe with Flowers doth gorgeously aray.
Ouze having Ouleney past, as shee were waxed mad,
From her first stayder course immediatly doth gad;
And in Meandred Gyres doth whirle herselfe about,
That, this way, here, and there, backe, forward, in, and out,
And like a wanton Girle, oft doubling in her gate,
In Labyrinth-like turnes, and twinings intricate,
Through those rich fields doth runne, till lastly in her pride,
The Shires Hospitious towne, shee in her course divide,
Where shee her spacious breast in glorious bredth displayes;
And varying her cleere forme a thousand sundry wayes,
Streakes through the verdant Meads; but farre she hath not gone,
When Ivell a cleare Nymph from Shefford sallying on,
Comes deftly dauncing in through many a daintie Slade,
Crown'd with a goodly Bridge, arriv'd at Bickleswade,
Encouraged the more her Mistris to pursue,
In whose cleere face the Sunne delights himselfe to view:
To mixe her selfe with Ouze, as on she thus doth make,
And lovingly at last hath hapt to overtake;
Shee in her Chrystall Armes her soveraigne Ouze doth cling,
Which Flood in her Allie, as highly glorying,
Shoots forward to Saint Neots, into those nether grounds,
Towards Huntingdon, and leaves the lov'd Bedfordian bounds.
Scarce is she entred yet upon this second Sheere,
Of which she soveraigne is, but that two Fountaines cleere,
At Harlweston neere hand, th'one salt, the other sweet,
At her first entrance, thus her greatnesse gently greet.
Once were we two faire Nymphs, who fortunatly prov'd,
The pleasures of the Woods, and faithfully belov'd

Of two such Sylvan gods, by hap that found us here;
For then their Sylvan kind most highly honoured were,
When this whole Countries face was Forresty, and we
Liv'd loosely in the Weilds, which now thus peopled be.
Oft interchang'd we sighs, oft amorous lookes we sent,
Oft whispering our deare loves, our thoughts oft did we vent
Amongst the secret shades, oft in the groves did play,
And in our sports our joyes, and sorrowes did bewray.
Oft cunningly we met, yet coyly then imbrac't,
Still languish'd in desire, yet liv'd we ever chast.
And quoth the saltish Spring, as one day mine and I,
Set to recount our loves, from his more tender eye
The brinish teares drop'd downe, on mine impearced breast,
And instantly therein so deeply were imprest,
That brackish I became: he finding me depriv'd
Of former freshnesse quite, the cause from him deriv'd,
On me bestow'd this gift, my sweetnesse to requite,
That I should ever cure the dimnesse of the sight.
And, quoth the fresher Spring, the Wood-god me that woo'd,
As one day by my brim, surpriz'd with love he stood,
On me bestow'd this gift, that ever after I
Should cure the painfull Itch, and lothsome Leprosie.
Held on with this discourse, shee on not farre hath runne,
But that shee is ariv'd at goodly Huntingdon;
Where shee no sooner viewes her darling and delight,
Proud Portholme, but became so ravish'd with the sight,
That shee her limber armes lasciviously doth throw
About the Islets waste, who b'ing imbraced so,
Her Flowry bosome shewes to the inamored Brooke;
On which when as the Ouze amazedly doth looke
On her brave Damask'd breast, bedeck'd with many a flowre
(That grace this goodly Mead) as though the Spring did powre
Her full aboundance downe, whose various dyes so thicke,
Are intermixt as they by one another sticke,
That to the gazing eye that standeth farre, they show
Like those made by the Sunne in the Celestiall Bow.
But now t'advaunce this Flood, the Fates had brought to passe,
As shee of all the rest the onely River was:
That but a little while before that fatall warre,
Twixt that divided Blood of Yorke and Lancaster,
Neere Harleswood, above in her Bedfordian trace,
By keeping backe her streame, for neere three furlongs space,
Laying her Bosome bare unto the publique view,
Apparantly was prov'd by that which did ensue,
In her Prophetique selfe, those troubles to foresee:
Wherefore (even as her due) the Destinies agree,
Shee should the glory have our civill fights to sing,
When swelling in her bankes, from her aboundant Spring,

Her sober silence shee now resolutely breakes,
In language fitting warre, and thus to purpose speakes.
With that most fatall field, I will not here begin,
Where Norman William first the Conqueror, did win
The day at Hastings, where the valiant Harold slaine,
Resign'd his Crowne, whose soyle the colour doth retaine,
Of th'English blood there shed, as th'earth still kept the skarre:
Which since not ours begot, but an invasive warre,
Amongst our home-fought fields, hath no discription here:
In Normandy nor that, that same day fortie yeare,
That Bastard William brought a Conquest on this Ile,
Twixt Robert his eld'st sonne, and Henry, who the while,
His Brothers warlike tents in Palestine were pight,
In England here usurp'd his eld'st borne brothers right;
Which since it forraine was, not strucke within this land,
Amongst our civill fights here numbred shall not stand.
But Lincolne Battell now we as our first will lay,
Where Maud the Empresse stood to trie the doubtfull day,
With Stephen, when he here had welneere three yeares raign'd,
Where both of them their right couragiously maintain'd,
And marshalling their Troups, the King his person put,
Into his well-arm'd Maine, of strong and valiant Foot:
The Wings that were his Horse, in th'one of them he plac'd
Young Alan that brave Duke of Britaine, whom he grac'd
With th'Earles of Norfolke, and Northampton, and with those,
He Mellent in that wing, and Warren did dispose.
The other no whit lesse, that this great day might sted;
The Earle of Aubemerle, and valiant Ipres led.
The Empresse powers again, but in two Squadrons were:
The Vaward Chester had, and Gloucester the Reare;
Then were there valiant Welsh, and desperate men of ours,
That when supplies should want, might reinforce their powers.
The Battels joyne, as when two adverse Seas are dasht
Against each others waves, that all the plaines were washt
With showers of sweltring blood, that downe the furrowes ran,
Ere it could be discern'd which either lost or wan.
Earle Baldwin, and Fitzurse those valiant Knights, were seene
To charge the Empresse Horse, as though dread Mars had beene
There in two sundry shapes; the day that beautious was,
Twinckled as when you see the Sunne-beames in a glasse,
That nimbly being stirr'd, flings up the trembling flame
At once, and on the earth reflects the very same.
With their resplendent swords, that glistred gainst the Sunne;
The honour of the day, at length the Empresse wonne.
King Stephen prisoner was, and with him many a Lord,
The common Souldiers put together to the sword.
The next, the Battell neere Saint Edmundsbury fought,
By our Fitz-Empresse force, and Flemings hither brought

By th'Earle of Leister, bent to move intestine strife,
For yong King Henries cause, crown'd in his fathers life;
Which to his kingly Syre much care and sorrow bred,
In whose defiance then that Earle his Ensignes spred,
Back'd by Hugh Bigots power, the Earle of Norfolke then,
By bringing to his ayd the valiant Norfolke men.
Gainst Bohun, Englands great high Constable that swayd
The Royall forces, joyn'd with Lucy for his ayd
Chiefe Justice, and with them the German powers, to expell
The Earles of Cornewall came, Gloster, and Arundell,
From Bury, that with them Saint Edmonds Banner bring,
Their Battels in aray; both wisely ordering
The Armies chanc'd to meet upon the Marshy ground,
Betwixt Saint Edmunds towne, and Fornham (fitly found)
The bellowing Drummes beat up a thunder for the charge,
The Trumpets rend the ayre, the Ensignes let at large,
Like waving flames farre off, to either hoste appeare:
The bristling Pykes doe shake, to threat their comming neere;
All clouded in a mist, they hardly could them view,
So shaddowed with the Shafts from either side that flew.
The Wings came wheeling in, at joyning of whose forces,
The either part were seene to tumble from their horses,
Which emptie put to rout, are paunch'd with Gleaves and Pyles,
Lest else by running loose, they might disranke their Fyles.
The Bilmen come to blowes, that with the cruell thwacks,
The ground lay strew'd with Male, and shreds of tatterd Jacks:
The playnes like to a shop, lookt each where to behold,
Where limbes of mangled men on heaps lay to be sold;
Sterne discontented Warre did never yet appeare
With a more threatning brow, then it that time did there.
O Leicester (alas) in ill time wast thou wonne
To ayd this gracelesse youth, the most ingratefull sonne
Against his naturall Syre, who crown'd him in his dayes,
Whose ill-requited love did him much sorrow raise,
As Le'ster by this warre against King Henry show'd,
Upon so bad a cause, O courage ill bestow'd;
Who had thy quarrell beene, as thou thy selfe was skild
In brave and martiall feats, thou evermore hadst fild
This Ile with thy high deeds, done in that bloody field:
But Bigot and this Lord, inforc'd at length to yeeld
Them to the other part, when on that fatall plaine,
Of th'English and the Dutch, ten thousand men lay slaine.
As for the second Fight at Lincolne, betwixt those
Who sided with the French, by seeking to depose
Henry the sonne of John, then young, and to advaunce
The Daulphin Lewes, sonne to Philip King of France,
Which Lincolne Castle, then most straightly did besiege;
And William Marshall Earle of Pembroke for his Liege,

(Who led the faithfull Lords) although so many there,
Or in the conflict slaine, or taken prisoners were;
Yet for but a surprize, no field appointed fight,
Mongst our set Battels here, may no way claime a right,
The Field at Lewes then, by our third Henry fought,
Who Edward his brave sonne unto that Conflict brought;
With Richard then the King of Almaine, and his sonne
Young Henry, with such Lords as to his part he wonne,
With him their Soveraigne Liege, their lives that durst engage.
And the rebellious league of the proud Barronage,
By Symon Mounford Earle of Le'ster their chiefe Head,
And th'Earle of Gloster, Clare, against King Henry led;
For th'ancient Freedomes here that bound their lives to stand,
The Aliens to expulse, who troubled all the land,
Whilst for this dreadfull day, their great designes were meant;
From Edward the young Prince, defiances were sent
To Mountfords valiant sonnes, Lord Henry, Sim, and Guy,
And calling unto him a Herauld, quoth he, Flie
To th'Earle of Leisters Tents, and publikely proclame
Defiance to his face, and to the Montfords name,
And say to his proud sonnes, say boldly thus from me;
That if they be the same, that they would seeme to be,
Now let them in the field be by their Band-roules knowne,
Where as I make no doubt, their valour shall be showne.
Which if they dare to doe, and still uphold their pride,
There will we vent our spleenes, where swords shall it decide.
To whom they thus replide, Tell that brave man of Hope,
He shall the Mountfords find in t'head of all their Troupe,
To answere his proud braves; our Bilbowes be as good
As his, our Armes as strong; and he shall find our blood
Sold at as deare a rate as his; and if we fall,
Tell him weele hold so fast, his Crowne shall goe withall.
The King into three fights his forces doth divide,
Of which his princely sonne the Vaward had to guide:
The second to the King of Almaine, and his sonne,
Young Henry he betooke, in the third Legion
Of Knights, and Men of Armes, in person he appeares.
Into foure severall Fights, the desperate Barons theirs.
I'th first those valiant youths, the sonnes of Leister came,
Of leading of the which, Lord Henry had the name:
The Earle of Gloster brought the second Battell on,
And with him were the Lords Mountchency, and Fitz-John:
The third wherein alone the Londoners were plac'd,
The stout Lord Segrave led; the greatest, and the last,
Brave Leicester himselfe, with courage undertooke.
The day upon the host affrightedly doth looke,
To see the dreadfull shocke, their first encounter gave,
As though it with the rore, the Thunder would out-brave.

Prince Edward all in gold, as he great Jove had beene:
The Mountfords all in Plumes, like Estriges were seene,
To beard him to his teeth, to th'worke of death they goe;
The crouds like to a Sea seemd waving to and fro.
Friend falling by his friend, together they expire:
He breath'd, doth charge afresh; he wounded, doth retyre.
The Mountfords with the Prince vye valour all the day,
Which should for Knightly deeds excell, or he, or they,
To them about his head, his glistring blade he throwes,
They waft him with their swords, as long with equall showes:
Now Henry, Simon then, and then the youngest Guy,
Kept by his brothers backe, thus stoutly doth reply,
What though I be but young, let death me overwhelme,
But I will breake my sword upon his plumed helme.
The younger Bohun there, to high atchievements bent,
With whom two other Lords, Lucy, and Hastings went,
Which charging but too home, all sorely wounded were,
Whom living from the field, the Barons strove to beare,
Being on their partie fixd; whilst still Prince Edward spurres;
To bring his Forces up to charge the Londoners,
T'whom cruell hate he bare, and joyning with their Force,
Of heavy-armed Foot, with his light Northerne Horse,
He putting them to flight, foure miles in chase them slew:
But ere he could returne, the conquest wholly drew
To the stout Barons side: his father fled the field,
Into the Abbay there, constrained thence to yeeld.
The Lords Fitz-warren slaine, and Wilton that was then
Chiefe Justice (as some say) with them five thousand men;
And Bohun that great Earle of Her'ford overthrowne,
With Bardolfe, Somery, Patshull, and Percie knowne.
By their Coat-armours then, for Barons, prisoners ta'n;
Though Henry ware the Crowne, great Le'ster yet did raigne.
Now for the Conflict next, at Chesterfield that chanc'd
Gainst Robert that proud Earle of Darby, who advanc'd
His Ensignes gainst the King, (contrary to his oath)
Upon the Barons part, with the Lord Devell, both
Surpriz'd by Henry Prince of Almain with his power,
By comming at so strange an unexpected hower:
And taking them unarmd; since meerely a defeat,
With our well-ordered fights, we will not here repeat.
The fatall Battell then at fertile Evsham struck,
Though with the selfe same hands, not with the selfe same luck:
For both the King and Prince at Lewes prisoners taken,
By fortune were not yet so utterly forsaken;
But that the Prince was got from Le'ster, and doth gather
His friends, by force of Armes yet to redeeme his father;
And th'Earle of Glo'ster wonne, who through the Mountfords pride
Disgrac'd, came with his power to the Emperiall side.

When now those Lords, which late at Lewes wonne the day,
The Sacrament receiv'd, their Armes not downe to lay,
Untill the King should yeeld th'old Charter to maintaine.
King Henry and his sonne Prince Edward swore againe,
They would repeale those Lawes that were at Oxford made,
Or through this bloody warre to their destruction wade.
But since the King remain'd in puissant Lei'sters power,
The remnant of his friends, whom death did not devoure
At Lewes Battell late, and durst his part partake.
The Prince excites againe, an Armie up to make,
Whom Roger Bigot, Earle of Norfolke doth assist,
Englands high Marshall then, and that great Martialist,
Old Henry Bohun, Earle of Her'ford, in this warre,
Gray, Basset, and Saint-John, Lisle, Percie, Latimer,
All Barons, which to him their utmost strengths doe lay,
With many a Knight for power their equall every way;
And William Valence, Earle of Pembroke, who had fled
From Lewes field, to France, thence with fresh succour sped.
Young Humphrey Bohun still, doth with great Le'ster goe,
Who for his Countries cause becomes his fathers foe.
Fitz-John, Gray, Spencer, Strange, Rosse, Segrave, Vessey, Gifford,
Wake, Lucy, Vipount, Vaux, Clare, Marmion, Hastings, Clifford.
In that blacke night before his sad and dismall day,
Were apparitions strange, as drad Heaven would bewray
The horrors to ensue, O most amazing sight!
Two Armies in the Ayre, discerned were to fight,
Which came so neere to earth, that in the morne they found
The prints of horses feet remaining on the ground,
Which came but as a show, the time to entertaine,
Till th'angry Armies joyn'd, to act the bloody Sceane.
Shrill shouts, and deadly cries, each way the ayre do fill,
And not a word was heard from either side, but kill:
The father gainst the sonne, the brother gainst the brother,
With Gleaves, Swords, Bills, and Pykes, were murthering one another.
The full luxurious earth, seemes surfitted with blood,
Whilst in his Unckles gore th'unnaturall Nephew stood;
Whilst with their charged Staves, the desperate horsmen meet,
They heare their kinsmen groane under their Horses feet.
Dead men, and weapons broke, doe on the earth abound;
The Drummes bedash'd with braines, doe give a dismall sound.
Great Le'ster there expir'd, with Henry his brave sonne,
When many a high exployt they in that day had done.
Scarce was there noble House, of which those times could tell,
But that some one thereof, on this, or that side fell;
Amongst the slaughtered men, that there lay heap'd on pyles:
Bohuns, and Beauchamps were, Basets, and Mandeviles:
Segraves, and Saint-Johns seeke, upon the end of all,
To give those of their names their Christian buriall.

Ten thousand on both sides were ta'n and slaine that day:
Prince Edward gets the gole, and beares the Palme away.
All Edward Long shankes time, her civill warres did cease,
Who strove his Countries bounds by Conquest to increase.
But in th'insuing raigne of his most riotous sonne,
As in his fathers dayes, a second warre begun;
When as the stubborne heires of the stout Barons dead,
Who for their Countries cause, their blood at Evsham shed,
Not able to endure the Spencers hatefull pride,
The father and the sonne, whose counsels then did guide
Th'inconsiderate King, conferring all his graces,
On them who got all gifts, and bought and sold all places,
Them raising, to debase the Baronage the more
For Gavaston, whom they had put to death before.
Which urg'd too farre, at length to open Armes they brake,
And for a speedy warre, they up their powers doe make.
Upon King Edwards part, for this great Action bent,
His brother Edmund came, the valiant Earle of Kent,
With Richmount, Arundell, and Pembroke, who engage,
Their powers, (three powerfull Earles) against the Baronage.
And on the Barons side, great master of the warre,
Was Thomas (of the Blood) the Earle of Lancaster,
With Henry Bohun, Earle of Hereford, his Peere,
With whom (of great command and Martialists) there were
Lyle, Darcy, Denvile, Teis, Beach, Bradburne, Bernvile, Knovile,
With Badlesmer, and Bercks, Fitz-william, Leyburne, Lovell,
Tuchet, and Talbot stout, doe for the Barons stand,
Mandute, and Mowbray, with great Clifford that command
Their Tenants to take Armes, that with their Landlords runne;
With these went also Hugh, and Henry Willington;
Redoubted Damory, as Audley, Elmesbridge, Wither,
Earles, Barons, Knights, Esquiers, embodied all together,
At Burton upon Trent who having gathered head,
Towards them with all his power the King in person sped;
Who at his neere approach (upon his March) discri'd,
That they against his power the Bridge had fortifi'd:
Which he by strong assault, assayes from them to win,
Where as a bloody fight doth instantly begin,
When he to beat them off, assayes them first by shot;
And they to make that good, which they before had got,
Defend them with the like, like Haylestones from the skie,
From Crosse-bowes, and the Long, the light-wingd arrowes flie:
But friended with the Flood, the Barons hold their strength,
Forcing the King by Boats, and pyles of wood at length,
T'attempt to land his force upon the other side.
The Barons, that the more his stratagems defide,
Withstand them in the streame, when as the troubled flood,
(With in a little time) was turned all to blood;

And from the Boats and Bridge, the mangled bodies feld,
The poore affrighted Fish, their watry walks expeld.
While at the Bridge the fight still strongly doth abide,
The King had learnt to know, that by a skilfull guide,
He by a Fourd not farre might passe his power of Horse,
Which quickly he performes, which drave the Barons force
From the defended Bridge, t'affront th'approching foe,
Imbattelling themselves, when to the shocke they goe,
(On both sides so assaild) till th'water, and the shore
Of one complexion were, distaind with equall gore.
Oft forc'd to change their fights, being driven from their ground,
That when by their much losse, too weake themselves they found,
Th'afflicted Barons flie, yet still together keepe.
The King his good successe, not suffring so to sleepe,
Pursues them with his power, which Northward still doe beare;
And seldome scapes a day, but he doth charge their Reare:
Till come to Burrough Bridge, where they too soone were staid
By Andrew Herckley, Earle of Carleill, with fresh ayd
Being lately thither come, King Edwards part to take.
The Barons range their fights, still good their ground to make;
But with long Marches tyerd, their wearied breath they draw,
After the desperat'st fight the Sunne yet ever saw,
Brave Bohun there was slaine, and Lancaster forsaken
Of Fortune, is surpriz'd; the Barons prisoners taken.
For those Rebellions, Stirres, Commotions, Uprores, here
In Richard Burdeaux raigne, that long so usuall were;
As that the first by Straw, and Tyler, with their Rout
Of Rebels brought from Kent, most insolent and stout,
By entring London, thought the Iland to subdue:
The first of which, the Maior of London bravely slew;
Walworth, which wonne his name much honour by the deed:
As they of Suffolke next, those Rascals that succeed,
By Litster led about, their Captaine who enstil'd
Himselfe the Commons King, in hope to have exil'd
The Gentry from those parts, by those that were his owne,
By that brave Bishop (then) of Norwitch overthrowne.
By such unruly Slaves, and that in Essex rais'd
By Thomas that stout Duke of Glo'ster, strongly ceaz'd,
As that at Radcot bridge, where the last named Peere,
With foure brave Earles his friends, encountred Robert Vere
Then Duke of Ireland cald, by Richard so created,
And gainst those Lords maintain'd, whom they most deadly hated;
Since they but Garboyles were, in a deformed masse,
Not ordered fitting warre, we lightly overpasse.
I chuse the Battell next of Shrewsbury to chant,
Betwixt Henry the fourth, the sonne of John of Gant,
And the stout Percies, Henry Hotspurre and his Eame
The Earle of Wor'ster, who the rightfull Diademe

Had from King Richard reft, and heav'd up to his Seat
This Henry, whom (too soone) they found to be too great,
Him seeking to depose, and to the Rule preferre
Richards proclaimed Heire, their cosen Mortimer,
Whom Owen Glendour then in Wales a prisoner staid,
Whom to their part they wonne, and thus their plot they laid,
That Glendour should have Wales, along as Severne went,
The Percies all the North, that lay beyond the Trent;
And Mortimer from thence the South to be his share;
Which Henry having heard, doth for the warre prepare,
And down to Cheshire makes, (where gathering powers they were)
At Shrewsbury to meet, and doth affront them there:
With him his peerelesse sonne, the princely Henry came,
With th'Earle of Stafford, and of Gentlemen of name,
Blunt, Shyrley, Clifton, men that very powerfull were,
With Cockayne, Calverly, Massy, and Mortimer,
Gausell, and Wendsley, all in Friends and Tenants strong,
Resorting to the King still as he past along;
Which in the open field before the ranged fights,
He with his warlike Sonne, there dub'd his Mayden Knights.
Th'Earle Dowglasse for this day doth with the Percies stand,
To whom they Berwicke gave, and in Northumberland
Some Seigniories and Holds, if they the Battell got,
Who brought with him to Field full many an angry Scot,
At Holmdon Battell late that being overthrowne,
Now on the King and Prince hop'd to regaine their owne;
With almost all the power of Cheshire got together,
By Venables, (there great) and Vernon mustred thether.
The Vaward of the King, great Stafford tooke to guide.
The Vaward of the Lords upon the other side,
Consisted most of Scots, which joyning, made such spoyle,
As at the first constrain'd the English to recoyle,
And almost brake their Rankes, which when King Henry found,
Bringing his Battell up, to reinforce the ground,
The Percies bring up theirs, againe to make it good.
Thus whilst the either Host in opposition stood,
Brave Dowglasse with his spurres, his furious Courser strake,
His Lance set in his rest, when desperatly he brake
In, where his eye beheld th'Emperiall Ensigne pight,
Where soone it was his chance, upon the King to light,
Which in his full carreere he from his Courser threw;
The next Sir Walter Blunt, he with three other slew,
All armed like the King, which he dead sure accounted;
But after when hee saw the King himselfe remounted:
This hand of mine, quoth he, foure Kings this day hath slaine,
And swore out of the earth he thought they sprang againe,
Or Fate did him defend, at whom he onely aym'd.
When Henry Hotspurre, so with his high deeds inflam'd,

Doth second him againe, and through such dangers presse,
That Dowglasse valiant deeds he made to seeme the lesse,
As still the people cryed, A Percy Espirance.
The King which saw then time, or never to advance
His Battell in the Field, which neere from him was wonne,
Ayded by that brave Prince, his most couragious sonne,
Who bravely comming on, in hope to give them chase,
It chanc'd he with a shaft was wounded in the face;
Whom when out of the fight, his friends would beare away,
He strongly it refus'd, and thus was heard to say,
Time never shall report, Prince Henry left the field,
When Harry Percy staid, his traytrous sword to weeld.
Now rage and equall wounds, alike inflame their bloods,
And the maine Battels joyne, as doe two adverse floods
Met in some narrow Arme, shouldring as they would shove
Each other from their path, or would their bankes remove.
The King his traytrous foes, before him downe doth hew,
And with his hands that day, neere fortie persons slue:
When conquest wholly turnes to his victorious side,
His power surrounding all, like to a furious tyde;
That Henry Hotspurre dead upon the cold earth lyes,
Stout Wor'ster taken was, and doughtie Douglasse flyes.
Five thousand from both parts left dead upon the ground,
Mongst whom the kings fast friend, great Staffords coarse was found;
And all the Knights there dub'd the morning but before,
The evenings Sunne beheld there sweltred in their gore.
Here I at Bramham More, the Battell in should bring,
Of which Earle Percie had the greatest managing,
With the Lord Bardolfe there, against the Counties power,
Fast cleaving to his friend, even to his utmost houre:
In Flanders, France, and Wales, who having been abroad
To raise them present powers, intending for a Road
On England, for the hate he to King Henry bore;
His sonne and brothers blood augmenting it the more,
Which in his mightie spirit still rooted did remaine,
By his too much default, whom he imputed slaine
At Shrewsbury before, to whom if he had brought
Supplies, (that bloody field, when they so bravely fought)
They surely it had wonne; for which to make amends,
Being furnished with men, amongst his forraine friends,
By Scotland entred here, and with a violent hand
Upon those Castles ceaz'd within Northumberland
His Earledome, (which the King, who much his truth did doubt,
Had taken to himselfe, and put his people out)
Toward Yorkshire comming on, where (soone repaid his owne)
At Bramhams fatall More, was fowly overthrowne:
Which though it were indeed a long and mortall fight,
Where many men were maim'd, and many slaine outright:

Where that couragious Earle, all hopes there seeing past,
Amongst his murthered troups (even) fought it to the last:
Yet for it was atchiev'd by multitudes of men,
Which with Ralfe Roksby rose, the Shreefe of Yorkshire then,
No well proportion'd fight, we of description quit,
Amongst our famous fields; nor will we here admit
That of that Rakehel Cades, and his rebellious crue,
In Kent and Sussex raisd, at Senok fight that slue
The Staffords with their power, that thither him pursu'd,
Who twice upon Black heath, back'd with the Commons rude,
Incamp'd against the King: then goodly London tooke,
There ransoming some rich, and up the prisons broke,
His sensuall beastly will, for Law that did preferre,
Beheaded the Lord Say, then Englands Treasurer,
And forc'd the King to flight, his person to secure,
The Muse admits not here, a rabble so impure.
But brings that Battell on of that long dreadfull warre,
Of those two Houses nam'd of Yorke and Lancaster,
In faire Saint Albans fought, most fatally betwixt
Richard then Duke of Yorke, and Henry cald the sixt,
For that ill-gotten Crowne, which him his Grandsire left,
That likewise with his life, he from King Richard reft,
When underhand the Duke doth but promoue his claime,
Who from the elder sonne, the Duke of Clarence came,
For which he raised Armes, yet seem'd but to abet
The people, to plucke downe the Earle of Somerset,
By whom (as they gave out) we Normandy had lost,
And yet he was the man that onely rul'd the roast.
With Richard Duke of Yorke, (into his faction wonne)
Salsbury and Warwicke came, the father and the sonne;
The Nevils nobler name, that have renown'd so farre.
So likewise with the King in this great action are,
The Dukes of Somerset, and Buckingham, with these
Were thrice so many Earles, their stout accomplices,
As Pembroke great in power, and Stafford with them stand
With Devonshire, Dorset, Wilt, and fierce Northumberland,
With Sidley, Bernes, and Rosse, three Barons with the rest,
When Richard Duke of Yorke, then marching from the west;
Towards whom, whilst with his power King Henry forward set,
Unluckily as't hapt, they at Saint Albans met;
Where taking up the Street, the buildings them enclose,
Where Front doth answer Front, & strength doth strength oppose;
Whilst like two mightie walls, they each to other stand,
And as one sinketh downe under his enemies hand,
Another thrusting in, his place doth still supply,
Betwixt them whilst on heaps the mangled bodies lie:
The Staules are overthrowne with the unweldy thrust,
The windowes with the shot, are shivered all to dust.

The Winters Sleet or Hayle was never seene so thicke,
As on the houses sides the bearded arrowes sticke,
Where Warwicks courage first most Comet-like appeard,
Who with words full of Spirit, his fighting Souldiers cheerd;
And ever as he saw the slaughter of his men,
He with fresh forces fil'd the places up agen.
The valiant Marchmen thus the battell still maintaine,
That when King Henry found on heaps his Souldiers slaine,
His great Commanders cals, who when they sadly saw,
The honour of the day would to the Yorkists draw,
Their persons they put in, as for the last to stand;
The Duke of Somerset, Henry Northumberland,
Of those brave warlike Earles, the second of that name,
The Earle of Stafford, sonne to th'Duke of Buckingham,
And John Lord Clifford then, which shed their noble gore
Under the Castles signe, (of which not long before,
A Prophet bad the Duke of Somerset beware)
With many a valiant Knight, in death that had his share:
So much great English blood, for others lawlesse guilt,
Upon so little ground before was never spilt.
Proud Yorke hath got the gole, the King of all forsaken,
Into a cottage got, a wofull prisoner taken.
The Battell of Blore-heath, the place doth next supply,
Twixt Richard Nevill, that great Earle of Salisbury,
Who with the Duke of Yorke, had at Saint Albans late,
That glorious Battell got with uncontrouled Fate:
And James Lord Audley stir'd by that revengefull Queene,
To stop him on his way, for the inveterate spleene
Shee bare him, for that still he with the Yorkists held,
Who comming from the North, (by sundry wrongs compeld
To parley with the King) the Queene that time who lay
In Staffordshire, and thought to stop him on his way,
That valiant Tuchet stir'd, in Cheshire powerfull then,
T'affront him in the field, where Cheshire Gentlemen
Divided were, th'one part made valiant Tuchet strong,
The other with the Earle rose as he came along,
Incamping both their powers, divided by a Brooke,
Whereby the prudent Earle, this strong advantage tooke:
For putting in the field his Army in aray,
Then making as (with speed) he meant to march away,
He caus'd a flight of Shafts to be discharged first.
The enemy who thought that he had done his worst,
And cowardly had fled in a disordred Rout,
Attempt to wade the Brooke, he wheeling (soone) about,
Set fiercely on that part, which then were passed over;
Their Friends then in the Reare, not able to recover
The other rising banke, to lend the Vaward ayd.
The Earle who found the plot take right that he had layd,

On those that forward prest, as those that did recoyle,
As hungry in revenge, there made a ravenous spoyle:
There Dutton, Dutton kils; A Done doth kill a Done;
A Booth, a Booth; and Leigh by Leigh is overthrowne;
A Venables, against a Venables doth stand;
And Troutbeck fighteth with a Troutbeck hand to hand;
There Molineux doth make a Molineux to die,
And Egerton, the strength of Egerton doth trie.
O Chesshire wert thou mad, of thine owne native gore
So much untill this day thou never shedst before!
Above two thousand men upon the earth were throwne,
Of which the greatest part were naturally thine owne.
The stout Lord Audley slaine, with many a Captaine there;
To Salsbury it sorts the Palme away to beare.
Then faire Northampton next, thy Battell place shall take,
Which of th'Emperiall warre, the third fought Field doth make,
Twixt Henry cald our sixt, upon whose partie came
His neere and deare Allies, the Dukes of Buckingham,
And Somerset, the Earle of Shrewsbury of account,
Stout Vicount Beaumount, and the yong Lord Egremount,
Gainst Edward Earle of March, sonne to the Duke of Yorke,
With Warwicke, in that warre, who set them all at worke,
And Falkonbridge with him, not much unlike the other;
A Nevill nobly borne, his puisant fathers brother,
Who to the Yorkists claime, had evermore been true,
And valiant Bourcher, Earle of Essex, and of Eau.
The King from out the towne, who drew his Foot and Horse,
As willingly to give full field-roomth to his Force,
Doth passe the River Nen, neere where it downe doth runne
From his first fountaines head, is neere to Harsington,
Advised of a place, by Nature strongly wrought,
Doth there encamp his power: the Earle of March who sought
To proove by dint of sword, who should obtaine the day,
From Tawcester traynd on his powers in good aray.
The Vaward Warwicke led, (whom no attempt could feare;
The Middle March himselfe, and Falkonbridge the Reare.
Now July entred was, and ere the restlesse Sunne,
Three houres ascent had got, the dreadfull fight begun
By Warwicke, who a straight from Vicount Beaumont tooke,
Defeating him at first, by which hee quickly brooke
In, on th'Emperiall host, which with a furious charge,
He forc'd upon the field, it selfe more to enlarge.
Now English Bowes, and Bills, and Battle-axes walke,
Death up and downe the field in gastly sort doth stalke.
March in the flower of Youth, like Mars himselfe doth beare;
But Warwicke as the man, whom Fortune seem'd to feare,
Did for him what he would, that wheresoere he goes,
Downe like a furious storme, before him all he throwes:

So Shrewsbury againe of Talbots valiant straine,
(That fatall Scourge of France) as stoutly doth maintaine,
The party of the King, so princely Somerset,
Whom th'others knightly deeds, more eagerly doth whet,
Beares up with them againe: by Somerset opposd
At last King Henries host being on three parts enclosd,
And ayds still comming in upon the Yorkists side,
The Summer being then at height of all her pride,
The Husbandman, then hard upon his Harvest was:
But yet the cocks of Hay, nor swaths of new-shorne grasse,
Strew'd not the Meads so thick, as mangled bodies there,
When nothing could be seene, but horror every where:
So that upon the bancks, and in the streame of Nen,
Ten thousand well resolv'd, stout, native English men
Left breathlesse, with the rest great Buckingham is slaine,
And Shrewsbury whose losse those times did much complaine,
Egremont, and Beaumont, both found dead upon the Field,
The miserable King, inforc'd againe to yeeld.
Then Wakefield Battell next, we in our Bedroule bring,
Fought by Prince Edward, sonne to that oft-conquered King,
And Richard Duke of Yorke, still strugling for the Crowne,
Whom Salsbury assists, the man with whose renowne,
The mouth of Fame seem'd fild, there having with them then
Some few selected Welsh, and Southerne Gentlemen:
A handfull to those powers, with which Prince Edward came;
Of which amongst the rest, the men of noblest name,
Were those two great-borne Dukes, which still his right preferre
His cosen Somerset, and princely Excester,
The Earle of Wiltshire still, that on his part stucke close:
With those two valiant Peeres, Lord Clifford, and Lord Rosse,
Who made their March from Yorke to Wakefield, on their way
To meet the Duke, who then at Sandall Castle lay,
Whom at his (very) gate, into the Field they dar'd,
Whose long expected powers not fully then prepar'd,
That March his valiant sonne, should to his succours bring.
Wherefore that puissant Lord, by speedy mustring
His Tenants and such friends, as he that time could get,
Five thousand in five dayes, in his Battalion set
Gainst their twice doubled strength; nor could the Duke be stayd,
Till he might from the South be seconded with ayd;
As in his martiall pride, disdaining his poore foes,
So often us'd to winne, he never thought to lose.
The Prince, which still provok'd th'incensed Duke to fight,
His maine Battalion rang'd in Sandals loftie sight,
In which he, and the Dukes, were seene in all their pride:
And as Yorkes powers should passe, he had on either side
Two wings in ambush laid, which at the place assign'd
His Rereward should inclose, which as a thing divin'd,

Just caught as he forecast; for scarse his armie comes
From the descending banks, and that his ratling Drummes
Excites his men to charge; but Wiltshire with his force,
Which were of light-arm'd Foot, and Rosse with his light Horse,
Came in upon their backes, as from a mountaine throwne,
In number to the Dukes, by being foure to one.
Even as a Rout of wolves, when they by chance have caught
A Beast out of the Heard, which long time they have sought;
Upon him all at once couragiously doe set,
Him by the Dewlaps some, some by the flanke doe get:
Some climbing to his eares, doe never leave their hold,
Till falling on the ground, they have him as they would,
With many of his kind, which, when he us'd to wend,
What with their hornes & hoofes, could then themselves defend.
Thus on their foes they fell, and downe the Yorkists fall;
Red Slaughter in her armes encompasseth them all.
The first of all the fights in this unnaturall warre,
In which blind Fortune smild on wofull Lancaster.
Heere Richard Duke of Yorke, downe beaten, breath'd his last,
And Salsbury so long with conquest still that past,
Inforced was to yeeld; Rutland a younger sonne
To the deceased Duke, as he away would runne,
(A child scarse twelve yeares old) by Clifford there surpriz'd,
Who whilst he thought with teares his rage to have suffiz'd,
By him was answered thus, Thy father hath slaine mine,
And for his blood (young Boy) Ile have this blood of thine,
And stab'd him to the heart: thus the Lancastrians raigne,
The Yorkist in the field on heaps together slaine.
The Battell at that Crosse, which to this day doth beare
The great and ancient name of th'English Mortimer,
The next shall heare have place, betwixt that Edward fought,
Entitled Earle of March, (revengefully that sought
To wreake his fathers blood, at Wakefield lately shed
But then he Duke of Yorke, his father being dead)
And Jasper Tudor Earle of Pembroke, in this warre,
That stood to underprop the House of Lancaster,
Halfe brother to the King, that strove to hold his Crowne,
With Wiltshire, whose high prowesse had bravely beaten downe
The Yorkists swelling pride in that successefull warre
At Wakefield, whose greatst power of Welsh and Irish are.
The Dukes were Marchers most, which still stucke to him close,
And meeting on the plaine, by that forenamed Crosse;
As either Generall there for his advantage found,
(For wisely they surveyd the fashion of the ground)
They into one maine fight their either Forces make,
When to the Duke of Yorke (his spirits as to awake)
Three sonnes at once appear'd, all severally that shone,
Which in a little space were joyned all in one.

Auspicious to the Duke, as after it fell out,
Who with the weaker power, (of which he seem'd to doubt)
The proud Lancastrian part had quickly put to chase,
Where plainly it should seeme, the Genius of the place,
The very name of March should greatly favour there,
A Title to this Prince deriv'd from Mortimer:
To whom this Trophy rear'd, much honored had the soyle.
The Yorkists here enrich'd with the Lancastrian spoyle,
Are Masters of the day; foure thousand being slaine,
The most of which were those, there standing to maintaine
The title of the King. Where Owen Tudors lot
Was to be taken then; who this young Earle begot
On Katherin the bright Queene, the fift King Henries Bride,
Who too untimely dead, this Owen had affide.
But he a Prisoner then, his sonne and Ormond fled,
At Hereford was made the shorter by the head;
When this most warlike Duke, in honour of that signe,
Which of his good successe so rightly did divine,
And thankfull to high heaven, which of his cause had care,
Three Sunnes for his device still in his Ensigne bare.
Thy second Battell now, Saint Albans I record,
Struck twixt Queene Margrets power, to ransome backe her Lord,
Ta'n prisoner at that towne, when there those factions fought,
Whom now the part of Yorke had thither with them brought,
Whose force consisted most of Southerne men, being led
By Thomas Howard Duke of Norfolke, and the head
Of that proud faction then, stout Warwicke still that swayd,
In every bloody field (the Yorkists onely ayd)
When eithers power approch'd, and they themselves had fixt,
Upon the South and North, the towne them both betwixt,
Which first of all to take, the Yorkists had forecast,
Putting their Vaward on, and their best Archers plac'd
The Market-sted about, and them so fitly layd,
That when the foe came up, they with such terror playd
Upon them in the Front, as forc'd them to retreit.
The Northerne mad with rage upon the first defeat,
Yet put for it againe, to enter from the North,
Which when great Warwicke heard, he sent his Vaward forth,
T'oppose them in what place so ere they made their stand,
Where in too fit a ground, a Heath too neere at hand,
Adjoyning to the towne, unluckily they light,
Where presenly began a fierce and deadly fight.
But those of Warwicks part, which scarce foure thousand were,
To th'Vaward of the Queenes, that stood so stoutly there,
Though still with fresh supplies from her maine Battell fed;
When they their courage saw so little them to sted,
Deluded by the long expectance of their ayd,
By passages too straight, and close ambushments stayd:

Their succours that forslow'd, to flight themselves betake,
When after them againe, such speed the Northerne make,
Being followed with the force of their maine Battell strong,
That this disordred Rout, these breathlesse men among,
They entred Warwicks Hoste, which with such horrour strooke
The Southerne, that each man began about to looke
A way how to escape, that when great Norfolke cri'd,
Now as you favour Yorke, and his just cause, abide.
And Warwicke in the Front even offred to have stood,
Yet neither of them both, should they have spent their blood,
Could make a man to stay, or looke upon a foe:
Where Fortune it should seeme, to Warwicke meant to show,
That shee this tide of his could turne, when ere she would.
Thus when they saw the day was for so little sould;
The King, which (for their ends) they to the field had brought,
Behind them there they leave, but as a thing of naught,
Which serv'd them to no use: who when his Queene and sonne,
There found in Norfolkes tent, the Battell being done,
With many a joyfull teare, each other they imbrace;
And whilst blind Fortune look'd with so well pleas'd a face:
Their swords with the warme blood of Yorkists so inbrude,
Their foes but lately fled, couragiously pursude.
Now followeth that blacke Sceane, borne up so wondrous hie,
That but a poore dumbe shew before a Tragedie,
The former Battels fought, have seem'd to this to be;
O Towton, let the blood Palme-Sunday spent on thee,
Affright the future times, when they the Muse shall heare,
Deliver it so to them; and let the ashes there
Of fortie thousand men, in that long quarrell slaine,
Arise out of the earth, as they would live againe,
To tell the manlike deeds, that bloody day were wrought
In that most fatall field, (with various fortunes fought)
Twixt Edward Duke of Yorke, then late proclaimed King,
Fourth of that royall name, and him accompanying,
The Nevills, (of that warre maintaining still the streame)
Great Warwicke, and with him his most couragious Eame,
Stout Falconbridge, the third, a firebrand like the other,
Of Salisbury surnam'd, that Warwicks bastard brother.
Lord Fitzwater, who still the Yorkists power assists,
Blount, Wenlock, Dinham, Knights approved Martialists.
And Henry the late King, to whom they still durst stand,
His true as powerfull friend, the great Northumberland,
With Westmerland, his claime who ever did preferre
His kinsman Somerset, his cosen Excester,
Dukes of the Royall line, his faithfull friends that were,
And little lesse then those, the Earle of Devonshire,
Th'Lord Dacres, and Lord Wels, both wise and warlike wights,
With him of great command, Nevill and Trolop, Knights.

Both armies then on foot, and on their way set forth,
King Edward from the South, King Henry from the North.
The later crowned King doth preparation make,
From Pomfret (where he lay) the passage first to take
O'r Aier at Ferybridge, and for that service sends
A most selected troupe of his well-chosen friends,
To make that passage good, when instantly began
The dire and ominous signes, the slaughter that foreran.
For valiant Clifford there, himselfe so bravely quit,
That comming to the Bridge (ere they could strengthen it)
From the Lancastrian power, with his light troupe of Horse,
And early in the morne defeating of their force,
The Lord Fitzwater slew, and that brave Bastard sonne
Of Salsbury, themselves who into danger runne:
For being in their beds, suspecting nought at all;
But hearing sudden noyse, suppos'd some broyle to fall
Mongst their misgovern'd troups, unarmed rushing out,
By Cliffords Souldiers soone incompassed about,
Were miserably slaine: which when great Warwicke heares,
As he had felt his heart transpersed through his eares,
To Edward mad with rage, imediatly he goes,
And with distracted eyes, in most sterne manner showes
The slaughter of those Lords; this day alone, quoth he,
Our utter ruine shall, or our sure rising be.
When soone before the Host, his glittering sword he drew,
And with relentlesse hands his springly Courser slew.
Then stand to me (quoth he) who meaneth not to flie;
This day shall Edward winne, or here shall Warwicke die.
Which words by Warwicke spoke, so deeply seem'd to sting
The much distempered breast of that couragious King,
That straight he made proclaim'd, that every fainting heart,
From his resolved host had licence to depart:
And those that would abide the hazard of the fight,
Rewards and titles due to their deserved right:
And that no man, that day, a prisoner there should take;
For this the upshot was, that all must marre or make.
A hundred thousand men in both the Armies stood,
That native English were: O worthy of your Blood
What conquest had there been? But Ensignes flie at large,
And trumpets every way sound to the dreadfull charge.
Upon the Yorkists part, there flew the irefull Beare:
On the Lancastrian side, the Cressant waving there.
The Southerne on this side, for Yorke a Warwicke crie,
A Percy for the right, the Northerne men reply.
The two maine Battels joyne, the foure large Wings doe meet;
What with the shouts of men, and noyse of horses feet,
Hell through the troubled earth, her horrour seem'd to breath;
A thunder heard above, an earth-quake felt beneath:

As when the Evening is with darknesse overspread,
Her Star-befreckled face with Clouds invelloped,
You oftentimes behold, the trembling lightning flie,
Which suddenly againe, but turning of your eye,
Is vanished away, or doth so swiftly glide,
That with a trice it touch t'Horizons either side;
So through the smoke of dust, from wayes, and fallowes raisd,
And breath of horse and men, that both together ceasd
The ayre one every part, sent by the glimmering Sunne,
The splendor of their Armes doth by reflection runne:
Till heapes of dying men, and those already dead,
Much hindred them would charge, and letted them that fled.
Beyond all wonted bounds, their rage so farre extends,
That sullen night begins, before their fury ends.
Ten howers this fight endur'd, whilst still with murthering hands,
Expecting the next morne, the weak'st unconquered stands;
Which was no sooner come, but both begin againe
To wrecke their friends deare blood, the former evening slaine.
New Battels are begun, new fights that newly wound,
Till the Lancastrian part, by their much lesning found
Their long expected hopes were utterly forlorne,
When lastly to the foe, their recreant backs they turne.
Thy Channell then, O Cock, was fild up with the dead,
Of the Lancastrian side, that from the Yorkists fled,
That those of Edwards part, that had the Reare in chase,
As though upon a Bridge, did on their bodies passe.
That Wharfe to whose large banks thou contribut'st thy store,
Had her more Christall face discoloured with the gore
Of fortie thousand men, that up the number made,
Northumberland the great, and Westmerland there layd
Their bodies: valiant Wels, and Dacres there doe leave
Their carkases, (whose hope too long) did them deceive.
Trolop and Nevill found massacred in the field,
The Earle of Wiltshire forc'd to the sterne foe to yeeld.
King Henry from fayre Yorke, upon this sad mischance
To Scotland fled, the Queene sayld over into France,
The Duke of Somerset, and Excester doe flie,
The rest upon the earth together breathlesse lie.
Muse, turne thee now to tell the Field at Hexam struck,
Upon the Yorkists part, with the most prosp'rous luck
Of any yet before, where to themselves they gain'd
Most safetie, yet their powers least damage there sustain'd,
Twixt John Lord Mountacute, that Nevill, who to stand
For Edward, gathered had out of Northumberland
A sort of valiant men, consisting most of Horse,
Which were againe suppli'd with a most puisant force,
Sent thither from the South, and by King Edward brought
In person downe to Yorke, to ayd if that in ought

His Generall should have need, for that he durst not trust
The Northerne, which so oft to him had been unjust:
Whilst he himselfe at Yorke, a second power doth hold,
To heare in this rough warre, what the Lancastrians would.
And Henry with his Queene, who to their powers had got,
The lively daring French, and the light hardy Scot,
To enter with them here, and to their part doe get,
Their faithfull lov'd Allie, the Duke of Somerset,
And Sir Ralfe Percie, then most powerfull in those parts,
Who had beene reconcil'd to Edward, but their hearts
Still with King Henry stay'd, to him and ever true,
To whom by this revolt, they many Northerne drew:
Sir William Taylboys, (cald of most) the Earle of Kime,
With Hungerford, and Rosse, and Mullins, of that time
Barons of high account, with Nevill, Tunstall, Gray,
Hussy, and Finderne, Knights, men bearing mighty sway.
As forward with his force, brave Mountacute was set,
It hap'd upon his way at Hegly More he met
With Hungerford, and Rosse, and Sir Ralph Percy, where,
In signe of good successe (as certainly it were)
They and their utmost force were quickly put to slight;
Yet Percy as he was a most couragious Knight,
Ne'r boudg'd till his last breath, but in the field was slaine.
Proud of this first defeat, then marching forth againe,
Towards Livells, a large Waste, which other plaines out-braves,
Whose Verge fresh Dowell still is watring with her waves,
Whereas his posting Scouts, King Henries power discri'd,
Tow'rds whom with speedy march, this valiant Generall hied,
Whose haste there likewise had such prosperous event,
That lucklesse Henry yet, had scarcely cleer'd his Tent,
His Captaines hardly set his Battels, nor enlarg'd
Their Squadrons on the field, but this great Nevill charg'd:
Long was this doubtfull fight on either side maintain'd,
That rising whilst this falls, this loosing whilst that gain'd:
The ground which this part got, and there as Conquerors stood,
The other quickly gaine, and firmely make it good,
To either as blind Chance, her favors will dispose;
So to this part it eb'd, and to that side it flowes.
At last, till whether 'twere that sad and horrid sight,
At Saxton that yet did their fainting spirits affright,
With doubt of second losse, and slaughter, or the ayd
That Mountacute receav'd; King Henries power dismayd:
And giving up the day, dishonourably fled,
Whom with so violent speed the Yorkists followed,
That had not Henry spur'd, and had a Courser swift,
Besides a skilfull guide, through woods and hilles to shift,
He sure had been surpriz'd, as they his Hench-men tooke,
With whom they found his Helme; with most disastrous lucke,

To save themselves by flight, ne'r more did any strive,
And yet so many men ne'r taken were alive.
Now Banbury we come thy Battell to report,
And show th'efficient cause, as in what wondrous sort
Great Warwicke was wrought in to the Lancastrian part,
When as that wanton King so vex'd his mightie heart:
Whilst in the Court of France, that Warriour he bestow'd,
(As potent here at home, as powerfull else abroad)
A marriage to intreat with Bona bright and sheene,
Of the Savoyan Blood, and sister to the Queene,
Which whilst this noble Earle negotiated there,
The widdow Lady Gray, the King espoused here.
By which the noble Earle in France who was disgrac'd,
(In England his revenge doth but too quickly hast)
T'excite the Northerne men doth secretly begin,
(With whom he powerfull was) to rile, that comming in,
He might put in his hand, (which onely he desir'd)
Which rising before Yorke were likely to have fierd
The Citie, but repuls'd, and Holdorn them that led,
Being taken, for the cause made shorter by the head.
Yet would not they disist, but to their Captaines drew
Henry the valiant sonne of John the Lord Fitz-Hugh,
With Coniers that brave Knight, whose valour they preferre,
With Henry Nevill, sonne to the Lord Latimer,
By whose Allies and friends, they every day grew strong,
And so in proud aray tow'rds London march along.
Which when King Edward saw the world began to side
With Warwicke, till himselfe he might of power provide,
To noble Pembroke sends, those Rebels to withstand.
Six thousand valiant Welsh, who mustring out of hand,
By Richard Harberts ayd, his brother them doth bring,
And for their greater strength (appointed by the King)
Th'Lord Stafford (of his house) of Powick named then,
Eight hundred Archers brought, the most selected men
The Marches could make out: these having Severne crost,
And up to Cotswould clome, they heard the Northern host,
Being at Northampton then, it selfe tow'rds Warwicke wayd,
When with a speedy march, the Harberts that forlayd
Their passage, charg'd their Reare with neere two thousand horse,
That the Lancastrian part suspecting all their force
Had followed them againe, their armie bring about,
Both with such speed and skill, that e're the Welsh got out,
By having charg'd too farre, some of their Vaward lost,
Beat to their armie backe; thus as these Legions coast,
On Danemore they are met, indifferent for this warre,
Whereas three easie hils that stand Trianguler,
Small Edgcoat overlooke; on that upon the West
The Welsh encampe themselves; the Northerne them possest

Of that upon the South, whilst, (by warres strange event)
Yong Nevill, who would brave the Harberts in their Tent,
Leading a troupe of Youth, (upon that fatall plaine)
Was taken by the Welsh, and miserably slaine;
Of whose untimely death, his friends the next day tooke
A terrible revenge, when Stafford there forsooke
The army of the Welsh, and with his Archers bad
Them fight that would for him; for that proud Pembroke had
Displac'd him of his Inne, in Banbury where he
His Paramore had lodg'd; where since he might not be,
He backward shapes his course, and leaves the Harberts there,
T'abide the brunt of all: with outcries every where
The clamorous Drummes & Fifes to the rough charge do sound,
Together horse and man come tumbling to the ground:
Then limbs like boughs were lop'd, from shoulders armes doe flie;
They fight as none could scape, yet scape as none could die.
The ruffling Northern Lads, and the stout Welshmen tri'd it;
Then Head-pieces hold out, or braines must sore abide it.
The Northern men Saint George for Lancaster doe crie:
A Pembroke for the King, the lustie Welsh replie;
When many a gallant youth doth desperatly assay,
To doe some thing that might be worthy of the day:
Where Richard Harbert beares into the Northern prease,
And with his Poleaxe makes his way with such successe,
That breaking through the Rankes, he their maine Battell past,
And quit it so againe, that many stood aghast,
That from the higher ground beheld him wade the crowd,
As often ye behold in tempests rough and proud,
O'rtaken with a storme, some Shell or little Crea,
Hard labouring for the land, on the high-working Sea,
Seemes now as swallowed up, then floating light and free
O'th top of some high wave; then thinke that you it see
Quite sunke beneath that waste of waters, yet doth cleere
The Maine, and safely gets some Creeke or Harbor neere:
So Harbert cleer'd their Host; but see th'event of warre,
Some Spialls on the hill discerned had from farre
Another Armie come to ayd the Northerne side,
When they which Claphams craft so quickly not espide,
Who with five hundred men about Northampton raisd,
All discontented spirits, with Edwards rule displeasd,
Displaying in the field great Warwicks dreaded Beare:
The Welsh who thought the Earle in person had been there,
Leading a greater power (disheartened) turne the backe
Before the Northerne host, that quickly goe to wracke.
Five thousand valiant Welsh are in chase o'rthrowne,
Which but an houre before had thought the day their owne.
Their Leaders (in the flight) the high-borne Harberts t'ane,
At Banbury must pay for Henry Nevill slaine.

Now Stamford in due course, the Muse doth come to tell,
Of thine owne named field, what in the fight befell,
Betwixt brave youthfull Wells, from Lincolnshire that led
Neere twentie thousand men, tow'rd London making head,
Against the Yorkists power, great Warwicke to abet,
Who with a puisant force prepared forth to set,
To joyne with him in Armes, and joyntly take their chance.
And Edward with his friends, who likewise doe advance
His forces, to refell that desperate daring foe;
Who for he durst himselfe in open Armes to show,
Nor at his dread command them downe againe would lay.
His father the Lord Wells, who he suppos'd might sway
His so outragious sonne, with his lov'd law-made brother,
Sir Thomas Dymock, thought too much to rule the other,
He strangely did to die, which so incens'd the spleene
Of this couragious youth, that he to wreake his teene
Upon the cruell King, doth every way excite
Him to an equall field, that com'n where they might smite
The Battell: on this plaine it chanc'd their Armies met:
They rang'd their severall fights, which once in order set,
The loudly-brawling Drummes, which seemed to have feard
The trembling ayre at first, soone after were not heard,
For out-cries, shreekes, and showts, whilst noyse doth noyse confound.
No accents touch the eare, but such as death doe sound:
In thirsting for revenge, whilst fury them doth guide:
As slaughter seemes by turnes to sease on either side.
The Southerne expert were, in all to warre belong,
And exercise their skill, the Marchmen stout and strong,
Which to the Battell sticke, and if they make retreat,
Yet comming on againe, the foe they backe doe beat,
And Wels for Warwicke crie, and for the rightfull Crowne;
The other call a Yorke, to beat the Rebels downe:
The worst that warre could doe, on either side she showes,
Or by the force of Bils, or by the strength of Bowes;
But still by fresh supplies, the Yorkists power encrease:
And Wels, who sees his troups so overborne with prease,
By hazarding too farre into the boystrous throng,
Incouraging his men the adverse troupes among,
With many a mortall wound, his wearied breath expir'd:
Which sooner knowne to his, then his first hopes desir'd,
Ten thousand on the earth before them lying slaine,
No hope left to repaire their ruin'd state againe,
Cast off their Countries coats, to hast their speed away,
(Of them) which Loose-coat field is cald (even) to this day.
Since needsly I must sticke upon my former text,
The bloody Battell fought, at Barnet followeth next,
Twixt Edward, who before he setled was to raigne,
By Warwicke hence expuls'd; but here ariv'd againe,

From Burgundy, brought in munition, men and pay,
And all things fit for warre, expecting yet a day.
Whose brother George came in, with Warwicke that had stood,
Whom nature wrought at length t'adhere to his owne blood:
His brother Richard Duke of Gloster, and his friend;
Lord Hastings, who to him their utmost powers extend;
And Warwick, whose great heart so mortall hatred bore
To Edward, that by all the Sacraments he swore,
Not to lay downe his Armes, untill his sword had rac'd,
That proud King from his Seat, that so had him disgrac'd:
And Marquesse Mountacute, his brother, that brave stem
Of Nevils noble Stock, who joyned had to them,
The Dukes of Somerset, and Excester, and take
The Earle of Oxford in; the Armies forward make,
And meeting on the plaine, to Barnet very neere,
That to this very day, is called Gladmore there.
Duke Richard to the field, doth Edwards Vaward bring;
And in the middle came that most couragious King,
With Clarence his reclaim'd, and brother then most deare;
His friend Lord Hastings had the guiding of the Reare,
(A man of whom the King most highly did repute.)
On puisant Warwicks part, the Marquesse Mountacute
His brother, and his friend the Earle of Oxford led
The right wing; and the left which most that day might sted,
The Duke of Excester; and he himselfe doe guide
The middle fight (which was the Armies onely pride)
Of Archers most approv'd, the best that he could get,
Directed by his friend, the Duke of Somerset.
O Sabboth ill bestow'd, O drery Easter day,
In which (as some suppose) the Sunne doth use to play,
In honour of that God for sinfull man that dy'd,
And rose on that third day, that Sunne which now doth hide
His face in foggy mists; nor was that morning seene,
So that the space of ground those angry hosts betweene,
Was overshadowed quite with darknesse, which so cast
The armies on both sides, that they each other past,
Before they could perceive advantage, where to fight;
Besides the envious mist so much deceiv'd their sight,
That where eight hundred men, which valiant Oxford brought,
Ware Comets on their coats: great Warwicks force which thought
They had King Edwards beene, which so with Sunnes were drest,
First made their shot at them, who by their friends distrest,
Constrayned were to flie, being scattered here and there.
But when this direfull day at last began to cleere,
King Edward then beholds that height of his first hopes,
Whose presence gave fresh life to his oft-fainting troupes,
Prepar'd to scourge his pride, there daring to defie
His mercie, to the host proclaiming publikely

His hatefull breach of faith, his perjury, and shame,
And what might make him vile; so Warwicke heard that name
Of Yorke, which in the field he had so oft advanc'd,
And to that glorious height, and greatnesse had inhanc'd,
Then cried against his power, by those which oft had fled,
Their swist pursuing foe, by him not bravely led,
Upon the enemies backe, their swords bath'd in the gore
Of those from whom they ran, like heartlesse men before,
Which Warwicks nobler name injuriously defide,
Even as the irefull host then joyned side to side.
Where cruell Richard charg'd the Earles maine battell, when
Proud Somerset therein, with his approoved men
Stood stoutly to the shocke, and flang out such a flight
Of shafts, as welneere seem'd t'eclipse the welcom'd light,
Which forc'd them to fall off, on whose retreit againe,
That great Battalion next approcheth the fayre plaine,
Wherein the King himselfe in person was to trie,
Proud Warwicks utmost strength: when Warwicke by and by,
With his left wing came up, and charg'd so home and round,
That had not his light horse by disvantagious ground
Been hindred, he had strucke the heart of Edwards host:
But finding his defeat, his enterprise so lost,
He his swift Currers sends, to will his valiant brother,
And Oxford, in command being equall to the other,
To charge with the right wing, who bravely up doe beare;
But Hastings that before raught thither with his Reare,
And with King Edward joynd, the host too strongly arm'd.
When every part with spoyle, with rape, with fury charm'd,
Are prodigall of blood, that slaughter seemes to swill
It selfe in humane gore, and every one cries kill.
So doubtfull and so long the battell doth abide,
That those, which to and fro, twixt that and London ride,
That Warwicke winnes the day for certaine newes doe bring,
Those following them againe, sayd certainly the King,
Untill great Warwicke found his armie had the worse,
And sore began to faint, alighting from his horse,
In with the formost puts, and wades into the throng;
And where he saw death stern'st, the murthered troupes among,
He ventures, as the Sunne in a tempestuous day,
With darknesse threatned long, yet sometimes doth display
His cheerefull beames, which scarce appeare to the cleere eye,
But suddenly the clouds, which on the winds doe flie,
Doe muffle him againe within them, till at length,
The storme (prevailing still with an unusuall strength)
His cleerenesse quite doth close, and shut him up in night:
So mightie Warwicke fares in this outragious fight.
The cruell Lyons thus inclose the dreaded Beare,
Whilst Montacute, who strives (if any helpe there were)

To rescue his belov'd and valiant brother, fell:
The losse of two such spirits at once, time shall not tell;
The Duke of Somerset, and th'Earle of Oxford fled,
And Excester being left for one amongst the dead,
At length recovering life, by night escap'd away,
Yorke never safely sat, till this victorious day.
Thus Fortune to his end this mightie Warwicke brings
This puisant setter up, and plucker downe of Kings.
He who those battels wonne, which so much blood had cost,
At Barnets fatall fight, both Life and Fortune lost.
Now Tewksbury it rests, thy storry to relate,
Thy sad and dreadfull fight, and that most direfull Fate
Of the Lancastrian Line, which hapned on that day,
Fourth of that fatall Month, that still-remembred May:
Twixt Edmund that brave Duke of Somerset, who fled
From Barnets bloody field, (againe there gathering head)
And Marquesse Dorset bound in blood to ayd him there,
With Thomas Courtney Earle of powerfull Devonshire:
With whom King Henries sonne, young Edward there was seene,
To claime his doubtlesse right, with that undaunted Queene
His mother, who from France with succours came on land
That day, when Warwicke fell at Barnet, which now stand,
Their fortune yet to trie, upon a second fight.
And Edward who imploy'd the utmost of his might,
The poore Lancastrian part (which he doth eas'ly feele,
By Warwicks mightie fall, already faintly reele)
By Battell to subvert, and to extirpe the Line;
And for the present act, his army doth assigne
To those at Barnet field so luckily that sped;
As Richard late did there, he here the Vaward led,
The Maine the King himselfe, and Clarence tooke to guide;
The Rearward as before by Hastings was supplide.
The Army of the Queene, into three Battels cast,
The first of which the Duke of Somerset, and (fast
To him) his brother John doe happily dispose;
The second, which the Prince for his owne safety chose
The Barons of Saint John, and Wenlocke; and the third,
To Courtney that brave Earle of Devonshire referd.
Where in a spacious field they set their Armies downe;
Behind, hard at their backes, the Abbey, and the Towne,
To whom their foe must come, by often banks and steepe,
Through quickset narrow Lanes, cut out with ditches deepe,
Repulsing Edwards power, constraining him to proove
By thundring Cannon shot, and Culvering to remoove
Them from that chosen ground, so tedious to assayle;
And with the shot came shafts, like stormy showres of Hayle:
The like they sent againe, which beat the other sore,
Who with the Ordnance strove the Yorkists to outrore,

And still make good their ground, that whilst the Peeces play,
The Yorkists hasting still to hand-blowes, doe assay,
In strong and boystrous crowds to scale the combrous Dykes;
But beaten downe with Bills, with Poleaxes, and Pykes,
Are forced to fall off; when Richard there that led
The Vaward, saw their strength so little them to sted,
As he a Captaine was, both politique and good,
The stratagems of warre, that rightly understood,
Doth seeme as from the field his forces to withdraw.
His sudden, strange retire, proud Somerset that saw,
(A man of haughtie spirit, in honour most precise;
In action yet farre more adventurous then wise)
Supposing from the field for safetie he had fled,
Straight giveth him the chase; when Richard turning head,
By his incounter let the desperate Duke to know,
Twas done to traine him out, when soone began the show
Of slaughter every where; for scarce their equall forces
Began the doubtfull fight, but that three hundred horses,
That out of sight this while on Edwards part had stayd,
To see, that neere at hand no ambushes were layd,
Soone charg'd them on the side, disordring quite their Ranks,
Whilst this most warlike King had wonne the climing Banks,
Upon the equall earth, and comming bravely in
Upon the adverse power, there likewise doth begin
A fierce and deadly fight, that the Lancastrian side,
The first and furious shocke not able to abide
The utmost of their strength, were forced to bestow,
To hold what they had got; that Somerset below,
Who from the second force, had still expected ayd,
But frustrated thereof, even as a man dismaid,
Scarce shifts to save himselfe his Battell overthrowne;
But faring as a man that frantique had beene growne,
With Wenlock hap'd to meet (preparing for his flight)
Upbraiding him with tearmes of basenesse and despight,
That cow'rdly he had faild to succour him with men:
Whilst Wenlock with like words requiteth him agen,
The Duke (to his sterne rage, as yeelding up the raines)
With his too pondrous Axe pasht out the Barons braines.
The partie of the Queene in every place are kild,
The Ditches with the dead, confusedly are fild,
And many in the flight, i'th neighbouring Rivers drown'd,
Which with victorious wreaths, the conquering Yorkists crownd.
Three thousand of those men, on Henries part that stood,
For their presumption paid the forfeit of their blood.
John Marquesse Dorset dead, and Devonshire that day
Drew his last vitall breath, as in that bloody fray,
Delues, Hamden, Whittingham, and Leuknor, who had there,
Their severall brave commands, all valiant men that were,

Found dead upon the earth. Now all is Edwards owne,
And through his enemies tents he march'd into the towne,
Where quickly he proclaimes, to him that foorth could bring
Young Edward, a large Fee, and as he was a King,
His person to be safe. Sir Richard Crofts who thought
His prisoner to disclose, before the King then brought
That faire and goodly Youth; whom when proud Yorke demands,
Why thus he had presum'd by helpe of traytrous hands
His kingdome to disturbe, and impiously display'd
His Ensignes: the stout Prince, as not a jot dismay'd,
With confidence replies, To claime his ancient right,
Him from his Grandsires left; by tyranny and might,
By him his foe usurp'd: with whose so bold reply,
Whilst Edward throughly vext, doth seeme to thrust him by;
His second brother George, and Richard neere that stood,
With many a cruell stab let out his princely blood;
In whom the Line direct of Lancaster doth cease,
And Somerset himselfe surprized in the prease;
With many a worthy man, to Gloster prisoners led,
There forfeited their lives: Queene Margaret being fled
To a religious Cell, (to Tewksbury, too neere)
Discoverd to the King, with sad and heavy cheere,
A prisoner was convey'd to London, wofull Queene,
The last of all her hopes, that buried now had seene.
But of that outrage here, by that bold Bastard sonne
Of Thomas Nevill, nam'd Lord Falkonbridge, which wonne
A rude rebellious Rout in Kent and Essex rais'd,
Who London here besieg'd, and Southwarke having seas'd,
Set fire upon the Bridge: but when he not prevaild,
The Suburbs on the East he furiously assayl'd;
But by the Cities power was lastly put to flight:
Which being no set Field, nor yet well ordred fight,
Amongst our Battels here, may no way reckoned be.
Then Bosworth here the Muse now lastly bids for thee,
Thy Battell to describe, the last of that long warre,.
Entit'led by the name of Yorke and Lancaster;
Twixt Henry Tudor Earle of Richmond onely left
Of the Lancastian Line, who by the Yorkists reft
Of libertie at home, a banish'd man abroad,
In Britany had liv'd; but late at Milford Road,
Being prosperously ariv'd, though scarce two thousand strong,
Made out his way through Wales, where as he came along.
First Griffith great in Blood, then Morgan next doth meet
Him, with their severall powers, as offring at his feet
To lay their Lands, and lives; Sir Rice ap Thomas then,
With his brave Band of Welsh, most choyce and expert men,
Comes lastly to his ayd; at Shrewsbury ariv'd,
(His hopes so faint before, so happily reviv'd)

He on for England makes, and neere to Newport towne,
The next ensuing night setting his Army downe,
Sir Gilbert Talbot still for Lancaster that stood,
(To Henry neere Alli'd in friendship as in Blood)
From th'Earle of Shrewsbury his Nephew (under age)
Came with two thousand men, in warlike Equipage,
Which much his power increas'd; when easily setting on,
From Lichfield, as the way leads foorth to Atherston,
Brave Bourcher and his friend stout Hungerford, whose hopes
On Henry long had laine, stealing from Richards troups,
(Wherewith they had been mix'd) to Henry doe appeare,
Which with a high resolve, most strangely seem'd to cheere,
His oft-appauled heart, but yet the man which most,
Gave sayle to Henries selfe, and fresh life to his host,
The stout Lord Stanley was, who for he had affide
The mother of the Earle, to him so neere allide:
The King who fear'd his truth, (which he to have, compeld)
The yong Lord Strange his sonne, in hostage strongly held,
Which forc'd him to fall off, till he fit place could finde,
His sonne in law to meet; yet he with him combinde
Sir William Stanley, knowne to be a valiant Knight,
T'assure him of his ayd. Thus growing tow'rds his hight,
A most selected Band of Chesshire Bow-men came,
By Sir John Savage led, besides two men of name:
Sir Brian Sanford, and Sir Simon Digby, who
Leaving the tyrant King, themselves expresly show
Fast friends to Henries part, which still his power increast:
Both Armies well prepar'd, towards Bosworth strongly preast,
And on a spacious Moore, lying Southward from the towne;
Indifferent to them both, they set their Armies downe
Their Souldiers to refresh, preparing for the fight:
Where to the guiltie King, that black fore-running night,
Appeare the dreadfull ghosts of Henry and his sonne,
Of his owne brother George, and his two nephewes done
Most cruelly to death; and of his wife and friend,
Lord Hastings, with pale hands prepar'd as they would rend
Him peece-meale; at which oft he roreth in his sleepe.
No sooner gan the dawne out of the East to peepe,
But Drummes and Trumpets chide, the Souldiers to their Armes,
And all the neighboring fields are covered with the swarmes
Of those that came to fight, as those that came to see,
(Contending for a Crowne) whose that great day should be.
First, Richmond rang'd his fights, on Oxford, and bestowes
The leading, with a Band of strong and Sinewy Bowes
Out of the Army pick'd; the Front of all the field,
Sir Gilbert Talbot next, he wisely tooke to weeld,
The right Wing, with his strengths, most Northern men that were.
And Sir John Savage, with the power of Lancashire,

And Chesshire (Chiefe of men) was for the left Wing plac'd:
The Middle Battell he in his faire person grac'd,
With him the noble Earle of Pembroke, who commands
Their Countrey-men the Welsh, (of whom it mainly stands,
For their great numbers found to be of greatest force)
Which but his guard of Gleaves, consisted all of Horse.
Into two severall fights the King contriv'd his strength,
And his first Battell cast into a wondrous length,
In fashion of a wedge, in poynt of which he set
His Archery, thereof and to the guidance let
Of John the noble Duke of Norfolke, and his sonne
Brave Surrey: he himselfe the second bringing on,
Which was a perfect square; and on the other side,
His Horsemen had for wings, which by extending wide,
The adverse seem'd to threat, with an unequall power.
The utmost poynt ariv'd of this expected hower,
He to Lord Stanley sends, to bring away his ayd;
And threats him by an Oath, if longer he delayd
His eldest sonne young Strange imediatly should die,
To whom stout Stanley thus doth carelessely reply:
Tell thou the King Ile come, when I fit time shall see,
I love the Boy, but yet I have more sonnes then he.
The angry Armies meet, when the thin ayre was rent,
With such re-ecchoing shouts, from eithers Souldiers sent,
That flying o'r the field the Birds downe trembling dropt.
As some old building long that hath been underpropt,
When as the Timber fayles, by the unweldy fall,
Even into powder beats, the Roofe, and rotten wall,
And with confused clouds of smouldring dust doth choke
The streets and places neere; so through the mistie smoke,
By Shot and Ordnance made, a thundring noyse was heard.
When Stanley that this while his succours had deferd,
Both to the cruell King, and to the Earle his sonne,
When once he doth perceive the Battell was begun,
Brings on his valiant Troups, three thousand fully strong,
Which like a cloud farre off, that tempest threatned long,
Falls on the Tyrants host, which him with terrour strooke,
As also when he sees, he doth but vainly looke
For succours from the great Northumberland, this while,
That from the Battell scarce three quarters of a mile,
Stood with his power of Horse, nor once was seene to stirre:
When Richard (that th'event no longer would deferre,
The two maine Battels mix'd, and that with wearied breath,
Some laboured to their life, some laboured to their death,
(There for the better fought) even with a Spirit elate,
As one that inly scorn'd the very worst that Fate
Could possibly impose, his Launce set in his Rest,
Into the thick'st of Death, through threatning perill prest,

To where he had perceiv'd the Earle in person drew,
Whose Standard-Bearer he, Sir William Brandon slew,
The pile of his strong staffe into his arme-pit sent;
When at a second shocke, downe Sir John Cheney went,
Which scarce a Launces length before the Earle was plac'd,
Untill by Richmonds Guard, invironed at last,
With many a cruell wound, was through the body gride.
Upon this fatall field, John Duke of Norfolke dide;
The stout Lord Ferrers fell, and Ratcliffe, that had long
Of Richards counsels been, found in the field among
A thousand Souldiers that on both sides were slaine,
O Red-more, it then seem'd, thy name was not in vaine,
When with a thousands blood the earth was coloured red.
Whereas th'Emperiall Crowne was set on Henries head,
Being found in Richards Tent, as he it there did winne;
The cruell Tyrant stript to the bare naked skin,
Behind a Herauld truss'd, was backe to Le'ster sent,
From whence the day before he to the Battell went.
The Battell then at Stoke, so fortunatly strucke,
(Upon King Henries part, with so successefull lucke,
As never till that day he felt his Crowne to cleave
Unto his temples close, when Mars began to leave
His fury, and at last to sit him downe was brought)
I come at last to sing, twixt that seventh Henry fought;
With whom, to this brave Field the Duke of Bedford came,
With Oxford his great friend, whose praise did him inflame
To all Atchievements great, that fortunate had bin
In every doubtfull fight, since Henries comming in,
With th'Earle of Shresbury, a man of great command,
And his brave sonne Lord George, for him that firmly stand.
And on the other side, John Duke of Suffolks sonne,
(John Earle of Lincolne cald) who this sterne warre begun,
Subborning a lewd Boy, a false Imposter, who
By Simonds a worse Priest, instructed what to doe;
Upon him tooke the name of th'Earle of Warwicke, heire
To George the murthered Duke of Clarence, who (for feare
Lest some that favoured Yorke, might under hand maintaine)
King Henry in the Tower, did at that time detaine.
Which practise set on foot, this Earle of Lincolne sayld
To Burgundy, where he with Margaret prevayld,
Wife to that warlike Charles, and his most loved Aunt,
Who vexed that a proud Lancastrian should supplant
The lawfull Line of Yorke, whence she her blood deriv'd;
Wherefore for Lincolnes sake shee speedily contriv'd,
And Lovell, that brave Lord, before him sent to land
Upon the same pretence, to furnish them a Band
Of Almanes, and to them for their stout Captaine gave
The valiant Martin Swart, the man thought scarce to have

His match for Martiall feats, and sent them with a Fleet
For Ireland, where shee had appoynted them to meet,
With Simonds that lewd Clerke, and Lambert, whom they there
The Earle of Warwicke cald, and publish'd every where
His title to the Crowne, in Divelin, and proclaime
Him Englands lawfull King, by the fift Edwards name:
Then joyning with the Lord Fitz-Gerald, to their ayd
Who many Irish brought, they up their Ankres wayd,
And at the rocky Pyle of Fowdray put to shore
In Lancashire; their power increasing more and more,
By Souldiers sent them in from Broughton (for supply)
A Knight that long had been of their confederacy;
Who making thence, direct their marches to the South.
When Henry saw himselfe so farre in dangers mouth,
From Coventry he came, still gathering up his Host,
Made greater on his way, and doth the Countrey coast,
Which way he understood his enemies must passe:
When after some few dayes (as if their Fortunes was)
At Stoke, a village neere to Newarke upon Trent,
Each in the others sight pitcht downe their warlike Tent.
Into one Battell soone, the Almans had disposd
Their Army, in a place upon two parts inclosd
With Dells, and fenced Dykes, (as they were expert men.)
And from the open fields King Henries Host agen,
In three faire severall fights came equally devided;
The first of which, and fitst, was given to be guided
By Shrewsbury, which most of Souldiers choice consisted:
The others plac'd as Wings, which ever as they listed,
Came up as need requir'd, or fell backe as they found
Just cause for their retire; when soone the troubled ground,
On her black bosome felt the thunder, which awooke
Her Genius, with the shock that violently shooke
Her intrayles; this sad day when there ye might have seene
Two thousand Almains stand, of which each might have beene
A Leader for his skill, which when the charge was hot,
That they could hardly see the very Sunne for shot,
Yet they that motion kept that perfect Souldiers should;
That most couragious Swart there might they well behold,
With most unusuall skill, that desperate fight maintaine,
And valiant De la Poole, most like his princely straine,
Did all that courage could, or noblesse might befit;
And Lovell that brave Lord, behind him not a whit,
For martiall deeds that day: stout Broughton that had stood
With Yorke (even) from the first, there lastly gave his blood
To that well-foughten Field: the poore Trowz'd Irish there,
Whose Mantles stood for Mayle, whose skinns for Corslets were,
And for their weapons had but Irish Skaines and Darts,
Like men that scorned death, with most resolved hearts,

Give not an inch of ground, but all in pieces hewen,
Where first they fought, they fell; with them was overthrowne
The Leader Geralds hope, amidst his men that fought,
And tooke such part as they, whom he had thither brought.
This of that field be told, There was not one that fled,
But where he first was plac'd, there found alive or dead.
If in a foughten field, a man his life should loose,
To dye as these men did, who would not gladly choose,
Which full foure thousand were. But in this tedious Song,
The too laborious Muse hath taried all too long.
As for the Black-Smiths Rout, who did together rise,
Encamping on Blackheath, t'annull the Subsidies
By Parliment then given, or that of Cornwall call'd,
Inclosures to cast downe, which overmuch enthrald
The Subject: or proud Kets, who with the same pretence
In Norfolke rais'd such stirres, as but with great expence
Of blood was not appeas'd; or that begun in Lent
By Wyat and his friends, the Mariage to prevent,
That Mary did intend with Philip King of Spaine:
Since these but Ryots were, nor fit the others straine,
Shee here her Battels ends: and as Shee did before,
So travelling along upon her silent shore,
Waybridge a neighbouring Nymph, the onely remnant left
Of all that Forrest kind, by Times injurious theft
Of all that tract destroy'd, with wood which did abound,
And former times had seene the goodliest Forrest ground,
This Iland ever had: but she so left alone,
The ruine of her kind, and no man to bemoane.
The deepe intranced Flood, as thinking to awake,
Thus from her shady Bower shee silently bespake.
O Flood in happy plight, which to this time, remainst,
As still along in state to Neptunes Court thou strainst;
Revive thee with the thought of those forepassed howers,
When the rough Wood-gods kept, in their delightfull Bowers
On thy embroydered bankes, when now this Country fild,
With villages, and by the labouring plowman tild,
Was Forrest, where the Firre, and spreading Poplar grew.
O let me yet the thought of those past times renew,
When as that woody kind, in our umbragious Wyld,
Whence every living thing save onely they exild,
In this their world of wast, the soveraigne Empire swayd.
O who would ere have thought, that time could have decayd
Those trees whose bodies seem'd by their so massie weight,
To presse the solid earth, and with their wondrous height
To climbe into the Clouds, their Armes so farre to shoot,
As they in measuring were of Acres, and their Root,
With long and mightie spurnes to grapple with the land,
As Nature would have sayd, that they should ever stand:

So that this place where now this Huntingdon is set,
Being an easie hill where mirthfull Hunters met,
From that first tooke the name. By this the Muse arives
At Elies Iled Marge, by having past Saint Ives,
Unto the German Sea shee hasteth her along,
And here shee shutteth up her two and twentieth Song,
In which shee quite hath spent her vigor, and must now,
As Workmen often use, a while sit downe and blow;
And after this short pause, though lesning of her height,
Come in another Key, yet not without delight.

THE THREE AND TWENTIETH SONG

THE ARGUMENT

From furious Fights Invention comes,
Deafned with noyse of ratling Drummes,
And in the Northamptonian bounds,
Shews Whittlewoods, and Sacies grounds;
Then to Mount Hellidon doth goe,
(Whence Charwell, Leame, and Nen doe flow)
The Surface, which of England sings,
And Nen downe to the Washes brings;
Then whereas Welland makes her way,
Shewes Rockingham, her rich aray:
A Course at Kelmarsh then shee takes,
Where shee Northamptonshire forsakes.

On tow'ds the Mid-lands now, th'industrious Muse doth make,
The Northamptonian earth, and in her way doth take;
As fruitfull every way, as those by Nature, which
The Husbandman by Art, with Compost doth inrich,
This boasting of her selfe; that walke her Verge about,
And view her well within, her breadth, and length throughout:
The worst foot of her earth, is equall with their best,
With most aboundant store, that highliest thinke them blest.
When Whittlewood betime th'unwearied Muse doth win
To talke with her awhile; at her first comming in,
The Forrest thus that greets: With more successefull Fate,
Thrive then thy fellow Nymphs, whose sad and ruinous state
We every day behold, if any thing there be,
That from this generall fall, thee happily may free,
'Tis onely for that thou dost naturally produce
More Under wood, and Brake, then Oke for greater use:
But when this ravenous Age, of those hath us bereft,
Time wanting this our store, shall sease what thee is left.

For what base Averice now inticeth men to doe,
Necessitie in time shall strongly urge them too;
Which each divining Spirit most cleerely doth foresee.
Whilst at this speech perplext, the Forrest seem'd to be,
A Water-nymph, neere to this goodly Wood-nymphs side,
(As tow'rds her soveraigne Ouze, shee softly downe doth slide)
Tea, her delightsome streame by Tawcester doth lead;
And sporting her sweet selfe in many a daintie Mead,
Shee hath not sallied farre, but Sacy soone againe
Salutes her; one much grac'd amongst the Sylvan traine:
One whom the Queene of Shades, the bright Diana oft
Hath courted for her lookes, with kisses smooth and soft,
On her faire Bosome lean'd, and tenderly imbrac't,
And cald her, her Deare heart, most lov'd, and onely chast:
Yet Sacie after Tea, her amourous eyes doth throw,
Till in the bankes of Ouze the Brooke her selfe bestow.
Where in those fertill fields, the Muse doth hap to meet
Upon that side which sits the West of Watling-street,
With Helidon a Hill, which though it bee but small,
Compar'd with their proud kind, which we our Mountaines call;.
Yet hath three famous Floods, that out of him doe flow,
That to three severall Seas, by their assistants goe;
Of which the noblest, Nen, to fayre Northampton hies,
By Owndle sallying on, then Peterborough plyes
Old Medhamsted: where her the Sea-mayds intertaine,
To lead her through the Fen into the German Maine,
The second, Charwell is, at Oxford meeting Thames,
Is by his King convayd into the Celtick streames.
Then Leame as least, the last, to mid-land Avon hasts,
Which Flood againe it selfe, into proud Severne casts:
As on th'Iberian Sea, her selfe great Severne spends;
So Leame the Dower she hath, to that wide Ocean lends.
But Helidon wax'd proud, the happy Sire to be
To so renowned Floods, as these fore-named three,
Besides the Hill of note, neere Englands midst that stands,
Whence from his Face, his backe, or on his either hands,
The Land extends in bredth, or layes it selfe in length.
Wherefore, this Hill to shew his state and naturall strength,
The surface of this part determineth to show,
Which we now England name, and through her tracts to goe.
But being plaine and poore, professeth not that hight,
As Falkon-like to sore, till lesning to the sight.
But as the sundry soyles, his style so altring oft,
As full expressions fit, or Verses smooth and soft,
Upon their severall Scites, as naturally to straine,
And wisheth that these Floods, his tunes to entertaine,
The ayre with Halcion calmes, may wholly have possest,
As though the rough winds tyerd, were eas'ly layd to rest.

Then on the worth'est tract up tow'rds the mid-dayes Sun,
His undertaken taske, thus Hellidon begun.
From where the kingly Thames his stomacke doth discharge,
To Devonshire, where the land her bosome doth inlarge;
And with the In-land ayre, her beauties doth releeve,
Along the Celtick Sea, cald oftentimes the Sleeve:
Although upon the coast, the Downes appeare but bare,
Yet naturally within the Countries wooddy are.
Then Cornwall creepeth out into the westerne Maine,
As (lying in her eye) shee poynted still at Spaine:
Or as the wanton soyle, disposd to lustfull rest,
Had layd her selfe along on Neptunes amorous breast.
With Denshire, from the firme, that Beake of land that fils,
What Landskip lies in Vales, and often rising hils,
So plac'd betwixt the French, and the Sabrinian Seas,
As on both sides adorn'd with many harborous Bayes,
Who for their Trade to Sea, and wealthy Mynes of Tinne,
From any other Tract, the praise doth clearely winne.
From Denshire by those shores, which Severne oft Surrounds,
The Soyle farre lower sits, and mightily abounds
With sundry sort of Fruits, as well-growne Grasse and Corne,
That Somerset may say, her batning Mores doe scorne
Our Englands richest earth, for burthen should them staine;
And on the selfe same Tract, up Severns streame againe,
The Vale of Evsham layes her length so largely forth,
As though shee meant to stretch her selfe into the North,
Where still the fertill earth depressed lyes and low,
Till her rich Soyle it selfe to Warwickshire doe show.
Hence somewhat South by East, let us our course incline,
And from these setting shores so meerely Maratine,
The Iles rich In-land parts, lets take with us along,
To set him rightly out, in our well-ordred Song;
Whose prospects to the Muse their sundry scites shall show,
Where shee from place to place, as free as ayre shall flow,
Their superficies so exactly to descry,
Through Wiltshire, poynting how the Plaine of Salisbury
Shootes foorth her selfe in length, and layes abroad a traine
So large, as though the land serv'd scarsely to containe
Her vastnesse, North from her, himselfe proud Cotswould vaunts,
And casts so sterne a looke, about him that he daunts,
The lowly Vales, remote that sit with humbler eyes.
In Barckshire, and from thence into the Orient lies
That most renowned Vale of White-horse, and by her,
So Buckingham againe doth Alsbury preferre,
With any English Earth, along upon whose pale,
That mounting Countrie then, which maketh her a Vale,
The chaulky Chilterne, runnes with Beeches crown'd about,
Through Bedfordshire that beares, till his bald front he shoot,

Into that foggy earth towards Ely, that doth grow
Much Fenny, and surrounds with every little flow.
So on into the East, upon the In-land ground,
From where that Christall Colne most properly doth bound,
Rough Chilterne, from the soyle, where in rich London sits,
As being faire and flat it naturally befits
Her greatnesse every way, which holdeth on along
To the Essexian earth, which likewise in our Song,
Since in one Tract they lye, we here together take,
Although the severall Shires, by sundry soyles doe make
It different in degrees; for Middlesex of Sands
Her soyle composeth hath; so are th'Essexian lands,
Adjoyning to the same, that sit by Isis side,
Which London over-lookes: but as she waxeth wide,
So Essex in her Tydes, her deepe-growne Marshes drownds,
And to Inclosures cuts her drier upland grounds,
Which lately woody were, whilst men those woods did prize;
Whence those fayre Countries lie, upon the pleasant rise,
(Betwixt the mouth of Thames, and where Ouze roughly dashes
Her rude unweildy waves, against the queachy Washes)
Suffolke and Norfolke neere, so named of their Scites,
Adorned every way with wonderfull delights,
To the beholding eye, that every where are seene,
Abounding with rich fields, and pastures fresh and greene,
Faire Havens to their shores, large Heaths within them lie,
As Nature in them strove to shew varietie.
From Ely all along upon that Easterne Sea,
Then Lincolneshire her selfe, in state at length doth lay,
Which for her fatning Fennes, her Fish, and Fowle may have
Preheminence, as she that seemeth to out-brave
All other Southerne Shires, whose head the Washes feeles,
Till wantonly she kicke proud Humber with her heeles.
Up tow'rds the Navell then, of England from her Flanke,
Which Lincolneshire we call, so levelled and lanke.
Northampton, Rutland then, and Huntingdon, which three
Doe shew by their full Soyles, all of one piece to be,
Of Nottingham a part, as Lester them is lent,
From Bevers batning Vale, along the banks of Trent.
So on the other side, into the Set againe,
Where Severne tow'rds the Sea from Shrewsbury doth straine,
Twixt which and Avons banks (where Arden when of old,
Her bushy curled front, she bravely did uphold,
In state and glory stood) now of three severall Shires,
The greatest portions lie, upon whose earth appeares
That mightie Forrests foot, of Worstershire a part,
Of Warwickeshire the like, which sometime was the heart
Of Arden that brave Nymph, yet woody here and there,
Oft intermixt with Heaths, whose Sand and Gravell beare,

A Turfe more harsh and hard, where Stafford doth partake,
In qualitie with those, as Nature strove to make
Them of one selfe same stuffe, and mixture, as they lye,
Which likewise in this Tract, we here together tye.
From these recited parts to th'North, more high and bleake,
Extended ye behold, the Mooreland and the Peake,
From eithers severall scite, in eithers mightie waste,
A sterner lowring eye, that every way doe cast
On their beholding Hills, and Countries round about;
Whose soyles as of one shape, appearing cleane throughout.
For Moreland which with Heath most naturally doth beare,
Her Winter livery still, in Summer seemes to weare;
As likewise doth the Peake, whose dreadfull Caverns found,
And Lead-mines, that in her, doe naturally abound,
Her superficies makes more terrible to show:
So from her naturall fount, as Severne downe doth flow,
The high Sallopian hills lift up their rising sayles;
Which Country as it is the near'st alli'd to Wales,
In Mountaines, so it most is to the same alike.
Now tow'rds the Irish Seas a little let us strike,
Where Cheshire, (as her choyce) with Lancashire doth lie
Along th'unlevel'd shores; this former to the eye,
In her complexion showes blacke earth with gravell mixt,
A Wood-land and a plaine indifferently betwixt,
A good fast-feeding grasse, most strongly that doth breed:
As Lancashire no lesse excelling for her seed,
Although with Heath, and Fin, her upper parts abound;
As likewise to the Sea, upon the lower ground,
With Mosses, Fleets, and Fells, she showes most wild and rough,
Whose Turfe, and square cut Peat, is fuell good ynough.
So, on the North of Trent, from Nottingham above,
Where Sherwood her curld front, into the cold doth shove,
Light Forrest land is found, to where the floting Don,
In making tow'rds the Maine, her Doncaster hath won,
Where Yorkshire's layd abroad, so many a mile extent,
To whom preceding times, the greatest circuit lent,
A Province, then a Shire, which rather seemeth: so
It incidently most varietie doth show.
Heere stony stirrill grounds, there wondrous fruitfull fields,
Here Champaine, and there Wood, it in abundance yeelds:
Th'West-riding, and North, be mountainous and high,
But tow'rds the German Sea the East, more low doth lie.
This Ile hath not that earth, of any kind elsewhere,
But on this part or that, epitomized here.
Tow'rds those Scotch-Irish Iles, upon that Sea againe,
The rough Virgivian cald, that tract which doth containe
Cold Cumberland, which yet wild Westmerland excels,
For roughnesse, at whose point lies rugged Fournesse Fells,

Is fild with mighty Mores, and Mountaines, which doe make
Her wilde superfluous waste, as Nature sport did take
In Heaths, and high-cleev'd Hils, whose threatning fronts doe dare
Each other with their looks, as though they would out-stare
The Starry eyes of heaven, which to out-face they stand.
From these into the East, upon the other hand,
The Bishopricke, and fayre Northumberland doe beare
To Scotlands bordering Tweed, which as the North elsewhere,
Not very fertile are, yet with a lovely face
Upon the Ocean looke; which kindly doth imbrace
Those Countries all along, upon the Rising side,
Which for the Batfull Gleabe, by nature them denide,
With mightie Mynes of Cole, abundantly are blest,
By which this Tract remaines renown'd above the rest:
For what from her rich wombe, each habourous Road receives.
Yet Hellidon not here, his lov'd description leaves,
Though now his darling Springs desir'd him to desist;
But say all what they can, hee'll doe but what he list.
As he the Surface thus, so likewise will he show,
The Clownish Blazons, to each Country long agoe,
Which those unlettered times, with blind devotion lent,
Before the Learned Mayds our Fountaines did frequent,
To shew the Muse can shift her habit, and she now
Of Palatins that sung, can whistle to the Plow;
And let the curious tax his Clownry, with their skill
He recks not, but goes on, and say they what they will.
Kent first in our account, doth to it selfe apply,
(Quoth he) this Blazon first, Long Tayles and Libertie.
Sussex with Surrey say, Then let us lead home Logs.
As Hamshire long for her, hath had the tearme of Hogs.
So Dorsetshire of long, they Dorsers usd to call.
Cornwall and Devonshire crie, Weele wrastle for a Fall.
Then Somerset sayes, Set the Bandog on the Bull.
And Glostershire againe is blazon'd, Weigh thy Wooll.
As Barkshire hath for hers, Lets to't and tosse the Ball.
And Wiltshire will for her, Get home and pay for all.
Rich Buckingham doth beare the terme of Bread and Beefe,
Where if you beat a Bush, tis ods you start a Theefe.
So Hartford blazon'd is, The Club, and clowted Shoone,
Thereto, Ile rise betime, and sleepe againe at Noone.
When Middlesex bids, Up to London let us goe,
And when our Markets done, weele have a pot or two.
As Essex hath of old beene named, Calves and Styles,
Fayre Suffolke, Mayds and Milke, and Norfolke, Many Wyles.
So Cambridge hath been call'd, Hold Nets, and let us winne;
And Huntingdon, With Stilts weele stalke through thick and thinne.
Northamptonshire of long hath had this Blazon, Love,
Below the girdle all, but little else above.

An outcrie Oxford makes, The Schollers have been heere,
And little though they payd, yet have they had good cheere.
Quoth warlike Warwickshire, Ile binde the sturdy Beare.
Quoth Worstershire againe, And I will squirt the Peare.
Then Staffordshire bids Stay, and I will Beet the Fire,
And nothing will I aske, but good will for my hire.
Beane-belly Lestershire, her attribute doth beare.
And Bells and Bag-pipes next, belong to Lincolnshire.
Of Malt-horse, Bedfordshire long since the Blazon wan.
And little Rutlandshire is tearmed Raddleman.
To Darby is assign'd the name of Wooll and Lead.
As Nottinghams, of old (is common) Ale and Bread.
So Hereford for her sayes, Give me Woofe and Warpe.
And Shropshire saith in her, That Shinnes be ever sharpe,
Lay wood upon the fire, reach hither mee my Harpe,
And whilst the blacke Bowle walks, we merily will carpe.
Old Chesshire is well knowne to be the Chiefe of Men.
Faire Women doth belong to Lancashire agen.
The lands that over Ouze to Berwicke foorth doe beare,
Have for their Blazon had the Snaffle, Spurre, and Speare.
Now Nen extreamely griev'd those barbarous things to heare,
By Helidon her sire, that thus delivered were:
For as his eld'st, shee was to passed ages knowne,
Whom by Aufona's name the Romans did renowne.
A word by them deriv'd of Avon, which of long,
The Britans cald her by, expressing in their tongue
The full and generall name of waters; wherefore shee
Stood much upon her worth, and jealous grew to bee,
Lest things so low and poore, and now quite out of date,
Should happily impaire her dignitie and state.
Wherefore from him her syre imediatly she hasts;
And as shee foorth her course to Peterborough casts,
Shee falleth in her way with Weedon, where tis sayd,
Saint Werburge princely borne, a most religious Mayd,
From those peculier fields, by prayer the Wild-geese drove,
Thence through the Champaine shee lasciviously doth rove
Tow'rds faire Northampton, which, whilst Nen was Avon cald,
Resum'd that happy name, as happily instald
Upon her Northerne side, where taking in a Rill,
Her long impoverish'd banks more plenteously to fill,
She flourishes in state, along the fruitfull fields;
Where whilst her waters shee with wondrous pleasure yeelds,
To Wellingborough comes, whose Fountaines in shee takes,
Which quickening her againe, imediately shee makes
To Owndle, which receives contractedly the sound
From Avondale, t'expresse that Rivers lowest ground:
To Peterborough thence she maketh foorth her way,
Where Welland hand in hand, goes on with her to Sea;

When Rockingham, the Muse to her faire Forrest brings,
Thence lying to the North, whose sundry gifts she sings.
O deare and daintie Nymph, most gorgeously arayd,
Of all the Driades knowne, the most delicious Mayd,
With all delights adorn'd, that any way beseeme
A Sylvan, by whose state we verily may deeme
A Deitie in thee, in whose delightfull Bowers,
The Fawnes and Fayries make the longest dayes, but howers,
And joying in the Soyle, where thou assum'st thy seat,
Thou to thy Handmaid hast, (thy pleasures to away)
Faire Benefield, whose care to thee doth surely cleave,
Which beares a grasse as soft, as is the daintie sleave,
And thrum'd so thicke and deepe, that the proud Palmed Deere,
Forsake the closser woods, and make their quiet leyre
In beds of platted fogge, so eas'ly there they sit.
A Forrest and a Chase in every thing so fit
This Iland hardly hath, so neere allide that be,
Brave Nymph, such praise belongs to Benefield and thee.
Whilst Rockingham was heard with these Reports to ring,
The Muse by making on tow'rds Wellands ominous Spring,
With Kelmarsh there is caught, for coursing of the Hare,
Which scornes that any place, should with her Plaines compare:
Which in the proper Tearmes the Muse doth thus report;
The man whose vacant mind prepares him to the sport,
The Finder sendeth out, to seeke out nimble Wat,
Which crosseth in the field, each furlong, every Flat,
Till he this pretty Beast upon the Forme hath found,
Then viewing for the Course, which is the fairest ground,
The Greyhounds foorth are brought, for coursing then in case,
And choycely in the Slip, one leading forth a brace;
The Finder puts her up, and gives her Coursers law.
And whilst the eager dogs upon the Start doe draw,
Shee riseth from her seat, as though on earth she flew,
Forc'd by some yelping Cute to give the Greyhounds view,
Which are at length let slip, when gunning out they goe,
As in respect of them the swiftest wind were slow,
When each man runnes his Horse, with fixed eyes, and notes
Which Dog first turnes the Hare, which first the other coats,
They wrench her once or twice, ere she a turne will take,
Whats offred by the first, the other good doth make;
And turne for turne againe with equall speed they ply,
Bestirring their swift feet with strange agilitie:
A hardned ridge or way, when if the Hare doe win,
Then as shot from a Bow, she from the Dogs doth spin,
That strive to put her off, but when hee cannot reach her,
This giving him a Coat, about againe doth fetch her
To him that comes behind, which seemes the Hare to beare;
But with a nimble turne shee casts them both arrere:

Till oft for want of breath, to fall to ground they make her,
The Greyhounds both so spent, that they want breath to take her.
Here leave I whilst the Muse more serious things attends,
And with my Course at Hare, my Canto likewise ends.

THE FOURE AND TWENTIETH SONG

THE ARGUMENT

The fatall Welland from her Springs,
This Song to th'Ile of Ely brings:
Our ancient English Saints revives,
Then in an oblique course contrives,
The Rarities that Rutland showes,
Which with this Canto shee doth close.

This way, to that faire Fount of Welland hath us led,
At Nasby to the North, where from a second head
Runs Avon, which along to Severne shapes her course,
But pliant Muse proceed, with our new-handled sourse,
Of whom from Ages past, a prophecie there ran,
(Which to this ominous flood much feare and reverance wan)
That she alone should drowne all Holland, and should see
Her Stamford, which so much forgotten seemes to bee;
Renown'd for Liberall Arts, as highly honoured there,
As they in Cambridge are, or Oxford ever were;
Whereby shee in her selfe a holinesse suppos'd,
That in her scantled banks, though wandring long inclos'd,
Yet in her secret breast a Catalogue had kept
Of our religious Saints, which though they long had slept,
Yet through the chrystned world, for they had wonne such fame
Both to the British first, then to the English name,
For their abundant Faith, and sanctimony knowne,
Such as were hither sent, or naturally our owne,
It much her Genius grievd, to have them now neglected,
Whose pietie so much those zealous times respected.
Wherefore she with her selfe resolved, when that shee
To Peterborough came, where much shee long'd to be,
That in the wished view of Medhamsted, that Towne,
Which he the greatst of Saints doth by his Name renowne,
Shee to his glorious Phane an Offring as to bring,
Of her deare Countries Saints, the Martyrologe would sing:
And therefore all in haste to Harborough she hy'd,
Whence Lestershire she leaves upon the Northward side,
At Rutland then ariv'd, where Stamford her sustaines,
By Deeping drawing out, to Lincolneshire she leanes,

Upon her Bank by North, against this greater throng,
Northamptonshire to South still lyes with her along,
And now approching neere to this appointed place,
Where she and Nen make shew as though they would imbrace;
But onely they salute, and each holds on her way,
When holy Welland thus was wisely heard to say.
I sing of Saints, and yet my Song shall not be fraught
With Myracles by them, but fayned to be wrought,
That they which did their lives so palpably belye,
To times have much impeach'd their holinesse thereby:
Though fooles (I say) on them, such poore impostures lay,
Have scandal'd them to ours, farre foolisher then they,
Which thinke they have by this so great advantage got
Their venerable names from memory to blot,
Which truth can ne'r permit; and thou that art so pure,
The name of such a Saint that no way canst endure;
Know in respect of them to recompense that hate,
The wretchedst thing, and thou have both one death and date:
From all vaine worship too; and yet am I as free
As is the most precise, I passe not who hee bee.
Antiquitie I love, nor by the worlds despight,
I can not be remoov'd from that my deare delight.
This spoke, to her faire ayd her sister Nen shee winnes,
When shee of all her Saints, now with that man beginnes.
The first that ever told Christ crucified to us,
(By Paul and Peter sent) just Aristobulus,
Renown'd in holy Writ, a Labourer in the word,
For that most certaine Truth, opposing fire and sword,
By th'Britans murthered here, so unbeleeving then.
Next holy Joseph came, the mercifulst of men,
The Saviour of mankind, in Sepulchre that layd,
That to the Britans was th'Apostle; in his ayd
Saint Duvian, and with him Saint Fagan, both which were
His Scollers, likewise left their sacred Reliques here:
All Denizens of ours, t'advaunce the Christian state,
At Glastenbury long that were commemorate.
When Amphiball againe our Martyrdome began
In that most bloody raigne of Dioclesian:
This man into the truth, that blessed Alban led
(Our Proto-Martyr call'd) who strongly discipled
In Christian Patience, learnt his tortures to appease:
His fellow-Martyrs then, Stephen, and Socrates,
At holy Albans Towne, their Festivall should hold;
So of that Martyr nam'd, (which Verlam was of old.)
A thousand other Saints, whom Amphiball had taught,
Flying the Pagan foe, their lives that strictly sought,
Were slaine where Lichfield is, whose name doth rightly sound,
(There of those Christians slaine) Dead field, or burying ground.

Then for the Christian faith, two other here that stood,
And teaching, bravely seald their Doctrine with their blood:
Saint Julius, and with him Saint Aron, have their roome,
At Carleon suffring death by Dioclesians doome;
Whose persecuting raigne tempestuously that rag'd,
Gainst those here for the Faith, their utmost that ingag'd,
Saint Angule put to death, one of our holiest men,
At London, of that See, the godly Bishop then
In that our Infant Church, so resolute was he.
A second Martyr too grace Londons ancient See,
Though it were after long, good Voadine who reprov'd
Proud Vortiger his King, unlawfully that lov'd
Anothers wanton wife, and wrong'd his Nuptiall bed;
For which by that sterne Prince unjustly murthered,
As he a Martyr dy'd, is Sainted with the rest.
The third Saint of that See (though onely he confest)
Was Guithelme, unto whom those times that reverence gave,
As he a place with them eternally shall have.
So Melior may they bring, the Duke of Cornwalls sonne,
By his false brothers hands, to death who being done
In hate of Christian faith, whose zeale lest time should taint,
As he a Martyr was, they justly made a Saint.
Those godly Romans then (who as mine Authour saith)
Wanne good King Lucius first t'imbrace the Christian faith,
Fugatius, and his friend Saint Damian, as they were
Made Denizens of ours, have their remembrance here:
As two more (neere that time, Christ Jesus that confest,
And that most lively faith, by their good works exprest)
Saint Elvan with his pheere Saint Midwin, who to win
The Britans, (com'n from Rome, where Christned they had bin)
Converted to the Faith their thousands, whose deare grave,
That Glastenbury grac'd, there their memoriall have.
As they their sacred Bones in Britaine here bestow'd,
So Britaine likewise sent her Saints to them abroad:
Marsellus that just man, who having gathered in
The scattered Christian Flocke, instructed that had bin
By holy Joseph here; to congregate he wan
This justly named Saint, this never-wearied man,
Next to the Germans preach'd, till (voyd of earthly feare)
By his couragious death, he much renown'd Trevere.
Then of our Native Saints, the first that di'd abroad;
Beatus, next to him shall fitly be bestow'd,
In Switzerland who preach'd, whom there those Paynims slue,
When greater in their place, though not in Faith, ensue
Saint Lucius (call'd of us) the primer christned King,
Of th'ancient Britons then, who led the glorious ring
To all the Saxon Race, that here did him succeed,
Changing his regall Robe to a religious Weed,

His rule in Britaine left, and to Helvetia hied,
Where he a Bishop liv'd, a Martyr lastly died.
As Constantine the Great, that godly Emperour,
Here first the Christian Church that did to peace restore,
Whose ever blessed birth, (as by the power divine)
The Roman Empire brought into the British Line,
Constantinoples Crowne, and th'ancient Britans glory.
So other here we have to furnish up our Story,
Saint Melon welneere, when the British Church began,
(Even early in the raigne of Romes Valerian)
Here leaving us for Rome, from thence to Roan was cald,
To preach unto the French, where soone he was instauld
Her Bishop: Britaine so may of her Gudwall vaunt,
Who first the Flemmings taught, whose feast is held at Gaunt.
So others foorth she brought, to little Britaine vow'd,
Saint Wenlocke, and with him Saint Sampson, both alow'd
Apostles of that place, the first the Abbot sole
Of Tawrac, and the last sate on the See of Dole:
Where dying, Maglor then, thereof was Bishop made,
Sent purposely from hence, that people to perswade,
To keepe the Christian faith: so Golvin gave we thither,
Who sainted being there, we set them here together.
As of the weaker Sex, that ages have enshrin'd
Amongst the British Dames, and worthily divin'd:
The finder of the Crosse Queene Helena doth lead,
Who though Rome set a Crowne on her Emperiall head,
Yet in our Britaine borne, and bred up choicely here.
Emerita the next, King Lucius sister deare,
Who in Helvetia with her martyred brother di'd;
Bright Ursula the third, who undertooke to guide
Th'eleven thousand Mayds to little Britaine sent,
By Seas and bloody men devoured as they went:
Of which we find these foure have been for Saints preferd,
(And with their Leader still doe live incalenderd)
Saint Agnes, Cordula, Odillia, Florence, which
With wondrous sumptuous shrines those ages did inrich
At Cullen, where their Lives most clearely are exprest,
And yearely Feasts observ'd to them and all the rest.
But when it came to passe the Saxon powers had put
The Britans from these parts, and them o'r Severne shut,
The Christian Faith with her, then Cambria had alone,
With those that it receiv'd (from this now England) gone,
Whose Cambrobritans so their Saints as duely brought,
T'advance the Christian Faith, effectually that wrought,
Their David, (one deriv'd of th'royall British blood)
Who gainst Palagius false and damn'd opinions stood,
And turn'd Menevias name to Davids sacred See,
Th Patron of the Welsh deserving well to be:

With Cadock, next to whom comes Canock, both which were
Prince Brechans sonnes, who gave the name to Brecnocksheere;
The first a Martyr made, a Confessor the other.
So Clintanck, Brecknocks Prince, as from one selfe same mother,
A Saint upon that seat, the other doth ensue,
Whom for the Christian Faith a Pagan Souldier slue.
So Bishops can shee bring, which of her Saints shall bee,
As Asaph, who first gave that name unto that See;
Of Bangor, and may boast Saint David which her wan
Much reverence, and with these Owdock and Telean,
Both Bishops of Landaff, and Saints in their Succession;
Two other following these, both in the same profession,
Saint Dubric whose report old Carleon yet doth carry,
And Elery in Northwales, who built a Monastery,
In which himselfe became the Abot, to his praise,
And spent in Almes and Prayer the remnant of his dayes.
But leaving these Divin'd, to Decuman we come,
In Northwales who was crown'd with glorious Martyrdome.
Justinian, as that man a Sainted place deserv'd,
Who still to feed his soule, his sinfull body sterv'd:
And for that height in zeale, whereto he did attaine,
There by his fellow Monkes most cruelly was slaine.
So Cambria, Beno bare; and Gildas, which doth grace
Old Bangor, and by whose learn'd writings we imbrace,
The knowledge of those times; the fruits of whose just pen,
Shall live for ever fresh, with all truth-searching men:
Then other, which for hers old Cambria doth averre,
Saint Senan, and with him wee set Saint Deiferre,
Then Tather will we take, and Chyned to the rest,
With Baruk who so much the Ile of Bardsey blest
By his most powerfull prayer, to solitude that liv'd,
And of all worldly care his zealous Soule depriv'd.
Of these, some liv'd not long, some wondrous aged were,
But in the Mountaines liv'd, all Hermits here and there.
O more then mortall men, whose Faith and earnest prayers,
Not onely bare ye hence, but were those mightie stayres
By which you went to heaven, and God so clearely saw,
As this vaine earthly pompe had not the power to draw
Your elevated soules, but once to looke so low,
As those depressed paths, wherein base worldlings goe.
What mind doth not admire the knowledge of these men?
But zealous Muse returne unto thy taske agen.
These holy men at home, as here they were bestow'd,
So Cambria had such too, as famous were abroad.
Sophy King Gulicks sonne of Northwales, who had seene
The Sepulchre three times, and more, seven times had beene
On Pilgrimage at Rome, of Beniventum there
The painfull Bishop made; by him so place we here,

Saint Mackloue, from Northwales to little Britaine sent,
That people to convert, who resolutely bent,
Of Athelney in time the Bishop there became,
Which her first title chang'd, and tooke his proper name.
So she her Virgins had, and vow'd as were the best:
Saint Keyne Prince Brechans child, (a man so highly blest,
That thirtie borne to him all Saints accounted were.)
Saint Inthwar so apart shall with these other beare,
Who out of false suspect was by her brother slaine.
Then Winifrid, whose name yet famous doth remaine,
Whose Fountaine in Northwales intitled by her name,
For Mosse, and for the Stones that be about the same,
Is sounded through this Ile, and to this latter age
Is of our Romists held their latest Pilgrimage.
But when the Saxons here so strongly did reside,
And surely seated once, as owners to abide;
When nothing in the world to their desire was wanting,
Except the Christian Faith, for whose substantiall planting,
Saint Augustine from Rome was to this Iland sent;
And comming through large France, ariving first in Kent,
Converted to the faith King Ethelbert, till then
Unchristened that had liv'd, with all his Kentishmen,
And of their chiefest Towne, now Canterbury cald,
The Bishop first was made, and on that See instauld.
Foure other, and with him for knowledge great in name,
That in this mighty worke of our conversion came,
Lawrence, Melitus then, with Justus, and Honorius,
In this great Christian worke, all which had beene laborious,
To venerable age, each comming in degree,
Succeeded him againe in Canterbury See,
As Peter borne in France, with these and made our owne,
And Pauline whose great zeale, was by his Preaching showne.
The first to Abbots state, wise Austen did preferre,
And to the latter gave the See of Rochester;
All canoniz'd for Saints, as worthy sure they were,
For establishing the Faith, which was received here.
Few Countries where our Christ had ere been preached then,
But sent into this Ile some of their godly men.
From Persia led by zeale, so Ive this Iland sought,
And neere our Easterne Fennes a fit place finding, taught
The Faith: which place from him the name alone derives,
And of that sainted man since called is Saint-Ives;
Such reverence to her selfe that time Devotion wan.
So Sun-burnt Affrick sent us holy Adrian,
Who preacht the Christian Faith here nine and thirtie yeere,
An Abbot in this Isle, and to this Nation deare,
That in our Countrey two Provinciall Synods cald,
T'reforme the Church that time with Heresies enthrald.

So Denmarke Henry sent t'encrease our holy store,
Who falling in from thence upon our Northerne shore
In th'Isle of Cochet liv'd, neere to the mouth of Tyne,
In Fasting as in Prayer, a man so much divine, of
That onely thrice a weeke on homely cates he fed,
And three times in the weeke himselfe he silenced,
That in remembrance of this most abstenious man,
Upon his blessed death the English men began,
By him to name their Babes, which it so frequent brings,
Which name hath honoured been by many English Kings.
So Burgundy to us three men most reverent bare,
Amongst our other Saints, that claime to have their share,
Of which was Felix first, who in th'East-Saxon raigne,
Converted to the faith King Sigbert: him againe
Ensueth Anselme, whom Augusta sent us in,
And Hugh, whose holy life, to Christ did many win,
By Henry th'Empresse sonne holpe hither, and to have
Him wholly to be ours, the See of Lincolne gave.
So Lumbardy to us, our reverent Lanfranck lent,
For whom into this land King William Conqueror sent,
And Canterburies See to his wise charge assign'd.
Nor France to these for hers was any whit behind,
For Grimbald shee us gave (as Peter long before,
Who with Saint Austen came, to preach upon this shore)
By Alsred hither cald, who him an Abbot made,
Who by his godly life, and preaching did perswade,
The Saxons to beleeve the true and quickning word:
So after long againe she likewise did afford,
Saint Osmond, whom the See of Salsbury doth owne,
A Bishop once of hers, and in our conquest knowne,
When hither to that end their Norman William came,
Remigius then, whose mind, that worke of ours of fame,
Rich Lincolne Minster shewes, where he a Bishop sat,
Which (it should seeme) he built for men to wonder at.
So potent were the powers of Church-men in those dayes.
Then Henry nam'd of Bloys, from France who crost the Seas,
With Stephen Earle of Bloys his brother, after King,
In Winchesters rich See, who him establishing,
He in those troublous times in preaching tooke such paine,
As he by them was not canonized in vaine.
As other Countries here, their holy men bestow'd;
So Britaine likewise sent her Saints to them abroad,
And into neighbouring France, our most religious went,
Saint Clare that native was of Rochester in Kent,
At Volcasyne came vow'd the French instructing there,
So early ere the truth amongst them did appeare,
That more then halfe a God they thought that reverent man.
Our Judock, so in France such fame our Nation wan,

For holinesse, where long an Abbots life he led
At Pontoyse, and so much was honoured, that being dead,
And after threescore yeares (their latest period dated)
His body taken up, was solemnly translated.
As Ceofrid, that sometime of Wyremouth Abbot was,
In his returne from Rome, as he through France did passe,
At Langres left his life, whose holinesse even yet,
Upon his reverent grave, in memory doth sit.
Saint Alkwin so for ours, we English boast againe,
The Tutor that became to mightie Charlemaigne,
That holy man, whose heart was so with goodnesse fild,
As out of zeale he wan that mightie King to build
That Academy now at Paris, whose Foundation
Through all the Christian world hath so renown'd that Nation,
As well declares his wealth, that had the power to doe it,
As his most lively zeale, perswading him unto it.
As Simon cald the Saint of Burdeux, which so wrought,
By preaching there the truth, that happily he brought
The people of those parts, from Paganisme, wherein
Their unbeleeving soules so long had nuzled bin.
So in the Norman rule, two most religious were,
Amongst ours that in France dispersed here and there,
Preach'd to that Nation long, Saint Hugh, who borne our owne,
In our first Henries rule sate on the See of Roan,
Where reverenc'd he was long. Saint Edmund so againe,
Who banished from hence in our third Henries raigne,
There led an Hermits life neere Pontoyse, where before,
Saint Judock did the like) whose honour to restore,
Religious Lewes there interr'd with wondrous cost,
Of whose rich Funerall France deservedly may boast.
Then Main we adde to these, an Abbot here of ours,
To little Britaine sent, imploying all his powers
To bring them to the Faith, which he so well effected,
That since he as a Saint hath ever been respected.
As these of ours in France, so had wee those did show
In Germany, as well the Higher, as the Low,
Their Faith: In Freezeland first Saint Boniface our best,
Who of the See of Mentz, whilst there he sate possest,
At Dockum had his death, by faithlesse Frizians slaine,
Whose Anniversaries there did after long remaine.
So Wigbert full of faith, and heavenly wisedome went
Unto the selfe same place, as with the same intent;
With Eglemond a man as great with God as he;
As they agreed in life, so did their ends agree,
Both by Radbodius slaine, who ruld in Frizia then:
So in the sacred roule of our Religious men,
In Freeze that preach'd the faith we of Saint Lullus read,
Who in the See of Mentz did Boniface succeed;

And Willihad that of Bren, that sacred Seat supplide,
So holy that him there, they halfely deifide;
With Marchelme, and with him our Plechelme, holy men,
That to the Freezes now, and to the Saxons then,
In Germany abroad the glorious Gospell spread,
Who at their lives depart, their bodies gathered,
Were at old-Seell enshrin'd, their Obijts yearely kept:
Such as on them have had as many praises heap'd,
That in their lives the truth as constantly confest,
As th'other that their Faith by Martyrdome exprest.
In Freeze, as these of ours, their names did famous leave,
Againe so had we those as much renown'd in Cleave;
Saint Swibert, and with him Saint Willick, which from hence,
To Cleeve-land held their way, and in the Truths defence
Pawn'd their religious lives, and as they went together,
So one and selfe same place allotted was to either:
For both of them at Wert in Cleaveland seated were,
Saint Swibert Bishop was, Saint Willick Abbot there.
So Guelderland againe shall our most holy bring,
As Edilbert the sonne of Edilbald the King
Of our South-Saxon Rule, incessantly that taught
The Guelders, whose blest dayes unto their period brought,
Unto his reverent Corpse, old Harlem harbour gave;
So Werenfrid againe, and Otger both we have,
Who to those people preach'd, whose praise that country tells.
What Nation names a Saint, for vertue that excels
Saint German who for Christ his Bishoprick forsooke,
And in the Netherlands most humbly him betooke,
From place to place to passe, the secrets to reveale,
Of our deare Saviours death, and last of all to seale
His doctrine with his blood: In Belgia so abroad,
Saint Wynock in like sort, his blessed time bestow'd,
Whose reliques Wormshault (yet) in Flanders hath reserv'd,
Of these, th'rebellious flesh (to winne them heaven) that starv'd.
Saint Menigold, a man, who in his youth had beene
A Souldier, and the French, and German warres had seene,
A Hermit last became, his sinfull soule to save,
To whom good Arnulph, that most godly Emperour gave
Some ground not farre from Leedge, his Hermitage to set,
Whose floore when with his teares, he many a day had wet,
He for the Christian faith upon the same was slaine:
So did th'Erwaldi there most worthily attaine
Their Martyrs glorious Types, to Ireland first approov'd,
But after (in their zeale) as need requir'd remoov'd,
They to Westphalia went, and as they brothers were,
So they, the Christian faith together preaching there,
Th'old Pagan Saxons slew, out of their hatred deepe
To the true Faith, whose shrines brave Cullen still doth keepe.

So Adler one of ours, by England set apart
For Germany, and sent that people to convert,
Of Erford Bishop made, there also had his end.
Saint Liphard like wise to our Martyraloge shall lend,
Who having been at Rome on Pilgrimage, to see
The Reliques of the Saints, supposed there to bee,
Returning by the way of Germany, at last,
Preaching the Christian faith, as he through Cambray past,
The Pagan people slew, whose Reliques Huncourt hath;
These others so we had, which trode the selfe same path
In Germany, which shee most reverently imbrac'd.
Saint John a man of ours, on Salzburgs See was plac'd;
Saint Willibald of Eist the Bishop so became,
And Burchard English borne, the man most great of name,
Of Witzburg Bishop was, at Hohemburg that reard
The Monastery, wherein he richly was interd.
So Mastreight unto her Saint Willibord did call,
And seated him upon her See Episcopall,
As two Saint Lebwins there amongst the rest are brought;
Th'one o'r Isells banks the ancient Saxons taught:
At over Isell rests, the other did apply,
The Gueldres, and by them interd at Deventry.
Saint Wynibald againe, at Hidlemayne enjoy'd
The Abbacy, in which his godly time employ'd
In their Conversion there, which long time him withstood.
Saint Gregory then, with us sprung of the Royall blood,
And sonne to him whom we the elder Edward stile,
Both Court and Country left, which he esteemed vile,
Which Germany receav'd, where he at Myniard led
A strict Monastick life, a Saint alive and dead.
So had we some of ours for Italy were prest,
As well as these before, sent out into the East.
King Inas having done so great and wondrous things,
As well might be suppos'd the works of sundry Kings,
Erecting beautious Phanes, and Monuments so faire,
As Monarchs have not since beene able to repaire,
Of many that he built, the least, in time when they
Have (by weake mens neglect) been falne into decay:
This Realme by him enrich'd, he povertie profest,
In Pilgrimage to Rome, where meekly he deceast.
As Richard the deare sonne to Lothar King of Kent,
When he his happy dayes religiously had spent;
And feeling the approch of his declining age,
Desirous to see Rome in holy Pilgrimage,
Into thy Country com'n at Leuca, left his life,
Whose myracles there done, yet to this day are rife.
The Patron of that place, so Thuscany in thee,
At faire Mount-flascon still the memory shall bee

Of holy Thomas there most reverently interd,
Who sometime to the See of Hereford preferd;
Thence travailing to Rome, in his returne bereft
His life by sicknesse, there to thee his body left.
Yet Italy gave not these honors all to them
That visited her Rome, but from Jerusalem,
Some comming back through thee, and yeelding up their spirits,
On thy rich earth receiv'd their most deserved merits.
O Naples, as thine owne, in thy large Territory,
Though to our Countries praise, yet to thy greater glory,
Even to this day the Shrines religiously dost keepe,
Of many a blessed Saint which in thy lap doth sleepe!
As Eleutherius, com'n from visiting the Tombe,
Thou gav'st to him at Arke in thy Apulia roome
To set his holy Cell, where he an Hermite dy'd,
Canonized her Saint; so hast thou glorifide
Saint Gerrard, one of ours, (above the former grac'd)
In such a sumptuous Shrine at Galinaro plac'd;
At Sancto Padre so, Saint Fulke hath ever fame,
Which from that reverent man 't should seeme deriv'd the name,
His Reliques there reserv'd; so holy Ardwins Shrine
Is at Ceprano kept, and honoured as divine,
For Myracles, that there by his strong faith were wrought.
Mongst these selected men, the Sepulchre that sought,
And in thy Realme arriv'd, their blessed soules resign'd:
Our Bernards body yet at Arpine we may find,
Untill this present time, her patronizing Saint.
So Countries more remote, with ours we did acquaint,
As Richard for the fame his holinesse had wonne,
And for the wondrous things that through his Prayers were done,
From this his native home into Calabria cald,
And of Saint Andrewes there the Bishop was instauld,
For whom shee hath profest much reverence to this land:
Saint William with this man, a paralell may stand,
Through all the Christian world accounted so divine,
That travelling from hence to holy Palestine,
Desirous that most blest Jerusalem to see,
(In which the Saviours selfe so oft vouchsaft to be)
Priour of that holy house by Suffrages related,
To th'Sepulchre of Christ, which there was dedicated;
To Tyre in Syria thence remov'd in little space,
And in lesse time ordain'd Archbishop of that place;
That God inspired man, with heavenly goodnesse fild,
A Saint amongst the rest deservedly is held.
Yet Italy, nor France, nor Germany, those times
Imployd not all our men, but into colder Clymes,
They wandred through the world, their Countries that forsooke.
So Sigfrid sent fromhence, devoutly undertooke

Those Pagans wild and rude, of Gothia to convert,
Who having laboured long, with danger oft ingirt,
Was in his reverent age for his deserved fee,
By Olaus King of Goths, set on Vexovia's See.
To Norway, and to those great North-East Countries farre;
So Gotebald gave himselfe holding a Christian warre
With Paynims, nothing else but Heathenish Rites that knew.
As Suethia to her selfe these men most reverent drew,
Saint Ulfrid of our Saints, as famous there as any,
Nor scarcely find we one converting there so many.
And Henry in those dayes of Oxsto Bishop made,
The first that Swethen King, which ever did perswade,
On Finland to make warre, to force them by the sword,
When nothing else could serve to heare the powerfull word;
With Eskill thither sent, to teach that barbarous Nation,
Who on the Passion day, there preaching on the Passion,
T'expresse the Saviours love to mankind, taking paine,
By cruell Paynims hands was in the Pulpit slaine,
Upon that blessed day Christ dyed for sinfull man,
Upon that day for Christ, his Martyrs Crowne he wan.
So David drawne from hence into those farther parts,
By preaching, who to pearce those Paynims hardned hearts,
Incessantly proclaim'd Christ Jesus, with a crie
Against their Heathen gods, and blind Idolatry.
Into those colder Clymes to people beastly rude,
So others that were ours couragiously pursude,
The planting of the Truth, in zeale three most profound,
The relish of whose names by likelinesse of sound,
Both in their lives and deaths, a likelinesse might show,
As Unaman we name, and Shunaman that goe,
With Wynaman their friend, which martyred gladly were
In Gothland, whilst they taught with Christian patience there.
Nor those from us that went, nor those that hither came
From the remotest parts, were greater yet in name,
Then those residing here on many a goodly See,
(Great Bishops in account, now greater Saints that be)
Some such selected ones for pietie and zeale,
As to the wretched world, more clearely could reveale,
How much there might of God in mortall man be found
In charitable workes, or such as did abound,
Which by their good successe in aftertimes were blest,
Were then related Saints, as worthier then the rest.
Of Canterbury here with those I will begin,
That first Archbishops See, on which there long hath bin
So many men devout, as rais'd that Church so high,
Much reverence, and have wonne their holy Hierarchy:
Of which he first that did with goodnesse so inflame
The hearts of the devout (that from his proper name)

As one (even) sent from God, the soules of men to save
The title unto him, of Deodat they gave.
The Bishops Brightwald next, and Tatwin in we take,
Whom time may say, that Saints it worthily did make
Succeeding in that See directly even as they,
Here by the Muse are plac'd, who spent both night and day
By doctrine, or by deeds, instructing, doing good,
In raising them were falne, or strengthening them that stood.
Then Odo the Severe, who highly did adorne
That See, (yet being of unchristened parents borne,
Whose Country Denmarke was, but in East England dwelt)
He being but a child, in his cleere bosome felt
The most undoubted truth, and yet unbaptiz'd long;
But as he grew in yeares, in spirit so growing strong:
And as the Christian faith this holy man had taught,
He likewise for that Faith in Sundry battels fought.
So Dunstan as the rest arose through many Sees,
To this Arch-type at last ascending by degrees,
There by his power confirm'd, and strongly credit wonne,
To many wondrous things, which he before had done.
To whom when (as they say) the Devill once appear'd,
This man so full of faith, not once at all afeard,
Strong conflicts with him had, in myracles most great.
As Egelnoth againe much grac'd that sacred seat,
Who for his godly deeds surnamed was the Good,
Not boasting of his birth, though com'n of Royall blood:
For that, nor at the first, a Monkes meane Cowle despis'd,
With winning men to God, who never was suffic'd.
These men before exprest; so Eadsine next ensues,
To propagate the truth, no toyle that did refuse;
In Haralds time who liv'd, when William Conqueror came,
For holinesse of life, attain'd unto that fame,
That Souldiers fierce and rude, that pitty never knew,
Were suddenly made mild, as changed in his view.
This man with those before, most worthily related
Arch-saints, as in their Sees Arch-bishops consecrated.
Saint Thomas Becket then, which Rome so much did hery,
As to his Christned name it added Canterbury;
There to whose sumptuous Shrine the neere succeeding ages,
So mighty offrings sent, and made such Pilgrimages,
Concerning whom, the world since then hath spent much breath,
And many questions made both of his life and death:
If he were truely just, he hath his right; if no,
Those times were much to blame, that have him reckond so.
Then these from Yorke ensue, whose lives as much have grac'd
That See, as these before in Canterbury plac'd:
Saint Wilfrid of her Saints, we then the first will bring,
Who twice by Egfrids ire, the sterne Northumbrian King,

Expulst his sacred Seat, most patiently it bare,
The man for sacred gifts almost beyond compare.
Then Bosa next to him as meeke and humble hearted,
As the other full of grace, to whom great God imparted
His mercies sundry wayes, as age upon him came.
And next him followeth John, who likewise bare the name,
Of Beverley, where he most happily was borne,
Whose holinesse did much his native place adorne,
Whose Vigils had by those devouter times bequests
The Ceremonies due to great and solemne Feasts.
So Oswald of that seat, and Cedwall sainted were,
Both reverenc'd and renown'd Archbishops, living there
The former to that See, from Worcester transfer'd,
Deceased, was againe at Worcester inter'd:
The other in that See a sepucher they chose,
And did for his great zeale amongst the Saints dispose,
As William by descent com'n of the Conquerors straine,
Whom Stephen ruling here did in his time ordaine
Archbishop of that See, among our Saints doth fall,
Deriv'd from those two Seats, styld Archiepiscopall.
Next these Arch-Sees of ours, now London place doth take,
Which had those, of whom time Saints worthily did make.
As Ceda, (brother to that reverent Bishop Chad,
At Lichfield in those times, his famous seat that had)
Is Sainted for that See amongst our reverent men,
From London though at length remoov'd to Lestingen,
A monastery, which then he richly had begun.
Him Erkenwald ensues th'East English Offa's sonne,
His fathers kingly Court, who for a Crosiar fled,
Whose works such fame him wonne for holinesse, that dead,
Time him enshrin'd in Pauls, (the mother of that See)
Which with Revenues large, and Priviledges he
Had wondrously endow'd; to goodnesse so affected,
That he those Abbayes great, from his owne power erected
At Chertsey neere to Thames, and Barking famous long.
So Roger hath a roome in these our Sainted throng,
Who by his words and works so taught the way to heaven,
As that great name to him sure was not vainely given.
With Winchester againe proceed we, which shall store
Us with as many Saints, as any See (or more)
Of whom we yet have sung, (as Heada there we have)
Who by his godly life, so good instructions gave,
As teaching that the way to make men to live well,
Example us assur'd, did Preaching farre excell.
Our Swithen then ensues, of him why ours I say,
Is that upon his Feast, his dedicated day,
As it in Harvest haps, so Plow-men note thereby,
Th'ensuing fortie dayes be either wet or dry,

As that day falleth out, whose Myracles may wee
Beleeve those former times, he well might sainted bee.
So Frithstan for a Saint incalendred we find,
With Brithstan not a whit the holyest man behind,
Canoniz'd, of which two, the former for respect
Of vertues in him found, the latter did elect
To sit upon his See, who likewise dying there,
To Ethelbald againe succeeding did appeare,
The honour to a Saint, as challenging his due.
These formerly exprest, then Elpheg doth ensue;
Then Ethelwald, of whom this Almes-deed hath been told,
That in a time of dearth his Churches plate he sold,
T'releeve the needy poore; the Churches wealth (quoth he)
May be againe repayr'd, but so these cannot be.
With these before exprest, so Britwald forth she brought,
By faith and earnest prayer his myracles that wrought,
That such against the Faith, that were most stony-hearted,
By his religious life, have lastly been converted.
This man, when as our Kings so much decayed were,
As 'twas suppos'd their Line would be extinguisht here,
Had in his Dreame reveald, to whom All-doing heaven,
The Scepter of this land in after-times had given;
Which in Prophettick sort by him delivered was,
And as he stoutly spake, it truly came to passe.
So other Southerne Sees, here either lesse or more,
Have likewise had their Saints, though not alike in store.
Of Rochester, we have Saint Ithamar, being then
In those first times, first of our native English men
Residing on that Seat; so as an ayd to her,
But singly Sainted thus, we have of Chichester,
Saint Richard, and with him Saint Gilbert, which doe stand
Enrold amongst the rest of this our Mytred Band,
Of whom such wondrous things, for truths delivered are,
As now may seeme to stretch our strait beleefe too farre.
And Cimbert, of a Saint had the deserved right,
His yearely Obiits long, done in the Isle of Wight;
A Bishop, as some say, but certaine of what See,
It scarcely can be proov'd, nor is it knowne to me.
Whilst Sherburne was a See, and in her glory shone,
And Bodmin likewise had a Bishop of her owne,
Whose Diocesse that time contained Cornwall; these
Had as the rest their Saints, derived from their Sees:
The first, her Adelme had, and Hamond, and the last
Had Patrock, for a Saint that with the other past;
That were it fit for us but to examine now
Those former times, these men for Saints that did allow,
And from our reading urge, that others might as well
Related be for Saints, as worthy every deale.

This scruteny of ours, would cleere that world thereby,
And shew it to be voyd of partiality,
That each man holy cald, was not canoniz'd here,
But such whose lives by death had triall many a yeere.
That See at Norwich now establisht (long not stird)
At Eltham planted first, to Norwich then transferd
Into our bedroule here, her Humbert in doth bring,
(A Counsellour that was to that most martyred King
Saint Edmund) who in their rude massacre then slaine,
The title of a Saint, his Martyrdome doth gaine.
So Hereford hath had on her Cathedrall Seat,
Saint Leofgar, a man by Martyrdome made great,
Whom Griffith Prince of Wales, that Towne which did subdue,
(O most unhallowed deed) unmercifully slue.
So Worster, (as those Sees here sung by us before)
Hath likewise with her Saints renown'd our native shore:
Saint Egwin as her eld'st, with Woolstan as the other,
Of whom she may be proud, to say shee was the Mother,
The Churches Champions both, for her that stoutly stood.
Lichfield hath those no whit lesse famous, nor lesse good:
The first of whom is that most reverent Bishop Chad,
In those religious times for holinesse that had,
The name above the best that lived in those dayes,
That Stories have been stuft with his abundant praise;
Who on the See of Yorke being formerly instauld,
Yet when backe to that place Saint Wilfrid was recald,
The Seat to that good man he willingly resign'd,
And to the quiet Closse of Lichfield him confin'd.
So Sexulfe after him, then Owen did supply,
Her Trine of reverent men, renown'd for sanctitie.
As Lincolne to the Saints, our Robert Grosted lent,
A perfect godly man, most learn'd and eloquent,
Then whom no Bishop yet walkt in more upright wayes,
Who durst reproove proud Rome, in her most prosperous dayes,
Whose life, of that next age the Justice well did show,
Which we may boldly say, for this we clearely know,
Had Innocent the fourth the Churches Suffrage led,
This man could not at Rome have been Canonized.
Her sainted Bishop John, so Ely addes to these,
Yet never any one of all our severall Sees
Northumberland like thine, have to these times been blest,
Which sent into this Isle so many men profest,
Whilst Hagustald had then a Mother-Churches stile,
And Lindisferne of us now cald the Holy-Ile,
Was then a See before that Durham was so great,
And long ere Carleill came to be a Bishops seat.
Aidan, and Finan both, most happily were found
Northumberland in thee, even whilst thou didst abound

With Paganisme, which them thy Oswin that good King,
His people to convert did in from Scotland bring:
As Etta likewise hers, from Malrorse that arose,
Being Abbot of that place, whom the Northumbers chose
The Bishopricke of Ferne, and Hagustald to hold.
And Cuthbert of whose life such Myracles are told,
As Storie scarcely can the truth thereof maintaine,
Of th'old Scotch-Irish Kings descended from the straine,
To whom since they belong, I from them here must swerve,
And till I thither come, their holinesse reserve,
Proceeding with the rest that on those Sees have showne,
As Edbert after these borne naturally our owne.
The next which in that See Saint Cuthbert did succeed,
His Church then built of wood, and thatch'd with homely reed,
He builded up of stone, and covered fayre with Lead,
Who in Saint Cuthberts Grave they buried being dead,
As his sad people he at his departing wild.
So Higbald after him a Saint is likewise held,
Who when his proper See, as all the Northren Shore,
Were by the Danes destroyd, he not dismayd the more,
But making shift to get out of the cruell flame,
His Cleargie carrying foorth, preach'd wheresoere he came.
And Alwyn who the Church at Durham now, begun,
Which place before that time was strangely overrun
With shrubs, and men for corne that plot had lately eard,
Where he that goodly Phane to after ages reard,
And thither his late Seat from Lindisferne translated,
Which his Cathedrall Church by him was consecrated.
So Acca we account mongst those which have been cald
The Saints of this our See, which sate at Hagenstald,
Of which he Bishop was, in that good age respected,
In Calenders preserv'd, in th'Catalogues neglected,
Which since would seeme to shew the Bishops as they came:
Then Edilwald, which some (since) Ethelwoolph doe name,
At Durham by some men supposed to reside
More rightly, but by some at Carleill justifide,
The first which rul'd that See, which Beauclerke did preferre,
Much gracing him, who was his only Confessor.
Nor were they Bishops thus related Saints alone;
Northumberland, but thou (besides) hast many a one,
Religious Abbots, Priests, and holy Hermits then,
Canonized as well as thy great Mytred men:
Two famous Abbots first are in the ranke of these,
Whose Abbayes touch'd the walls of thy two ancient Seas.
Thy Roysill (in his time the tutillage that had
Of Cuthbert that great Saint, whose hopes then but a lad,
Exprest in riper yeares how greatly he might merit)
The man who had from God a prophesying Spirit,

Foretelling many things; and growing to be old,
His very hower of death, was by an Angell told.
At Malroyes this good man his Sainting well did earne,
Saint Oswald his againe at holy Lindisferne,
With Ive a godly Priest, suppos'd to have his lere
Of Cuthbert, and with him was Herbert likewise there
His fellow-pupill long, (who as mine Authour saith)
So great opinion had, of Cuthbert and his faith,
That at one time and place, he with that holy man,
Desir'd of God to dye, which by his prayer he wan.
Our venerable Bede so forth that Country brought,
And worthily so nam'd, who of those ages sought
The truth to understand, impartially which he
Delivered hath to time, in his Records that we,
Things left so farre behind, before us still may read,
Mongst our canoniz'd sort, who called is Saint Bede.
A sort of Hermits then, by thee to light are brought,
Who liv'd by Almes, and Prayer, the world respecting nought.
Our Edilwald the Priest, in Ferne (now holy Ile)
Which standeth from the firme to Sea nine English mile,
Sate in his reverent Cell, as Godrick thou canst show;
His head and beard as white as Swan or driven Snow,
At Finchall threescore yeeres, a Hermits life to lead;
Their solitary way in thee did Alrick tread,
Who in a Forrest neere to Carleill, in his age,
Bequeath'd himselfe to his more quiet Hermitage.
Of Wilgusse, so in thee Northumberland we tell,
Whose most religious life hath merited so well,
(Whose blood thou boasts to be of thy most royall straine)
That Alkwin, Master to that mightie Charlemaigne,
In Verse his Legend writ, who of our holy men,
He him the subject chose for his most learned pen.
So Oswyn, one of thy deare Country thou canst show,
To whom as for the rest for him we likewise owe
Much honour to thy earth, this godly man that gave,
Whose Reliques that great house of Lesting long did save,
To sinders till it sanke: so Benedict by thee,
We have amongst the rest, for Saints that reckoned bee,
Of Wyremouth worship'd long, her Patron buried there,
In that most goodly Church, which he himselfe did reare.
Saint Thomas so to us Northumberland thou lent'st,
Whom up into the South, thou from his Country sent'st;
For sanctitie of life, a man exceeding rare,
Who since that of his name so many Saints there are,
This man from others more, that times might understand,
They to his christened name added Northumberland.
Nor in one Country thus our Saints confined were,
But through this famous Isle dispersed here and there:

As Yorkshire sent us in Saint Robert to our store,
At Knarsborough most knowne, whereas he long before
His blessed time bestowd; then one as just as he,
(If credit to those times attributed may be)
Saint Richard with the rest deserving well a roome,
Which in that Country once, at Hampoole had a toombe.
Religious Alred so, from Rydall we receive,
The Abbot, who to all posteritie did leave,
The fruits of his staid faith, delivered by his Pen.
Not of the least desert amongst our holiest men,
One Eusac then we had, but where his life he led,
That doubt I, but am sure he was Canonized,
And was an Abbot too, for sanctity much fam'd.
Then Woolsey will we bring, of Westminster so nam'd,
And by that title knowne, in power and goodnesse great;
And meriting as well his Sainting, as his Seat.
So have we found three Johns, of sundry places here,
Of which (three reverent men) two famous Abbots were.
The first Saint Albans shew'd, the second Lewes had,
Another godly John we to these former add,
To make them up a Trine, (the name of Saints that wonn)
Who was a Yorkshire man, and Prior of Berlington.
So Biren can we boast, a man most highly blest
With the title of a Saint, whose ashes long did rest
At Dorchester, where he was honoured many a day;
But of the place he held, books diversly dare say,
As they of Gilbert doe, who founded those Divines,
Monasticks all that were, of him nam'd Gilbertines:
To which his Order here, he thirteene houses built,
When that most thankfull time, to shew he had not spilt
His wealth on it in vaine, a Saint hath made him here,
At Sempringham enshrin'd, a towne of Lincolneshire.
Of sainted Hermits then, a company we have,
To whom devouter times this veneration gave:
As Gwir in Cornwall kept his solitary Cage,
And Neoth by Hunstock there, his holy Hermitage,
As Guthlake, from his youth, who liv'd a Souldier long,
Detesting the rude spoyles, done by the armed throng,
The mad tumultuous world contemptibly forsooke,
And to his quiet Cell by Crowland him betooke,
Free from all publique crowds, in that low Fenny ground.
As Bertiline againe, was neere to Stafford found:
Then in a Forrest there, for solitude most fit,
Blest in a Hermits life, by there enjoying it.
An Hermit Arnulph so in Bedfordshire became,
A man austere of life, in honour of whose name,
Time after built a Towne, where this good man did live,
And did to it the name of Arnulphsbury give.

These men, this wicked world respected not a hayre,
But true Professors were of povertie and prayer.
Amongst these men which times have honoured with the Stile
Of Confessors, (made Saints) so every little while,
Our Martyrs have com'n in, who sealed with their blood,
That faith which th'other preach'd, gainst them that it withstood;
As Alnoth, who had liv'd a Herdsman, left his Seat,
Though in the quiet fields, whereas he kept his Neat,
And leaving that his Charge, he left the world withall,
An Anchorite and became, within a Cloystred wall,
Inclosing up himselfe, in prayer to spend his breath,
But was too soone (alas) by Pagans put to death.
Then Woolstan, one of these, by his owne kinsman slaine
At Evsham, for that he did zealously maintaine
The veritie of Christ. As Thomas, whom we call
Of Dover, adding Monke, and Martyr therewithall;
For that the barbarous Danes he bravely did withstand,
From ransacking the Church, when here they put on land,
By them was done to death, which rather he did chuse,
Then see their Heathen hands those holy things abuse.
Two Boyes of tender age, those elder Saints ensue,
Of Norwich William was, of Lincolne little Hugh,
Whom th'unbeleeving Jewes (rebellious that abide)
In mockery of our Christ at Easter crucifi'd,
Those times would every one should their due honour have,
His freedome or his life, for Jesus Christ that gave.
So Wiltshire with the rest her Hermit Ulfrick hath
Related for a Saint, so famous in the Faith,
That sundry ages since, his Cell have sought to find,
At Hasselburg, who had his Obiits him assign'd.
So had we many Kings most holy here at home,
As men of meaner ranke, which have attaind that roome:
Northumberland, thy seat with Saints did us supply
Of thy religious Kings; of which high Hierarchy
Was Edwin, for the Faith by Heathenish hands inthrald,
Whom Penda which to him the Welsh Cadwallyn cald,
Without all mercy slew: But he alone not dide
By that proud Mercian King, but Penda yet beside,
Just Oswald likewise slew, at Oswaldstree, who gave
That name unto that place, as though time meant to save
His memory thereby, there suffring for the Faith,
As one whose life deserv'd that memory in death.
So likewise in the Roule of these Northumbrian Kings,
With those that Martyrs were, so foorth that Country brings
Th'annoynted Oswin next, in Deira to ensue,
Whom Osway that bruit King of wild Bernitia slue:
Two kingdomes, which whilst then Northumberland remain'd
In greatnesse, were within her larger bounds contain'd;

This Kingly Martyr so, a Saint was rightly crown'd.
As Alkmond one of hers for sanctity renown'd,
King Alreds Christned sonne, a most religious Prince,
Whom when the Heathenish here by no meanes could convince,
(Their Paganisme a pace declining to the wane)
At Darby put to death, whom in a goodly Phane,
Cald by his glorious name, his corpse the Christians layd.
What fame deserv'd your faith, (were it but rightly wayd)
You pious Princes then, in godlinesse so great;
Why should not full-mouthd Fame your praises oft repeat?
So Ethelwolph her King, Northumbria notes againe,
In Martyrdomethe next, though not the next in raigne,
Whom his false Subjects slue, for that he did deface
The Heathenish Saxon gods, and bound them to embrace
The lively quickning Faith, which then began to spread.
So for our Saviour Christ, as these were martyred:
There other holy Kings were likewise, who confest,
Which those most zealous times have Sainted with the rest,
King Alfred that his Christ he might more surely hold,
Left his Northumbrian Crowne, and soone became encould,
At Malroyse, in the land, whereof he had been King.
So Egbert to that Prince, a Paralell we bring,
To Oswoolph his next heire, his kingdome that resign'd,
And presently himselfe at Lindisferne confin'd,
Contemning Courtly state, which earthly fooles adore:
So Ceonulph againe as this had done before,
In that religious house, a cloystred man became,
Which many a blessed Saint hath honoured with the name.
Nor those Northumbrian Kings the onely Martyrs were,
That in this seven-fold Rule the scepters once did beare,
But that the Mercian raigne, which Pagan Princes long,
Did terribly infest, had some her Lords among,
To the true Christian Faith much reverence which did add
Our Martyrologe to helpe: so happily shee had
Rufin, and Ulfad, sonnes to Wulphere, for desire
They had t'imbrace the Faith, by their most cruell Sire
Were without pittie slaine, long ere to manhood growne,
Whose tender bodies had their burying Rites at Stone.
So Kenelme, that the King of Mercia should have beene,
Before his first seven yeares he fully out had seene,
Was slaine by his owne Guard, for feare lest waxing old,
That he the Christian Faith undoubtedly would hold.
So long it was ere truth could Paganisme expell.
Then Fremund, Offa's sonne, of whom times long did tell,
Such wonders of his life and sanctitie, who fled
His fathers kingly Court, and after meekly led
An Hermits life in Wales, where long he did remaine
In Penitence and prayer, till after he was slaine

By cruell Oswayes hands, the most inveterate foe,
The Christian faith here found: so Etheldred shall goe
With these our martyred Saints, though onely he confest,
Since he of Mercia was, a King who highly blest,
Faire Bardncy, where his life religiously he spent,
And meditating Christ, thence to his Saviour went.
Nor our West-Saxon raigne was any whit behind
Those of the other rules (their best) whose zeale wee find,
Amongst those sainted Kings, whose fames are safeliest kept;
As Cedwall, on whose head such praise all times have heapt,
That from a Heathen Prince, a holy Pilgrim turn'd,
Repenting in his heart against the truth t'have spurn'd,
To Rome on his bare feet his patience exercis'd,
And in the Christian faith there humbly was baptiz'd.
So Ethelwoolph, who sat on Cedwalls ancient Seat,
For charitable deeds, who almost was as great,
As any English King, at Winchester enshrin'd,
A man amongst our Saints, most worthily devin'd.
Two other Kings as much our Martyrologe may sted,
Saint Edward, and with him comes in Saint Ethelred,
By Alfreda, the first, his Stepmother was slaine,
That her most loved sonne young Ethelbert might raigne:
The other in a storme, and deluge of the Dane,
For that he Christned was, receav'd his deadly bane;
Both which with wondrous cost, the English did interre,
At Wynburne this first Saint, the last at Winchester,
Where that West-Saxon Prince, good Alfred buried was
Among our Sainted Kings, that well deserves to passe.
Nor were these Westerne Kings of the old Saxon straine,
More studious in those times, or stoutlier did maintaine
The truth, then these of ours, the Angles of the East,
Their neer'st and deer'st Allies, which strongly did invest
The Island with their name, of whose most holy Kings,
Which justly have deserv'd their high Canonizings,
Are Sigfrid, whose deare death him worthily hath crownd,
And Edmund in his end, so wondrously renownd,
For Christs sake suffring death, by that blood-drowning Dane,
To whom those times first built that Citie and that Phane,
Whose ruines Suffolke yet can to her glory show,
When shee will have the world of her past greatnesse know.
As Ethelbert againe alur'd with the report
Of more then earthly pompe, then in the Mercian Court,
From the East-Angles went, whilst mighty Offa raign'd;
Where, for he christned was, and Christian-like abstain'd
To Idolatrize with them, fierce Quenred, Offa's Queene
Most treacherously him slew out of th'inveterate spleene
Shee bare unto the Faith, whom we a Saint adore.
So Edwald brother to Saint Edmund, sung before,

A Confessor we call, whom past times did interre,
At Dorcester by Tame, (now in our Calender.)
Amongst those kingdomes here, so Kent account shall yeeld
Of three of her best blood, who in this Christian Field
Were mighty, of the which, King Ethelbert shall stand
The first; who having brought Saint Augustine to land,
Himselfe first christned was, by whose example then,
The Faith grew after strong amongst his Kentishmen.
As Ethelbrit againe, and Ethelred his pheere,
To Edbald King of Kent, who naturall Nephewes were,
For Christ there suffring death, assume them places hye,
Amongst our martyred Saints, commemorate at Wye.
To these two brothers, so two others come againe,
And of as great discent in the Southsexian straine:
Arwaldi of one name, whom ere King Cedwall knew
The true and lively Faith, he tyranously slew:
Who still amongst the Saints have their deserved right,
Whose Vigils were observ'd (long) in the Isle of Wight.
Remembred too the more, for being of one name,
As of th'East-Saxon line, King Sebba so became
A most religious Monke, at London, where he led
A strict retyred life, a Saint alive and dead.
Related for the like, so Edgar we admit,
That King, who over eight did soly Monarch sit,
And with our holyest Saints for his endowments great,
Bestow'd upon the Church. With him we likewise seat
That sumptuous shrined King, good Edward, from the rest
Of that renowned name, by Confessor exprest.
To these our sainted Kings, remembred in our Song,
Those Mayds and widdowed Queenes, doe worthily belong,
Incloystred that became, and had the selfe same style,
For Fasting, Almes, and Prayer, renowned in our Isle,
As those that foorth to France, and Germany we gave,
For holy charges there; but here first let us have
Our Mayd-made-Saints at home, as Hilderlie, with her
We Theorid thinke most fit, for whom those times averre,
A Virgin strictlyer vow'd, hath hardly lived here.
Saint Wulfshild then we bring, all which of Barking were,
And reckoned for the best, which most that house did grace,
The last of which was long the Abbesse of that place.
So Werburg, Wulpheres child, (of Mercia that had been
A persecuting King) by Ermineld his Queene,
At Ely honoured is, where her deare mother late,
A Recluse had remain'd, in her sole widdowed state:
Of which good Audry was King Ina's daughter bright,
Reflecting on those times so cleare a Vestall light,
As many a Virgin-breast she fired with her zeale,
The fruits of whose strong faith, to ages still reveale

The glory of those times, by liberties she gave,
By which those Easterne Shires their Priviledges have.
Of holy Audries too, a sister here we have,
Saint Withburg, who her selfe to Contemplation gave,
At Deerham in her Cell, where her due howres she kept,
Whose death with many a teare in Norfolke was bewept.
And in that Isle againe, which beareth Elies name,
At Ramsey, Merwin so a Vayled Mayd became
Amongst our Virgin-Saints, where Elfled is enrold,
The daughter that is nam'd of noble Ethelwold,
A great East-Anglian Earle, of Ramsey Abbas long,
So of our Mayden-Saints, the Female sex among.
With Milburg, Mildred comes, and Milwid, daughters deere,
To Mervald, who did then the Mercian Scepter beare.
At Wenlock, Milburg dy'd, (a most religious mayd)
Of which great Abbay shee the first foundation layd:
And Thanet as her Saint (even to this age) doth herye
Her Mildred. Milwid was the like at Canterbury.
Nor in this utmost Isle of Thanet may we passe,
Saint Eadburg Abbesse there, who the deare daughter was,
To Ethelbert her Lord, and Kents first Christened King,
Who in this place most fitst we with the former bring,
Translated (as some say) to Flanders: but that I,
As doubtfull of the truth, here dare not justifie.
King Edgars sister so, Saint Edith, place may have
With these our Maiden-Saints, who to her Powlsworth gave
Immunities most large, and goodly livings layd.
Which Modwen, long before, a holy Irish mayd,
Had founded in that place, with most devout intent.
As Eanswine, Eadwalds child, one of the Kings of Kent,
At Foulkston found a place (given by her father there)
In which she gave her selfe to abstinence and prayer.
Of the West-Saxon rule, borne to three severall Kings,
Foure holy Virgins more the Muse in order brings:
Saint Ethelgive the child to Alfred, which we find,
Those more devouter times at Shaftsbury enshrin'd.
Then Tetta in we take, at Winburne on our way,
Which Cuthreds sister was, who in those times did sway
On the West-Saxon Seat, two other sacred Mayds,
As from their Cradels vow'd to bidding of their beads.
Saint Cuthburg, and with her Saint Quinburg, which we here
Succeedingly doe set, both as they Sisters were,
And Abbesses againe of Wilton, which we gather,
Our Virgin-Band to grace, both having to their father
Religious Ina, red with those which ruld the West,
Whose mothers sacred wombe with other Saints was blest,
As after shall be shew'd: an other Virgin vow'd,
And likewise for a Saint amongst the rest allow'd;

To th'elder Edward borne, bright Eadburg, who for she,
(As five related Saints of that blest name there be)
Of Wilton Abbasse was, they her of Wilton styl'd:
Was ever any Mayd more mercifull, more mild,
Or sanctimonious knowne: But Muse, on in our Song,
With other princely Mayds, but first with those that sprung
From Penda, that great King of Mercia; holy Tweed,
And Kinisdred, with these their sisters, Kinisweed,
And Eadburg, last not least, at Godmanchester all
Incloystred; and to these Saint Tibba let us call,
In solitude to Christ, that set her whole delight,
In Godmanchester made a constant Anchorite.
Amongst which of that house, for Saints that reckoned be,
Yet never any one more grac'd the fame then she.
Deriv'd of royall Blood, as th'other Elfled than
Neece to that mighty King, our English Athelstan,
At Glastenbury shrin'd; and one as great as shee,
Being Edward Out-lawes child, a Mayd that liv'd to see
The Conquerour enter here, Saint Christian (to us knowne)
Whose life by her cleere name divinely was foreshowne.
For holinesse of life, that as renowned were,
And not lesse nobly borne, nor bred, produce we here;
Saint Hilda, and Saint Hien, the first of noble name,
At Strenshalt, tooke her vow, the other sister came
To Colchester, and grac'd the rich Essexian shore:
Whose Reliques many a day the world did there adore.
And of our sainted Mayds, the number to supply,
Of Eadburg we allow, sometime at Alsbury,
To Redwald then a King of the East-Angles borne,
A Votresse as sincere as shee thereto was sworne.
Then Pandwine we produce, whom this our native Isle,
As forraine parts much priz'd, and higher did instyle,
The holyest English Mayd, whose Vigils long were held
In Lincolneshire; yet not Saint Frideswid exceld,
The Abbesse of an house in Oxford, of her kind
The wonder; nor that place, could hope the like to find.
Two sisters so we have, both to devotion plite,
And worthily made Saints; the elder Margarite,
Of Katsby Abbesse was, and Alice, as we read,
Her sister on that seat, did happily succeed,
At Abington, which first receiv'd their living breath.
Then those Northumbrian Nymphs, all vayld, as full of Faith,
That Country sent us in, t'increase our Virgin-Band,
Faire Elfled, Oswalds child, King of Northumberland,
At Strenshalt that was vaild. As mongst those many there,
O Ebba, whose cleere fame, time never shall out-weare,
At Coldingham, farre hence within that Country plac'd;
The Abbesse, who to keepe thy vayled Virgins chast,

Which else thou fearst the Danes would ravish, which possest
This Isle; first of thy selfe and then of all the rest,
The Nose and upper Lip from your fayre faces kerv'd,
And from pollution so your hallowed house preserv'd.
Which when the Danes perceiv'd, their hopes so farre deluded,
Setting the house on fire, their Martyrdome concluded.
As Leofron, whose faith with others rightly wayd,
Shall shew her not out-match'd by any English Mayd:
Who likewise when the Dane with persecution storm'd,
She here a Martyrs part most gloriously perform'd.
Two holy Mayds againe at Whitby were renown'd,
Both Abbesses thereof, and Confessors are crown'd;
Saint Ethelfrid, with her Saint Congill, as a payre
Of Abbesses therein, the one of which by prayer
The Wild-geese thence expeld, that Island which annoy'd,
By which their grasse and graine was many times destroy'd,
Which fall from off their wings, nor to the ayre can get
From the forbidden place, till they be fully set.
As these within this Isle in Cloysters were inclosd:
So we our Virgins had to forraine parts exposd;
As Eadburg, Ana's child, and Sethred borne our owne,
Were Abbesses of Bridge, whose zeale to France was knowne:
And Ercongate againe we likewise thither sent,
(Which Ercombert begot, sometime a King of Kent)
A Prioresse of that place; Burgundosora bare,
At Eureux the chaste rule, all which renowned are
In France, which as this Isle of them may freely boast.
So Germany some grac'd, from this their native coast.
Saint Walburg heere extract from th'royall English Line,
Was in that Country made Abbesse of Heydentine.
Saint Tecla to that place at Ochenford they chose:
From Wynburne with the rest (in Dorsetshire) arose
Chast Agatha, with her went Lioba along.
From thence, two not the least these sacred Mayds among,
At Biscopsen, by time encloystred and became.
Saint Lewen so attayn'd an everliving name
For Martyrdome, which shee at Wynokebergin wan,
Mayds seeming in their Sex t'exceed the holyest man.
Nor had our Virgins here for sanctitie the prize,
But widdowed Queenes as well, that being godly wise,
Forsaking second beds, the world with them forsooke,
To strict retyred lives, and gladly them betooke
To Abstinence and Prayer, and as sincerely liv'd.
As when the Fates of life King Ethelwold depriv'd,
That o'r the East-Angles raign'd, bright Heriswid his wife,
Betaking her to lead a strait Monasticke life,
Departing hence to France, receav'd the holy Vayle,
And lived many a day incloystred there at Kale.

Then Keneburg in this our Sainted front shall stand,
To Alfred the lov'd wife, King of Northumberland,
Daughter to Penda King of Mercia, who though he
Himselfe most Heathenish were, yet liv'd that age to see
Foure Virgins, and this Queene, his children, consecrated
Of Godmanchester all, and after Saints related.
As likewise of this Sex, with Saints that doth us store,
Of the Northumbrian Line so have we many more;
Saint Eanfled widdowed left, by Osway raigning there,
At Strenshalt tooke her Vaile, as Ethelburg the pheere
To Edwin, (rightly nam'd) the holy, which possest
Northumbers sacred seat, her selfe that did invest
At Lymming farre in Kent, which Country gave her breath.
So Edeth as the rest after King Sethricks death,
Which had the selfe same rule of Wilton Abbesse was,
Where two West-Saxon Queenes for Saints shall likewise passe,
Which in that selfe same house, Saint Edeth did succeed,
Saint Ethelwid, which here put on her hallowed weed,
King Alreds worthy wife, of Westsex; so againe
Did Wilfrid, Edgars Queene, (so famous in his raigne)
Then Eadburg, Ana's wife, received as the other,
Who as a Saint her selfe, so likewise was she mother
To two most holy Mayds, as we before have show'd
At Wilton, (which we say) their happy time bestow'd,
Though she of Barking was, a holy Nunne profest,
Who in her husbands time, had raigned in the West:
Th'East-Saxon Line againe, so others to us lent,
As Sexburg sometime Queene to Ercombert of Kent,
Though Ina's loved child, and Audryes sister knowne,
Which Ely in those dayes did for her Abbesse owne.
Nor to Saint Osith we lesse honour ought to give,
King Sethreds widdowed Queene, who (when death did deprive
Th'Essexian King of life) became enrould at Chich,
Whose Shrine to her there built, the world did long enrich.
Two holy Mercian Queenes so widdowed, Saints became,
For sanctity much like, not much unlike in name.
King Wulpheres widdowed Pheere, Queene Ermineld, whose life
At Ely is renown'd, and Ermenburg, the wife
To Mervald raigning there, a Saint may safely passe,
Who to three Virgin-Saints the vertuous mother was,
The remnant of her dayes, religiously that bare,
Immonastred in Kent, where first she breath'd the ayre.
King Edgars mother so, is for a Saint preferd,
Queene Algyue, who (they say) at Shipston was interd.
So Edward Outlawes wife, Saint Agatha, we bring,
By Salomon begot, that great Hungarian King;
Who when she saw the wrong to Edgar her deare sonne,
By cruell Harold first, then by the Conquerour done,

Depriv'd his rightfull crowne, no hope it to recover,
A Vestall habite tooke, and gave the false world over.
Saint Maud here not the least, though shee be set the last,
And scarcely over-matcht by any that is past,
Our Beauclearks Queene, and borne to Malcolme King of Scots,
Whose sanctity was seene to wipe out all the spots
Were laid upon her life, when shee her Cloyster fled,
And chastly gave her selfe to her lov'd husbands bed,
Whom likewise for a Saint those reverend ages chose,
With whom we at this time our Catalogue will close.
Now Rutland all this time, who held her highly wron'g,
That shee should for the Saints thus strangely be prolong'd,
As that the Muse such time upon their praise should spend,
Sent in her ambling Wash, faire Welland to attend
At Stamford, which her Streame doth eas'ly overtake,
Of whom her Mistresse Flood seemes wondrous much to make;
For that she was alone the darling and delight
Of Rutland, ravisht so with her beloved sight,
As in her onely childs, a mothers heart may be:
Wherefore that she the least, yet fruitfulst Shire should see,
The honourable ranke shee had amongst the rest,
The ever-labouring Muse her Beauties thus exprest.
Love not thy selfe the lesse, although the least thou art,
What thou in greatnesse wantst, wise Nature doth impart
In goodnesse of thy soyle; and more delicious mould,
Survaying all this Isle, the Sunne did nere behold.
Bring forth that British Vale, and be it ne'r so rare,
But Catmus with that Vale, for richnesse shall compare:
What Forrest-Nymph is found, how brave so ere she be,
But Lyfield shewes her selfe as brave a Nymph as shee?
What River ever rose from Banke, or swelling Hill,
Then Rutlands wandring Wash, a delicater Rill?
Small Shire that can produce to thy proportion good,
One Vale of speciall name, one Forrest, and one Flood.
O Catmus, thou faire Vale, come on in Grasse and Corne;
That Bever ne'r be sayd thy sister-hood to scorne,
And let thy Ocham boast, to have no litle grace,
That her they pleased Fates, did in thy bosome place,
And Lyfield, as thou art a Forrest, live so free,
That every Forrest-Nymph may praise the sports in thee.
And downe to Wellands course, O Wash, runne ever cleere,
To honour, and to be much honoured by this Shire.

And here my Canto ends, which kept the Muse so long,
That it may rather seeme a Volume, then a Song.

THE FIVE AND TWENTIETH SONG

THE ARGUMENT

Tow'rds Lincolnshire our Progresse layd,
Wee through deepe Hollands Ditches wade,
Fowling, and Fishing in the Fen;
Then come wee next to Kestiven,
And bringing Wytham to her fall,
On Lindsey light wee last of all,
Her Scite and Pleasures to attend,
And with the Isle of Axholme end.

Now in upon thy earth, rich Lincolnshire I straine,
At Deeping, from whose Street, the plentious Ditches draine,
Hemp-bearing Hollands Fen, at Spalding that doe fall
Together in their Course, themselves as emptying all
Into one generall Sewer, which seemeth to divide,
Low Holland from the High, which on their Easterne side
Th'in-bending Ocean holds, from the Norfolcean lands,
To their more Northern poynt, where Wainfleet drifted stands,
Doe shoulder out those Seas, and Lindsey bids her stay,
Because to that faire part, a challenge she doth lay.
From fast and firmer Earth, whereon the Muse of late,
Trod with a steady foot, now with a slower gate,
Through Quicksands, Beach, and Ouze, the Washes she must wade,
Where Neptune every day doth powerfully invade
The vast and queachy soyle, with Hosts of wallowing waves,
From whose impetuous force, that who himselfe not saves,
By swift and sudden flight, is swallowed by the deepe,
When from the wrathfull Tydes the foming Surges sweepe,
The Sands which lay all nak'd, to the wide heaven before,
And turneth all to Sea, which was but lately Shore,
From this our Southerne part of Holland, cal'd the Low,
Where Crowlands ruines yet, (though almost buried) show
Her mighty Founders power, yet his more Christian zeale,
Shee by the Muses ayd, shall happily reveale
Her sundry sorts of Fowle, from whose abundance she
Above all other Tracts, may boast her selfe to be
The Mistris, (and indeed) to sit without compare,
And for no worthlesse soyle, should in her glory share,
From her moyst seat of Flags, of Bulrushes and Reed,
With her just proper praise, thus Holland doth proceed.
Yee Acherusian Fens, to mine resigne your glory,
Both that which lies within the goodly Territory
Of Naples, as that Fen Thesposia's earth upon,
Whence that infernall Flood, the smutted Acheron
Shoves forth her sullen head, as thou most fatall Fen,

Of which Hetruria tells, the watry Thrasimen,
In History although thou highly seemst to boast,
That Haniball by thee o'rthrew the Roman Host.
I scorne th'Egyptian Fen, which Alexandria showes,
Proud Mareotis, should my mightinesse oppose,
Or Scythia, on whose face the Sunne doth hardly shine,
Should her Meotis thinke to match with this of mine,
That covered all with Snow continually doth stand.
I stinking Lerna hate, and the poore Libian Sand. Hollands Oration.
Marica that wise Nymph, to whom great Neptune gave
The charge of all his Shores, from drowning them to save,
Abideth with me still upon my service prest,
And leaves the looser Nymphs to wayt upon the rest:
In Summer giving earth, from which I spare my Peat,
And faster feedings by, for Deere, for Horse, and Neat.
My various Fleets for Fowle, O who is he can tell,
The species that in me for multitudes excell!
The Duck, and Mallard first, the Falconers onely sport,
(Of River-flights the chiefe, so that all other sort,
They onely Greene-Fowle tearme) in every Mere abound,
That you would thinke they sate upon the very ground,
Their numbers be so great, the waters covering quite,
That rais'd, the spacious ayre is darkened with their flight;
Yet still the dangerous Dykes, from shot doe them secure,
Where they from Flash to Flash, like the full Epicure
Waft, as they lov'd to change their Diet every meale;
And neere to them ye see the lesser dibling Teale
In Bunches, with the first that flie from Mere to Mere,
As they above the rest were Lords of Earth and Ayre.
The Gossander with them, my goodly Fennes doe show
His head as Ebon blacke, the rest as white as Snow,
With whom the Widgeon goes, the Golden-Eye, the Smeath,
And in odde scattred pits, the Flags, and Reeds beneath;
The Coot, bald, else cleane black, that whitenesse it doth beare
Upon the forehead star'd, the Water-Hen doth weare
Upon her little tayle, in one small feather set.
The Water-woosell next, all over black as Jeat,
With various colours, black, greene, blew, red, russet, white,
Doe yeeld the gazing eye as variable delight,
As doe those sundry Fowles, whose severall plumes they be.
The diving Dob-chick, here among the rest you see,
Now up, now downe againe, that hard it is to proove,
Whether under water most it liveth, or above:
With which last little Fowle, (that water may not lacke;
More then the Dob-chick doth, and more doth love the brack)
The Puffin we compare, which comming to the dish,
Nice pallats hardly judge, if it be flesh or fish.
But wherefore should I stand upon such toyes as these,

That have so goodly Fowles, the wandring eye to please.
Here in my vaster Pooles, as white as Snow or Milke,
(In water blacke as Stix) swimmes the wild Swanne, the Ilke,
Of Hollanders so tearm'd, no niggard of his breath,
(As Poets say of Swannes, which onely sing in death)
But oft as other Birds, is heard his tunnes to roat,
Which like a Trumpet comes, from his long arched throat,
And tow'rds this watry kind, about the Flashes brimme,
Some cloven-footed are, by nature not to swimme.
There stalks the stately Crane, as though he march'd in warre,
By him that hath the Herne, which (by the Fishy Carre)
Can fetch with their long necks, out of the Rush and Reed,
Snigs, Fry, and yellow Frogs, whereon they often feed:
And under them againe, (that water never take,
But by some Ditches side, or little shallow Lake
Lye dabling night and day) the pallat-pleasing Snite,
The Bidcocke, and like them the Redshanke, that delight
Together still to be, in some small Reedy bed,
In which these little Fowles in Summers time were bred.
The Buzzing Bitter sits, which through his hollow Bill,
A sudden bellowing sends, which many times doth fill
The neighbouring Marsh with noyse, as though a Bull did roare;
But scarcely have I yet recited halfe my store:
And with my wondrous flocks of Wild-geese come I then,
Which looke as though alone they peopled all the Fen,
Which here in Winter time, when all is overflow'd,
And want of sollid sward inforceth them abroad,
Th'abundance then is seene, that my full Fennes doe yeeld,
That almost through the Ifle, doe pester every field.
The Barnacles with them, which wheresoere they breed,
On Trees, or rotten Ships, yet to my Fennes for feed
Continually they come, and chiefe abode doe make,
And very hardly forc'd my plenty to forsake:
Who almost all this kind doe challenge as mine owne,
Whose like I dare averre, is elsewhere hardly knowne.
For sure unlesse in me, no one yet ever saw
The multitudes of Fowle, in Mooting time they draw:
From which to many a one, much profit doth accrue.
Now such as flying feed, next these I must pursue;
The Sea-meaw, Sea-pye, Gull, and Curlew heere doe keepe,
As searching every Shole, and watching every deepe,
To find the floating Fry, with their sharpe-pearcing sight,
Which suddenly they take, by stouping from their height.
The Cormorant then comes, (by his devouring kind)
Which flying o'r the Fen, imediately doth find
The Fleet best stor'd of Fish, when from his wings at full,
As though he shot himselfe into the thickned skull,
He under water goes, and so the Shoale pursues,

Which into Creeks doe flie, when quickly he doth chuse,
The Fin that likes him best, and rising, flying feeds.
The Ospray oft here seene, though seldome here it breeds,
Which over them the Fish no sooner doe espie,
But (betwixt him and them, by an antipathy)
Turning their bellies up, as though their death they saw,
They at his pleasure lye, to stuffe his glutt'nous maw.
The toyling Fisher here is tewing of his Net:
The Fowler is imployd his lymed twigs to set.
One underneath his Horse, to get a shoot doth stalke;
Another over Dykes upon his Stilts doth walke:
There other with their Spades, the Peats are squaring out,
And others from their Carres, are busily about,
To draw out Sedge and Reed, for Thatch and Stover fit,
That whosoever would a Landskip rightly hit,
Beholding but my Fennes, shall with more shapes be stor'd,
Then Germany, or France, or Thuscan can afford:
And for that part of me, which men high Holland call,
Where Boston seated is, by plenteous Wythams fall,
I peremptory am, large Neptunes liquid field,
Doth to no other tract the like aboundance yeeld.
For that of all the Seas invironing this Isle,
Our Irish, Spanish, French, how e'r we them enstyle,
The German is the great'st, and it is onely I,
That doe upon the same with most advantage lye.
What Fish can any shore, or British Sea-towne show,
That's eatable to us, that it doth not bestow
Abundantly thereon? the Herring king of Sea,
The faster feeding Cod, the Mackrell brought by May,
The daintie Sole, and Plaice, the Dabb, as of their blood;
The Conger finely sous'd, hote Summers coolest food;
The Whiting knowne to all, a generall wholesome Dish;
The Gurnet, Rochet, Mayd, and Mullet, dainty Fish;
The Haddock, Turbet, Bert, Fish nourishing and strong;
The Thornback, and the Scate, provocatiue among:
The Weaver, which although his prickles venom bee,
By Fishers cut away, which Buyers seldome see:
Yet for the Fish he beares, tis not accounted bad;
The Sea-Flounder is here as common as the Shad;
The Sturgeon cut to Keggs, (too big to handle whole)
Gives many a dainty bit out of his lusty Jole.
Yet of rich Neptunes store, whilst thus I ldely chat,
Thinke not that all betwixt the Wherpoole, and the Sprat,
I goe about to name, that were to take in hand,
The Atomy to tell, or to cast up the sand;
But on the English coast, those most that usuall are,
Wherewith the staules from thence doe furnish us for farre;
Amongst whose sundry sorts, since thus farre I am in,

Ile of our Shell-Fish speake, with these of Scale and Fin:
The Sperme-increasing Crab, much Cooking that doth aske,
The big-legg'd Lobster, fit for wanton Venus taske,
Voluptuaries oft take rather then for food,
And that the same effect which worketh in the blood
The rough long Oyster is, much like the Lobster limb'd:
The Oyster hote as they, the Mussle often trimd
With Orient Pearle within, as thereby nature show'd,
That she some secret good had on that Shell bestow'd:
The Scallop cordiall judgd, the dainty Wilk and Limp,
The Periwincle, Prawne, the Cockle, and the Shrimpe,
For wanton womens tasts or for weake stomacks bought.
When Kestiven this while that certainly had thought,
Her tongue would ne'r have stopt, quoth shee, O how I hate,
Thus of her foggy Fennes, to heare rude Holland prate,
That with her Fish and Fowle, here keepeth such a coyle,
As her unwholesome ayre, and more unwholesome soyle,
For these of which shee boasts, the more might suffred be;
When those her feathered flocks she sends not out to me,
Wherein cleare Witham they, and many a little Brooke,
(In which the Sunne it selfe may well be proud to looke)
Have made their Flesh more sweet by my refined food,
From that so ramish tast of her most fulsome mud,
When the toyld Cater home them to the Kitchen brings,
The Cooke doth cast them out, as most unsavory things.
Besides, what is she else, but a foule woosie Marsh,
And that shee calls her grasse, so blady is, and harsh,
As cuts the Cattels mouthes, constrain'd thereon to feed,
So that my poorest trash, which mine call Rush and Reed,
For litter scarcely fit, that to the dung I throw,
Doth like the Penny grasse, or the pure Clover show,
Compared with her best: and for her sundry Fish,
Of which she freely boasts, to furnish every Dish.
Did not full Neptunes fields so furnish her with store,
Those in the Ditches bred, within her muddy Moore,
Are of so earthy taste, as that the Ravenous Crow
Will rather starve, thereon her stomack then bestow.
From Stamford as along my tract tow'rd Lincolne straines,
What Shire is there can shew more valuable Vaines
Of soyle then is in mee? or where can there be found,
So faire and fertile fields, or Sheep-walks nere so sound?
Where doth the pleasant ayre resent a sweeter breath?
What Countrey can produce a delicater Heath,
Then that which her faire Name from Ancaster doth hold?
Through all the neighboring Shires, whose praise shall still be told,
Which Flora in the Spring doth with such wealth adorne,
That Bever needs not much her company to scorne,
Though shee a Vale lye low, and this a Heath sit hye,

Yet doth she not alone, allure the wondring eye
With prospect from each part, but that her pleasant ground
Gives all that may content, the well-breath'd Horse and Hound:
And from the Britans yet, to shew what then I was,
One of the Roman Wayes neere through my midst did passe:
Besides to my much praise, there hath been in my mould
Their painted Pavements found, and Armes of perfect gold.
They neere the Saxons raigne, that in this tract did dwell,
All other of this Isle, for that they would excell
For Churches every where, so rich and goodly rear'd
In every little Dorpe, that after-times have fear'd
T'attempt so mighty workes; yet one above the rest,
In which it may be thought, they strove to doe their best,
Of pleasant Grantham is, that Piramis so hye,
Rear'd (as it might be thought) to overtop the skie,
The Traveller that strikes into a wondrous maze,
As on his Horse he sits, on that proud height to gaze.
When Wytham that this while a listning eare had laid,
To hearken (for her selfe) what Kestiven had said,
Much pleasd with this report, for that she was the earth
From whom she onely had her sweet and seasoned birth,
From Wytham which that name derived from her Springs,
Thus as she trips along, this dainty Rivelet sings.
Ye easie ambling streames, which way soe'r you runne,
Or tow'rds the pleasant rise, or tow'rds the mid-day Sunne:
By which (as some suppose by use that have them tride)
Your waters in their course are neatly purifi'd.
Be what you are, or can, I not your Beauties feare,
When Neptune shall commaund the Naiades t'appeare.
In River what is found, in me that is not rare:
Yet for my wel-fed Pykes, I am without compare.
From Wytham mine owne Towne, first watred with my sourse,
As to the Easterne Sea, I hasten on my course.
Who sees so pleasant plaines, or is of fairer seene,
Whose Swains in Shepheards gray, and Gyrles in Lincolne greene?
Whilst some the rings of Bells, and some the Bag-pipes ply,
Dance many a merry Round, and many a Hydegy.
I envy, any Brooke should in my pleasure share,
Yet for my daintie Pykes, I am without compare.
No Land-floods can mee force to over-proud a height;
Nor am I in my Course, too crooked, or too streight:
My depths fall by descents, too long, nor yet too broad,
My Foards with Pebbles, cleare as Orient Pearles, are strowd;
My gentle winding Banks, with sundry Flowers are drest,
The higher rising Heaths, hold distance with my brest.
Thus to her proper Song, the Burthen still she bare;
Yet for my dainty Pykes, I am without compare.
By this to Lincolne com'n, upon whose loftie Scite,

Whilst wistly Wytham looks with wonderfull delight,
Enamoured of the state, and beautie of the place,
That her of all the rest especially doth grace,
Leaving her former Course, in which she first set forth,
Which seemed to have been directly to the North:
Shee runnes her silver front into the muddy Fen,
Which lyes into the East, in her deepe journey, when
Cleare Ban a pretty Brooke, from Lyndsey comming downe,
Delicious Wytham leads to holy Botulphs Towne,
Where proudly she puts in amongst the great resort,
That their appearance make in Neptunes watry Court.
Now Lyndsey all this while, that duely did attend,
Till both her Rivals thus had fully made an end
Of their so tedious talke, when lastly shee replyes;
Loe, bravely here she sits, that both your states defies.
Faire Lincolne is mine owne, which lies upon my South,
As likewise to the North, great Humbers swelling mouth
Encircles me, twixt which in length I bravely lye:
O who can me the best, before them both deny?
Nor Britaine in her Bounds, scarce such a Tract can show,
Whose shore like to the backe of a well-bended Bow,
The Ocean beareth out, and every where so thicke,
The Villages and Dorps upon my Bosome sticke,
That it is very hard for any to define,
Whether Up-land most I be, or most am Maratine.
What is there that compleat can any Country make,
That in large measure I, (faire Lindsey) not pertake,
As healthy Heaths, and Woods, faire Dales, and pleasant Hils,
All watred here and there, with pretty creeping Rills,
Fat Pasture, mellow Gleabe, and of that kind what can,
Give nourishment to beast, or benefit to man,
As Kestiven doth boast, her Wytham so have I,
My Ancum (onely mine) whose fame as farre doth flie,
For fat and daintie Eeles, as hers doth for her Pyke,
Which makes the Proverbe up, the world hath not the like.
From Razin her cleere Springs, where first she doth arive,
As in an even course, to Humber foorth doth drive,
Faire Barton shee salutes, which from her Scite out-braves
Rough Humber, when he strives to shew his sternest waves.
Now for my Bounds to speake, few Tracts (I thinke) there be,
(And search through all this Isle) to paralell with mee:
Great Humber holds me North, as I have said before)
From whom (even) all along, upon the Easterne shore,
The German Ocean lyes; and on my Southerne side,
Cleere Wytham in her course, me fairely doth divide
From Holland; and from thence the Fosdyke is my bound,
Which our first Henry cut from Lincolne, where he found,
Commodities by Trent, from Humber to convay:

So Nature, the cleere Trent doth fortunatly lay,
To ward me on the West, though farther I extend,
And in my larger bounds doe largely comprehend
Full Axholme, (which those neere, the fertile doe instile)
Which Idle, Don, and Trent, imbracing make an Isle.
But wherefore of my Bounds, thus onely doe I boast,
When that which Holland seemes to vaunt her on the most,
By me is overmatcht; the Fowle which shee doth breed:
Shee in her foggy Fennes, so moorishly doth feed,
That Phisick oft forbids the Patient them for food,
But mine more ayrie are, and make fine spirits and blood:
For neere this batning Isle, in me is to be seene,
More then on any earth, the Plover gray, and greene,
The Corne-land-loving Quayle, the daintiest of our bits,
The Rayle, which seldome comes, but upon Rich mens spits:
The Puet, Godwit, Stint, the pallat that allure,
The Miser and doe make a wastfull Epicure:
The Knot, that called was Canutus Bird of old,
Of that great King of Danes, his name that still doth hold,
His apetite to please, that farre and neere was sought,
For him (as some have sayd) from Denmarke hither brought
The Dotterell, which we thinke a very daintie dish,
Whose taking makes such sport, as man no more can wish;
For as you creepe, or cowre, or lye, or stoupe, or goe,
So marking you (with care) the Apish Bird doth doe,
And acting every thing, doth never marke the Net,
Till he be in the Snare, which men for him have set.
The big-boan'd Bustard then, whose body beares that size,
That he against the wind must runne, e're he can rise:
The Shouler, which so shakes the ayre with saily wings,
That ever as he flyes, you still would thinke he sings.
These Fowles, with other Soyles, although they frequent be,
Yet are they found most sweet and delicate in me.
Thus whilst shee seemes t'extoll in her peculiar praise,
The Muse which seem'd too slacke, in these too low-pitcht layes,
For nobler height prepares, her oblique course, and casts
A new Booke to begin, an end of this shee hasts.

THE SIXE AND TWENTIETH SONG

THE ARGUMENT

Three Shires at once this Song assayes,
By various and unusuall wayes.
At Nottingham first comming in,
The Vale of Bever doth begin;

Tow'rds Lester then her course shee holds,
And sayling o'r the pleasant Oulds,
Shee fetcheth Soare downe from her Springs,
By Charnwood, which to Trent shee brings,
Then showes the Braveries of that Flood,
Makes Sherwood sing her Robin Hood;
Then rouzes up the aged Peake,
And of her Wonders makes her speake:
Thence Darwin downe by Darby tends,
And at her fall, to Trent, it ends.

Now scarcely on this Tract the Muse had entrance made,
Enclining to the South, but Bevers batning Slade
Receiveth her to Guest, whose comming had too long
Put off her rightfull praise, when thus her selfe she sung.
Three Shires there are (quoth she) in me their parts that claime,
Large Lincolne, Rutland Rich, and th'Norths Eye Nottingham.
But in the last of these since most of me doth lye,
To that my most-lov'd Shire my selfe I must apply.
Not Evsham that proud Nymph, although she still pretend
Her selfe the first of Vales, and though abroad she send
Her awfull dread Command, that all should tribute pay
To her as our great Queene; nor White-horse, though her Clay
Of silver seeme to be, new melted, nor the Vale
Of Alsbury, whose grasse seemes given out by tale,
For it so Silken is, nor any of our kind,
Or what, or where they be, or howsoere inclind,
Me Bever shall outbrave, that in my state doe scorne,
By any of them all (once) to be overborne,
With theirs, doe but compare the Country where I lye,
My Hill, and Oulds will say, they are the Islands eye.
Consider next my Scite, and say it doth excell;
Then come unto my Soyle, and you shall see it swell,
With every Grasse and Graine, that Britaine forth can bring:
I challenge any Vale, to shew me but that thing
I cannot shew to her, (that truly is mine owne)
Besides I dare thus boast, that I as farre am knowne,
As any of them all, the South their names doth sound,
The spacious North doth mee, that there is scarcely found
A roomth for any else, it is so fild with mine,
Which but a little wants of making me divine:
Nor barren am of Brookes, for that I still reteine
Two neat and daintie Rills, the little Snyte, and Deane,
That from the lovely Oulds, their beautious parent sprong
From the Lecestrian fields, come on with me along,
Till both within one Banke, they on my North are meint,
And where I end, they fall, at Newarck, into Trent.
Hence wandring as the Muse delightfully beholds

The beautie of the large, and goodly full-flockd Oulds,
Shee on the left hand leaves old Lecester, and flyes,
Untill the fertile earth glut her insatiate eyes,
From Rich to Richer still, that riseth her before,
Untill shee come to cease upon the head of Soare,
Where Fosse, and Watling cut each other in their course
At Sharnford, where at first her soft and gentle sourse,
To her but shallow Bankes, beginneth to repayre,
Of all this beautious Isle, the delicatest ayre;
Whence softly sallying out, as loath the place to leave,
Shee Sence a pretty Rill doth courteously receive:
For Swift, a little Brooke, which certainly shee thought
Downe to the Banks of Trent, would safely her have brought,
Because their native Springs so neerely were allyde,
Her sister Soare forsooke, and wholly her applide
To Avon, as with her continually to keepe,
And wayt on her along to the Sabrinian deepe.
Thus with her hand-mayd Sence, the Soare doth eas'ly slide
By Lecester, where yet her ruines show her pride,
Demolisht many yeares, that of the great foundation
Of her long buried walls, men hardly see the station;
Yet of some pieces found, so sure the Cyment locks
The stones, that they remaine like perdurable rocks:
Where whilst the lovely Soare, with many a deare imbrace,
Is solacing her selfe with this delightfull place,
The Forrest, which the name of that brave Towne doth beare,
With many a goodly wreath, crownes her disheveld hayre,
And in her gallant Greene, her lusty Livery showes
Her selfe to this faire Flood, which mildly as shee flowes,
Reciprocally likes her length and breadth to see,
As also how shee keepes her fertile purlues free:
The Herds of Fallow Deere shee on the Launds doth feed,
As having in her selfe to furnish every need.
But now since gentle Soare, such leasure seemes to take,
The Muse in her behalfe this strong defence doth make,
Against the neighbour floods, for that which tax her so,
And her a Channell call, because she is so slow.
The cause is that shee lyes upon so low a Flat,
Where nature most of all befriended her in that,
The longer to enjoy the good she doth possesse:
For had those (with such speed that forward seeme to presse)
So many dainty Meads, and Pastures theirs to be,
They then would wish themselves to be as slow as she,
Who well may be compar'd to some young tender Mayd,
Entring some Princes Court, which is for pompe arayd,
Who led from roome to roome amazed is to see
The furnitures and states, which all Imbroyderies be,
The rich and sumptuous Beds, with Tester-covering plumes,

And various as the Sutes, so various the perfumes,
Large Galleries, where piece with piece doth seeme to strive,
Of Pictures done to life, Landskip, and Perspective,
Thence goodly Gardens sees, where Antique Statues stand
In Stone and Copper, cut by many a skilfull hand,
Where every thing to gaze, her more and more entices,
Thinking at once shee sees a thousand Paradices,
Goes softly on, as though before she saw the last,
She long'd againe to see, what she had slightly past.
So the enticing Soyle the Soare along doth lead,
As wondring in her selfe, at many a spacious Mead;
When Charnwood from the rocks salutes her wished sight,
(Of many a Wood-god woo'd) her darling and delight,
Whose beautie whilst that Soare is pawsing to behold
Cleere Wreakin comming in, from Waltham on the Ould,
Brings Eye, a pretty Brooke, to beare her silver traine,
Which on by Melton make, and tripping o'r the Plaine,
Here finding her surpriz'd with proud Mount-Sorrels sight,
By quickning of her Course, more eas'ly doth invite
Her to the goodly Trent, where as she goes along
By Loughborough, she thus of that faire Forrest sung.
O Charnwood, be thou cald the choycest of thy kind,
The like in any place, what Flood hath hapt to find?
No Tract in all this Isle, the proudest let her be,
Can shew a Sylvan Nymph, for beautie like to thee:
The Satyrs, and the Fawnes, by Dian set to keepe,
Rough Hilles, and Forrest holts, were sadly seene to weepe,
When thy high-palmed Harts the sport of Bowes and Hounds,
By gripple Borderers hands, were banished thy grounds.
The Driades that were wont about thy Lawnes to rove,
To trip from Wood to Wood, and scud from Grove to Grove,
On Sharpley that were seene, and Cadmans aged rocks,
Against the rising Sunne, to brayd their silver locks;
And with the harmelesse Elves, on Heathy Bardons height,
By Cynthia's colder beames to play them night by night,
Exil'd their sweet aboad, to poore bare Commons fled,
They with the Okes that liv'd, now with the Okes are dead.
Who will describe to life, a Forrest, let him take
Thy Surface to himselfe, nor shall he need to make
An other forme at all, where oft in thee is found
Fine sharpe but easie Hills, which reverently are crownd
With aged Antique Rocks, to which the Goats and Sheepe,
(To him that stands remoat) doe softly seeme to creepe,
To gnaw the little shrubs, on their steepe sides that grow;
Upon whose other part, on some descending Brow,
Huge stones are hanging out, as though they downe would drop,
Where under-growing Okes, on their old shoulders prop
The others hory heads, which still seeme to decline,

And in a Dimble neere, (even as a place divine,
For Contemplation fit) an Iuy-seeled Bower,
As Nature had therein ordayn'd some Sylvan power;
As men may very oft at great Assemblies see,
Where many of most choyce, and wondred Beauties be:
For Stature one doth seeme the best away to beare;
Another for her Shape, to stand beyond compare;
Another for the fine composure of a face:
Another short of these, yet for a modest grace
Before them all preferd; amongst the rest yet one,
Adjudg'd by all to bee, so perfect Paragon,
That all those parts in her together simply dwell,
For which the other doe so severally excell.
My Charnwood like the last, hath in her selfe alone,
What excellent can be in any Forrest showne,
On whom when thus the Soare had these high praises spent,
She easily slid away into her Soveraigne Trent,
Who having wandred long, at length began to leave
Her native Countries bounds, and kindly doth receive
The lesser Tame, and Messe, the Messe a daintie Rill,
Neere Charnwood rising first, where she begins to fill
Her Banks, which all her course on both sides doe abound
With Heath and Finny olds, and often gleaby ground,
Till Croxals fertill earth doth comfort her at last
When shee is entring Trent; but I was like t'ave past
The other Sence, whose source doth rise not farre from hers,
By Ancor, that her selfe to famous Trent prefers,
The second of that name, allotted to this Shire,
A name but hardly found in any place but here;
Nor is to many knowne, this Country that frequent.
But Muse returne at last, attend the princely Trent,
Who straining on in state, the Norths imperious Flood,
The third of England cald, with many a daintie Wood,
Being crown'd to Burton comes, to Needwood where she showes
Her selfe in all her pompe; and as from thence she flowes,
Shee takes into her Traine rich Dove, and Darwin cleere,
Darwin, whose fount and fall are both in Darbysheere;
And of those thirtie Floods, that wayt the Trent upon,
Doth stand without compare, the very Paragon.
Thus wandring at her will, as uncontrould shee ranges,
Her often varying forme, as variously and changes.
First Erwash, and then Lyne, sweet Sherwood sends her in;
Then looking wyde, as one that newly wak'd had bin,
Saluted from the North, with Nottinghams proud height,
So strongly is surpriz'd, and taken with the sight,
That shee from running wild, but hardly can refraine,
To view in how great state, as she along doth straine,
That brave exalted seat, beholdeth her in pride,

As how the large-spread Meads upon the other side,
All flourishing in Flowers, and rich embroyderies drest,
In which she sees her selfe above her neighbours blest.
As rap'd with the delights, that her this Prospect brings,
In her peculiar praise, loe thus the River sings.
What should I care at all, from what my name I take,
That Thirtie doth import, that thirty Rivers make;
My greatnesse what it is, or thirty Abbayes great,
That on my fruitfull Banks, times formerly did seat:
Or thirtie kinds of Fish, that in my Streames doe live,
To me this name of Trent did from that number give.
What reack I: let great Thames, since by his fortune he
Is Soveraigne of us all that here in Britaine be;
From Isis, and old Tame, his Pedigree derive:
And for the second place, proud Severne that doth strive,
Fetch her discent from Wales, from that proud Mountaine sprung,
Plinillimon, whose praise is frequent them among,
As of that princely Mayd, whose name she boasts to beare,
Bright Sabrin, which she holds as her undoubted heyre.
Let these imperious Floods draw downe their long discent
From these so famous Stocks, and only say of Trent,
That Moorelands barren earth me first to light did bring,
Which though she be but browne, my cleere complexiond Spring,
Gain'd with the Nymphs such grace, that when I first did rise,
The Naiades on my brim, danc'd wanton Hydagies,
And on her spacious breast, with Heaths that doth abound)
Encircled my faire Fount with many a lustie round:
And of the British Floods, though but the third I be,
Yet Thames, and Severne both in this come short of me,
For that I am the Mere of England, that divides
The North part from the South, on my so either sides,
That reckoning how these Tracts in compasse be extent,
Men bound them on the North, or on the South of Trent;
Their Banks are barren Sands, if but compar'd with mine,
Through my perspicuous Breast, the pearly Pebbles shine:
I throw my Christall Armes along the Flowry Vallies,
Which lying sleeke, and smooth, as any Garden-Allies,
Doe give me leave to play, whilst they doe Court my Streame,
And crowne my winding banks with many an Anademe:
My Silver-scaled Skuls about my Streames doe sweepe,
Now in the shallow foords, now in the falling Deepe:
So that of every kind, the new-spawn'd numerous Frie
Seeme in me as the Sands that on my Shore doe lye.
The Barbell, then which Fish, a braver doth not swimme,
Nor greater for the Ford within my spacious brimme,
Nor (newly taken) more the curious taste doth please;
The Greling, whose great Spawne is big as any Pease;
The Pearch with pricking Finnes, against the Pike prepar'd,

As Nature had thereon bestow'd this stronger guard,
His daintinesse to keepe, (each curious pallats proofe)
From his vile ravenous foe: next him I name the Ruffe,
His very neere Ally, and both for scale and Fin,
In taste, and for his Bayte (indeed) his next of kin;
The pretty slender Dare, of many cald the Dace,
Within my liquid glasse, when Phœbus lookes his face,
Oft swiftly as he swimmes, his silver belly showes,
But with such nimble slight, that ere yee can disclose
His shape, out of your sight like lightning he is shot.
The Trout by Nature markt with many a Crimson spot,
As though shee curious were in him above the rest,
And of fresh-water Fish, did note him for the best;
The Roche, whose common kind to every Flood doth fall;
The Chub, (whose neater name) which some a Chevin call,
Food to the Tyrant Pyke, (most being in his power)
Who for their numerous store he most doth them devoure;
The lustie Salmon then, from Neptunes watry Realme,
When as his season serves, stemming my tydefull Streame,
Then being in his kind, in me his pleasure takes,
(For whom the Fisher then all other Game forsakes)
Which bending of himselfe to th'fashion of a Ring,
Above the forced Weares, himselfe doth nimbly fling,
And often when the Net hath dragd him safe to land,
Is seene by naturall force to scape his murderers hand;
Whose graine doth rise in flakes, with fatnesse interlarded,
Of many a liquorish lip, that highly is regarded.
And Humber, to whose waste I pay my watry store,
Me of her Sturgeons sends, that I thereby the more
Should have my beauties grac'd, with some thing from him sent:
Not Ancums silvered Eele exceedeth that of Trent;
Though the sweet-smelling Smelt be more in Thames then me,
The Lamprey, and his Lesse, in Severne generall be;
The Flounder smooth and flat, in other Rivers caught,
Perhaps in greater store, yet better are not thought:
The daintie Gudgeon, Loche, the Minnow, and the Bleake,
Since they but little are, I little need to speake
Of them, nor doth it fit mee much of those to reck,
Which every where are found in every little Beck;
Nor of the Crayfish here, which creepes amongst my stones,
From all the rest alone, whose shell is all his bones:
For Carpe, the Tench, and Breame, my other store among,
To Lakes and standing Pooles, that chiefly doe belong,
Here scowring in my Foards, feed in my waters cleere,
Are muddy Fish in Ponds to that which they are heere.
From Nottingham, neere which this River first begun,
This Song, she the meane while, by Newarke having run,
Receiving little Snyte, from Bevers batning grounds,

At Gaynsborough goes out, where the Lincolnian bounds.
Yet Sherwood all this while not satisfi'd to show
Her love to princely Trent, as downward shee doth flow,
Her Meden and her Man, shee downe from Mansfield sends
To Idle for her ayd, by whom she recommends
Her love to that brave Queene of waters, her to meet,
When she tow'rds Humber comes, do humbly kisse her feet,
And clip her till shee grace great Humber with her fall.
When Sherwood somewhat backe, the forward Muse doth call;
For shee was let to know, that Soare had in her Song
So chanted Charnwoods worth, the Rivers that along,
Amongst the neighbouring Nymphs, there was no other Layes,
But those which seem'd to sound of Charnwood, and her praise:
Which Sherwood tooke to heart, and very much disdain'd,
(As one that had both long, and worthily maintain'd
The title of the great'st, and bravest of her kind)
To fall so farre below, one wretchedly confin'd
Within a furlongs space, to her large skirts compar'd:
Wherefore shee as a Nymph that neither fear'd, nor car'd
For ought to her might chance, by others love or hate,
With Resolution arm'd, against the power of Fate,
All selfe-praise set apart, determineth to sing
That lustie Robin Hood, who long time like a King
Within her compasse liv'd, and when he list to range
For some rich Booty set, or else his ayre to change,
To Sherwood still retyr'd, his onely standing Court,
Whose praise the Forrest thus doth pleasantly report.
The merry pranks he playd, would aske an age to tell,
And the adventures strange that Robin Hood befell,
When Mansfield many a time for Robin hath bin layd,
How he hath cosned them, that him would have betrayd;
How often he hath come to Nottingham disguisd,
And cunningly escapt, being set to be surprizd.
In this our spacious Isle, I thinke there is not one,
But he hath heard some talke of him and little John;
And to the end of time, the Tales shall ne'r be done,
Of Scarlock, George a Greene, and Much the Millers sonne,
Of Tuck the merry Frier, which many a Sermon made,
In praise of Robin Hood, his Out-lawes, and their Trade.
An hundred valiant men had this brave Robin Hood,
Still ready at his call, that Bow-men were right good,
All clad in Lincolne Greene, with Caps of Red and Blew,
His fellowes winded Horne, not one of them but knew,
When setting to their lips their little Beugles shrill,
The warbling Eccho's wakt from every Dale and Hill:
Their Bauldricks set with Studs, athwart their shoulders cast,
To which under their armes, their Sheafes were buckled fast,
A short Sword at their Belt, a Buckler scarse a span,

Who strooke below the knee, not counted then a man:
All made of Spanish Yew, their Bowes were wondrous strong;
They not an Arrow drew, but was a cloth-yard long.
Of Archery they had the very perfect craft,
With Broad-arrow, or But, or Prick, or Roving Shaft,
At Markes full fortie score, they us'd to Prick, and Rove,
Yet higher then the breast, for Compasse never strove;
Yet at the farthest marke a foot could hardly win:
At Long-buts, short, and Hoyles, each one could cleave the pin:
Their Arrowes finely pair'd, for Timber, and for Feather,
With Birch and Brazill peec'd, to flie in any weather;
And shot they with the round, the square, or forked Pyle,
The loose gave such a twang, as might be heard a myle.
And of these Archers brave, there was not any one,
But he could kill a Deere his swiftest speed upon,
Which they did boyle and rost, in many a mightie wood,
Sharpe hunger the fine sauce to their more kingly food.
Then taking them to rest, his merry men and hee
Slept many a Summers night under the Greenewood tree.
From wealthy Abbots chests, and Churles abundant store,
What often times he tooke, he shar'd amongst the poore:
No lordly Bishop came in lusty Robins way,
To him before he went, but for his Passe must pay:
The Widdow in distresse he graciously reliev'd,
And remedied the wrongs of many a Virgin griev'd:
He from the husbands bed no married woman wan,
But to his Mistris deare, his loved Marian
Was ever constant knowne, which wheresoere shee came,
Was soveraigne of the Woods, chiefe Lady of the Game:
Her Clothes tuck'd to the knee, and daintie braided haire,
With Bow and Quiver arm'd, shee wandred here and there,
Amongst the Forrests wild; Diana never knew
Such pleasures, nor such Harts as Mariana slew.
Of merry Robin Hood, and of his merrier men,
The Song had scarcely ceas'd, when as the Muse agen
Wades Erwash, (that at hand) on Sherwoods setting side,
The Nottinghamian Fields, and Derbian doth divide,
And Northward from her Springs, haps Scardale forth to find,
Which like her Mistris Peake, is naturally enclind
To thrust forth ragged Cleeves, with which she scattered lyes,
As busie Nature here could not her selfe suffice,
Of this oft-altring earth the sundry shapes to show,
That from my entrance here, doth rough and rougher grow,
Which of a lowly Dale, although the name it beare,
You by the Rocks might think that it a Mountaine were,
From which it takes the name of Scardale, which exprest,
Is the hard Vale of Rocks, of Chesterfield possest,
By her which is instild; where Rother from her rist,

Ibber, and Crawley hath, and Gunno, that assist
Her weaker wandring Streame tow'rds Yorkeshire as she wends,
So Scardale tow'rds the same, that lovely Iddle sends,
That helps the fertile Seat of Axholme to in-Isle:
But to th'unwearied Muse the Peake appeares the while,
A withered Beldam long, with bleared watrish eyes,
With many a bleake storme dim'd, which often to the Skies
Shee cast, and oft to th'earth bow'd downe her aged head,
Her meager wrinkled face, being sullyed still with lead,
Which sitting in the workes, and poring o'r the Mines,
Which shee out of the Oare continually refines:
For shee a Chimist was, and Natures secrets knew,
And from amongst the Lead, she Antimony drew,
And Christall there congeal'd, (by her enstyled Flowers)
And in all Medcins knew their most effectuall powers.
The spirits that haunt the Mynes, she could command and tame,
And bind them as she list in Saturns dreadfull name:
Shee Mil-stones from the Quarrs, with sharpned picks could get,
And dainty Whetstones make, the dull-edgd tooles to whet.
Wherefore the Peake as proud of her laborious toyle,
As others of their Corne, or goodnesse of their Soyle,
Thinking the time was long, till shee her tale had told,
Her Wonders one by one, thus plainly doth unfold.
My dreadfull daughters borne, your mothers deare delight,
Great Natures chiefest worke, wherein shee shew'd her might;
Yee darke and hollow Caves, the pourtratures of Hell,
Where Fogs, and misty Damps continually doe dwell;
O yee my onely Joyes, my Darlings, in whose eyes,
Horror assumes her seat, from whose abiding flyes
Thicke Vapours, that like Rugs still hang the troubled ayre,
Yee of your mother Peake, the hope and onely care:
O thou my first and best, of thy blacke Entrance nam'd
The Divels-Arse, in me, O be thou not asham'd,
Nor thinke thy selfe disgrac'd, or hurt thereby at all,
Since from thy horror first men us'd thee so to call:
For as amongst the Moores, the Jettiest blacke are deem'd
The beautifulst of them; so are your kind esteem'd,
The more ye gloomy are, more fearefull and obscure,
(That hardly any eye your sternnesse may endure)
The more yee famous are, and what name men can hit,
That best may ye expresse, that best doth yee befit:
For he that will attempt thy blacke and darksome jawes,
In midst of Summer meets with Winters stormy flawes,
Cold Dewes, that over head from thy foule roofe distill,
And meeteth under foot, with a dead sullen Rill,
That Acheron it selfe, a man would thinke he were
Imediately to passe, and stay'd for Charon there;
Thy Flore drad Cave, yet flat, though very rough it be,

With often winding turnes: then come thou next to me,
My prettie daughter Poole, my second loved child,
Which by that noble name was happily enstild,
Of that more generous stock, long honor'd in this Shire,
Of which amongst the rest, one being out-law'd here,
For his strong refuge tooke this darke and uncouth place,
An heyre-loome ever since, to that succeeding race:
Whose entrance though deprest below a mountaine steepe,
Besides so very strait, that who will see't, must creepe
Into the mouth thereof, yet being once got in,
A rude and ample Roofe doth instantly begin
To raise it selfe aloft, and who so doth intend
The length thereof to see, still going must ascend
On mightie slippery stones, as by a winding stayre,
Which of a kind of base darke Alablaster are,
Of strange and sundry formes, both in the Roofe and Floore,
As Nature show'd in thee, what ne'r was seene before.
For Elden thou my third, a Wonder I preferre
Before the other two, which perpendicular
Dive'st downe into the ground, as if an entrance were
Through earth to lead to hell, ye well might judge it here,
Whose depth is so immense, and wondrously profound,
As that long line which serves the deepest Sea to sound,
Her bottome never wrought, as though the vast descent,
Through this Terrestriall Globe directly poynting went
Our Antipods to see, and with her gloomy eyes,
To glote upon those Starres, to us that never rise;
That downe into this hole if that a stone yee throw,
An acres length from thence, (some say that) yee may goe,
And comming backe thereto, with a still listning eare,
May heare a sound as though that stone then falling were.
Yet for her Caves, and Holes, Peake onely not excells,
But that I can againe produce those wondrous Wells
Of Buckston, as I have, that most delicious Fount,
Which men the second Bath of England doe account,
Which in the primer raignes, when first this well began
To have her vertues knowne unto the blest Saint Anne,
Was consecrated then, which the same temper hath,
As that most daintie Spring, which at the famous Bath,
Is by the Crosse enstild, whose fame I much preferre,
In that I doe compare my daintiest Spring to her,
Nice sicknesses to cure, as also to prevent,
And supple their cleare skinnes, which Ladies oft frequent;
Most full, most faire, most sweet, and most delicious sourse.
To this a second Fount, that in her naturall course,
As mighty Neptune doth, so doth shee ebbe and flow,
If some Welsh Shires report, that they the like can show.
I answere those, that her shall so no wonder call,

So farre from any Sea, not any of them all.
My Caves, and Fountaines thus delivered you, for change.
A little Hill I have, a wonder yet more strange,
Which though it be of light, and almost dusty sand,
Unaltred with the wind, yet firmly doth it stand;
And running from the top, although it never cease,
Yet doth the foot thereof, no whit at all increase.
Nor is it at the top, the lower, or the lesse,
As Nature had ordain'd, that so its owne excesse,
Should by some secret way within it selfe ascend,
To feed the falling backe; with this yet doe not end
The wonders of the Peake, for nothing that I have,
But it a wonders name doth very justly crave:
A Forrest such have I, (of which when any speake,
Of me they it enstile, The Forrest of the Peake)
Whose Hills doe serve for Brakes, the Rocks for shrubs and trees,
To which the Stag pursu'd, as to the thicket flees;
Like it in all this Isle, for sternnesse there is none,
Where Nature may be said to show you groves of stone,
As she in little there, had curiously compyld
The modell of the vast Arabian stony Wyld.
Then as it is suppos'd, in England that there be
Seven wonders: to my selfe so have I here in me,
My seaven before rehearc'd, allotted me by Fate,
Her greatnesse, as therein ordain'd to imitate.
No sooner had the Peake her seven proud wonders sung,
But Darwin from her Fount, her mothers Hills among,
Through many a crooked way, opposd with envious Rocks,
Comes tripping downe tow'rds Trent, and sees the goodly Flocks
Fed by her mother Peake; and Heards, (for horne and haire,
That hardly are put downe by those of Lancashire,)
Which on her Mountaines sides, and in her Bottoms graze,
On whose delightfull Course, whilst Unknidge stands to gaze,
And looke on her his fill, doth on his tiptoes get,
He Nowstoll plainly sees, which likewise from the Set,
Salutes her, and like friends, to Heaven-Hill farre away,
Thus from their lofty tops, were plainly heard to say.
Faire Hill bee not so proud of thy so pleasant Scite,
Who for thou giv'st the eye such wonderfull delight,
From any Mountaine neere, that glorious name of Heaven,
Thy bravery to expresse, was to thy greatnesse given:
Nor cast thine eye so much on things that be above:
For sawest thou as we doe, our Darwin, thou wouldst love
Her more then any thing, that so doth thee allure;
When Darwin that by this her travell could endure,
Takes Now into her traine, (from Nowstoll her great Sire,
Which shewes to take her name) with many a winding Gyre.
Then wandring through the Wylds, at length the pretty Wye,

From her blacke mother Poole, her nimbler course doth plye
Tow'rds Darwin, and along from Bakewell with her brings
Lathkell a little Brooke, and Headford, whose poore Springs,
But hardly them the name of Riverets can affoord;
When Burbrook with the strength, that Nature hath her stor'd,
Although but very small, yet much doth Darwin sted.
At Worksworth on her way, when from the Mynes of Lead,
Browne Eclesborne comes in, then Amber from the East,
Of all the Darbian Nymphs of Darwin lov'd the best,
(A delicater Flood from fountaine never flow'd)
Then comming to the Towne, on which she first bestow'd
Her naturall British name, her Darby, so againe,
Her, to that ancient Seat, doth kindly intertaine,
Where Marten-Brooke, although an easie shallow Rill,
There offereth all she hath, her Mistris Banks to fill,
And all too little thinks that was on Darwin spent;
From hence as shee departs, in travailing to Trent,
Backe goes the active Muse, tow'rds Lancashire amaine,
Where matter rests ynough her vigor to maintaine,
And to the Northern Hills shall lead her on along,
Which now must wholly bee the subject of my Song.

THE SEAVEN AND TWENTIETH SONG

THE ARGUMENT

The circuit of this Shire exprest,
Erwell, and Ribble then contest;
The Muse next to the Mosses flies,
And to fayre Wyre her selfe applies.
The Fishy Lun then doth shee bring,
The praise of Lancashire to sing,
The Isle of Man maintaines her plea,
Then falling Eastward from that Sea,
On rugged Furnesse, and his Fells,
Of which this Canto lastly tells.

Scarce could the labouring Muse salute this lively Shire,
But strait such shouts arose from every Mosse and Mere,
And Rivers rushing downe, with such unusuall noyse,
Upon their peably sholes, seem'd to expresse their joyes,
That Mersey (in her course which happily confines
Brave Chesshire from this Tract, two County Palatines)
As ravish'd with the newes, along to Lerpoole ran,
That all the Shores which lye to the Vergivian,
Resounded with the shouts, so that from Creeke to Creeke,

So lowd the Ecchoes cry'd, that they were heard to shreeke
To Fournesse ridged Front, whereas the rocky Pile
Of Foudra is at hand, to guard the out-layd Isle
Of Walney, and those grosse and foggy Fells awooke;
Thence flying to the East, with their reverberance shooke
The Clouds from Pendles head, (which as the people say,
Prognosticates to them a happy Halcyon day)
Rebounds on Blackstonedge, and there by falling fils
Faire Mersey, making in from the Derbeian Hills.
But whilst the active Muse thus nimbly goes about,
Of this large Tract to lay the true Demensions out,
The neat Lancastrain Nymphes, for beauty that excell,
That for the Hornpipe round doe beare away the bell;
Some that about the Banks of Erwell make abode,
With some that have their seat by Ribbles silver road,
In great contention fell, (that mighty difference grew)
Which of those Floods deserv'd to have the soveraigne due;
So that all future spleene, and quarrels to prevent,
That likely was to rise about their long discent,
Before the neighbouring Nymphs, their right they meane to plead,
And first thus for her selfe the lovely Erwell sayd.
Yee Lasses, quoth this Flood, have long and blindly er'd,
That Ribble before me, so falsely have prefer'd,
That am a Native borne, and my descent doe bring,
From ancient Gentry here, when Ribble from her Spring,
An Alien knowne to be, and from the Mountaines rude
Of Yorkshire getting strength, here boldly dares intrude
Upon my proper Earth, and through her mighty fall,
Is not asham'd her selfe of Lancashire to call:
Whereas of all the Nymphes that carefully attend
My Mistris Merseys State, ther's none that doth transcend
My greatnesse with her grace, which doth me so preferre,
That all is due to me, which doth belong to her.
For though from Blackstonedge the Taume come tripping downe,
And from that long-ridg'd Rocke, her fathers high renowne,
Of Mersey thinks from me, the place alone to winne,
With my attending Brooks, yet when I once come in,
I out of count'nance quite doe put the Nymph, for note,
As from my Fountaine I tow'rds mightier Mersey float,
First Roch a dainty Rill, from Roch-dale her deare Dame,
Who honored with the halfe of her sterne mothers name,
Growes proud; yet glad her selfe into my Bankes to get,
Which Spodden from her Spring, a pretty Rivelet,
As her attendant brings, when Irck addes to my store,
And Medlock to their much, by lending somewhat more,
At Manchester doe meet, all kneeling to my State,
Where brave I show my selfe; then with a prouder gate,
Tow'rds Mersey making on, great Chatmosse at my fall,

Lyes full of Turfe, and Marle, her unctuous Minerall,
And Blocks as blacke as Pitch, (with boring-Augars found)
There at the generall Flood supposed to be drownd.
Thus chiefe of Merseys traine, away with her I runne,
When in her prosperous course shee watreth Warrington,
And her faire silver load in Lerpoole downe doth lay,
A Road none more renownd in the Vergivian Sea.
Yee lustie Lasses then, in Lancashire that dwell,
For Beautie that are sayd to beare away the Bell,
Your Countries Horn-pipe, yee so minsingly that tread,
As ye the Eg-pye love, and Apple Cherry-red;
In all your mirthfull Songs, and merry meetings tell,
That Erwell every way doth Ribble farre excell.
Her well-disposed speech had Erwell scarcely done,
But swift report therewith imediatly doth runne
To the Virgivian Shores, among the Mosses deepe,
Where Alt a neighboring Nymph for very joy doth weepe,
That Symonds-wood, from whence the Flood assumes her Spring,
Excited with the same, was lowdly heard to ring;
And over all the Moores, with shrill re-ecchoing sounds,
The drooping Fogs to drive from those grosse watry grounds,
Where those that toyle for Turffe, with peating Spades doe find
Fish living in that earth (contrary to their kind)
Which but that Pontus, and Heraclia likewise showes,
The like in their like earth, that with like moisture flowes,
And that such Fish as these, had not been likewise found,
Within farre firmer earth, the Paphlagonian ground,
A Wonder of this Isle, this well might have been thought.
But Ribbell that this while for her advantage wrought,
Of what shee had to say, doth well her selfe advise,
And to brave Erwels speech, thus boldly she replies.
With that, whereby the most thou thinkst me to disgrace,
That I an Alien am, (not rightly of this place)
My greatest glory is, and Lancashire therefore,
To Nature for my Birth, beholding is the more;
That Yorkshire, which all Shires for largenesse doth exceed,
A kingdome to be cald, that well deserves (indeed)
And not a Fountaine hath, that from her wombe doth flow
Within her spacious selfe, but that she can bestow;
To Lancaster yet lends, me Ribbell, from her store,
Which adds to my renowne, and makes her Bountie more.
From Penigents proud foot, as from my source I slide,
That Mountaine my proud Syre, in height of all his pride,
Takes pleasure in my Course, as in his first-borne Flood:
And Ingleborow Hill of that Olympian Brood,
With Pendle, of the North the highest Hills that be,
Doe wistly me behold, and are beheld of me,
These Mountaines make me proud, to gaze on me that stand:

So Long-ridge, once ariv'd on the Lancastrian Land,
Salutes me, and with smiles, me to his soyle invites,
So have I many a Flood, that forward me excites,
As Hodder, that from home attends me from my Spring;
Then Caldor comming downe, from Blackstonedge doth bring
Me eas'ly on my way, to Preston the greatst Towne,
Wherewith my Banks are blest; whereat my going downe,
Cleere Darwen on along me to the Sea doth drive,
And in my spacious fall no sooner I arrive,
But Savock to the North, from Longridge making way,
To this my greatnesse adds, when In my ample Bay,
Swart Dulas comming in, from Wiggin with her ayds,
Short Taud, and Dartow small, two little Country Mayds,
(In those low watry lands, and Moory Mosses bred)
Doe see mee safely layd in mighty Neptunes bed;
And cutting in my course, even through the very heart
Of this renowned Shire, so equally it part,
As Nature should have said, Loe thus I meant to doe;
This Flood divides this Shire thus equally in two.
Ye Mayds, the Horne-pipe then, so minsingly that tread,
As yee the Egg-pye love, and Apple Cherry-red;
In all your mirthfull Songs, and merry meetings tell,
That Ribbell every way, your Erwell doth excell.
Heere ended shee againe, when Mertons Mosse and Mere,
With Ribbels sole reply so much revived were,
That all the Shores resound the Rivers good successe,
And wondrous joy there was all over Andernesse,
Which straight convayd the newes into the upper land,
Where Pendle, Penigent, and Ingleborow stand
Like Gyants, and the rest doe proudly overlooke;
Or Atlas-like as though they onely undertooke
To under-prop high Heaven, or the wide Welkin dar'd,
Who in their Ribbles praise (be sure) no speeches spar'd;
That the loud sounds from them downe to the Forrests fell,
To Bowland brave in state, and Wyersdale, which as well,
As any Sylvan Nymphes, their beautious Scites may boast,
Whose Eccho's sent the same all round about the Coast,
That there was not a Nymph to Jollity inclind,
Or of the wooddy brood, or of the watry kind,
But at their fingers ends, they Ribbels Song could say,
And perfectly the Note upon the Bag-pipe play.
That Wyre, when once she knew how well these Floods had sped,
(When their reports abroad in every place was spred)
It vex'd her very heart, their eminence to see,
Their equall (at the least) who thought her selfe to be,
Determins at the last to Neptunes Court to goe,
Before his ample State, with humblenesse to show
The wrongs she had sustain'd by her proud sisters spight,

And offring them no wrong, to doe her greatnesse right;
Arising but a Rill at first from Wyersdales lap,
Yet still receiving strength from her full Mothers pap,
As downe to Seaward she, her serious course doth ply,
Takes Caldor comming in, to beare her company.
From Woolfcrags Cliffy foot, a Hill to her at hand,
By that fayre Forrest knowne, within her Verge to stand.
So Bowland from her breast sends Brock her to attend,
As she a Forrest is, so likewise doth shee send
Her child, on Wyresdales Flood, the dainty Wyre to wayt,
With her assisting Rills, when Wyre is once repleat:
Shee in her crooked course to Seaward softly slides,
Where Pellins mighty Mosse, and Mertons, on her sides
Their boggy breasts out lay, and Skipton downe doth crawle,
To entertaine this Wyer, attained to her fall:
When whilst each wandring flood seem'd setled to admire,
First Erwell, Ribbell then, and last of all this Wyre,
That mighty wagers would have willingly been layd,
(But that these matters were with much discretion staid)
Some broyles about these Brooks had surely been begun.
When Coker a coy Nymph, that cleerely seemes to shun
All popular applause, who from her Christall head,
In Wyresdale, neere where Wyre is by her fountaine fed,
That by their naturall birth, they seeme (in deed) to twin,
Yet for her sisters pride shee careth not a pin,
Of none, and being help'd, she likewise helpeth none,
But to the Irish Sea goes gently downe alone
Of any undisturbd, till comming to her Sound,
Endangered by the Sands, with many a loftie bound,
Shee leaps against the Tydes, and cries to Christall Lon,
The Flood that names the Towne, from whence the Shire begun,
Her title first to take, and loudly tells the Flood,
That if a little while she thus but trifling stood,
These pettie Brooks would bee before her still preferd.
Which the long-wandring Lon, with good advisement heard,
As shee comes ambling on from Westmerland, where first
Arising from her head, amongst the Mountaines nurst,
By many a pretty spring, that howerly getting strength,
Ariving in her Course in Lancashire at length,
To Lonsdale showes her selfe, and lovingly doth play
With her deare daughter Dale, which her frim Cheeke doth lay
To her cleere mothers Breast, as minsingly she traces,
And oft imbracing her, she oft againe imbraces,
And on her Darling smiles, with every little gale.
When Lac the most lov'd child of this delicious Dale,
And Wemming on the way, present their eithers Spring.
Next them she Henbourne hath, and Robourne, which do bring
Their bounties in one banke, their Mistris to preferre,

That shee with greater state may come to Lancaster,
Of her which takes the name, which likewise to the Shire,
The Soveraigne title lends, and eminency, where
To give to this her Towne, what rightly doth belong,
Of this most famous Shire, our Lun thus frames her Song.
First, that most precious thing, and pleasing most to man,
Who from him (made of earth) imediatly began,
His shee selfe woman, which the goodliest of this Isle,
This country hath brought forth, that much doth grace my stile;
Why should those Ancients else, which so much knowing were,
When they the Blazons gave to every severall Shire,
Fayre women as mine owne, have titled due to me?
Besides in all this Isle, there no such Cattell be,
For largenesse, Horne, and Haire, as these of Lancashire;
So that from every part of England farre and neere,
Men haunt her Marts for Store, as from her Race to breed.
And for the third, wherein she doth all Shires exceed,
Be those great race of Hounds, the deepest mouth'd of all
The other of this kind, which we our Hunters call,
Which from their bellowing throats upon a sent so roare,
That you would surely thinke, that the firme earth they tore
With their wide yawning chaps, or rent the Clouds in sunder,
As though by their lowd crie they meant to mocke the thunder.
Besides, her Natives have been anciently esteem'd,
For Bow-men neere our best, and ever have been deem'd
So loyall, that the Guard of our preceding Kings,
Of them did most consist; but yet mongst all these things,
Even almost ever since the English Crowne was set
Upon the lawfull head, of our Plantaginet,
In Honor, next the first, our Dukedome was allow'd,
And alwayes with the greatst, revenewes was endow'd:
And after when it hapt, France-conquering Edwards blood
Divided in it selfe, here for the Garland stood;
The right Lancastrian Line, it from Yorks Issue bare;
The Red-rose, our brave Badge, which in their Helmets ware,
In many a bloody field, at many a doubtfull fight,
Against the House of Yorke, which bare for theirs the White.
And for my selfe there's not the Tivy, nor the Wye,
Nor any of those Nymphs, that to the Southward lye,
For Salmon me excels; and for this name of Lun,
That I am Christned by, the Britaines it begun,
Which Fulnesse doth import, of waters still encrease:
To Neptune lowting low, when Christall Lun doth cease,
And Conder comming in, conducts her by the hand,
Till lastly shee salute the poynt of Sunderland,
And leaves our dainty Lun to Amphitrites care.
So blyth and bonny now the Lads and Lasses are,
That ever as anon the Bag-pipe up doth blow,

Cast in a gallant Round about the Harth they goe,
And at each pause they kisse, was never seene such rule
In any place but heere, at Boon-fire, or at Yeule;
And every village smokes at Wakes with lusty cheere,
Then Hey they cry for Lun, and Hey for Lancashire;
That one high Hill was heard to tell it to his brother,
That instantly againe to tell it to some other:
From Hill againe to Vale, from Vale to Hill it went,
The High-lands they againe, it to the lower sent,
The mud-exhausted Meres, and Mosses deepe among,
With the report thereof, each Road, and Harbor rung;
The Sea-Nymphs with their Song, so great a coyle doe keepe,
They cease not to resound it over all the Deepe,
And acted it each day before the Isle of Man,
Who like an Empresse sits in the Virgivian,
By her that hath the Calfe, long Walney, and the Pyle,
As Hand-mayds to attend on her their Soveraigne Isle,
To whom, so many though the Hebrides doe show,
Acknowlege, that to her they due subjection owe:
With Corne and Cattell stor'd, and what for hers is good,
(That we, nor Ireland, need not scorne her neighbourhood)
Her midst with Mountaines set, of which, from Sceafels height,
A cleere and perfect eye, the weather being bright,
(Be Neptunes visage ne'r so terrible and sterne)
The Scotch, the Irish Shores, and th'English may discerne;
And what an Empire can, the same this Island brings
Her Pedigrees to show, her right successive Kings,
Her Chronicles and can as easily rehearce,
And with all forraine parts to have had free commerce;
Her Municipiall Lawes, and Customes very old,
Belonging to her State, which strongly shee doth hold:
This Island, with the Song of Lun is taken so,
As shee hath speciall cause before all other, who
For her bituminous Turfe, squar'd from her Mossy ground,
And Trees farre under earth, (by daily digging found,
As for the store of Oats, which her blacke Gleabe doth beare,
In every one of these resembling Lancashire,
To her shee'l stoutly stick, as to her neerest kin,
And cries the day is ours, brave Lancashire doth win.
But yet this Isle of Man more seemes not to rejoyce
For Lancashires good luck, nor with a louder voyce
To sound it to the Shores; then Furnesse whose sterne face,
With Mountaines set like Warts, which Nature as a grace
Bestow'd upon this Tract, whose Browes doe looke so sterne,
That when the Nymphs of Sea did first her Front discerne,
Amazedly they fled, to Amphitrite's Bower.
Her grim aspect to see, which seem'd to them so sower,
As it malign'd the Rule which mighty Neptune bare,

Whose Fells to that grim god, most sterne and dreadfull are,
With Hills whose hanging browes, with Rocks about are bound,
Whose weighty feet stand fixt in that blacke beachy ground,
Whereas those scattered trees, which naturally pertake,
The fatnesse of the soyle (in many a slimy Lake,
Their roots so deeply sok'd) send from their stocky bough,
A soft and sappy Gum, from which those Tree-geese grow,
Call'd Barnacles by us, which like a Jelly first
To the beholder seeme, then by the fluxure nurst,
Still great and greater thrive, untill you well may see
Them turn'd to perfect Fowles, when dropping from the tree
Into the Meery Pond, which under them doth lye,
Waxe ripe, and taking wing, away in flockes doe flye;
Which well our Ancients did among our Wonders place:
Besides by her strong Scite, she doth receave this grace,
Before her neighbouring Tracts, (which Fournesse well may vaunt)
That when the Saxons here their forces first did plant,
And from the Inner-land the ancient Britains drave,
To their distrest estate it no lesse succour gave,
Then the trans-Severn'd Hills, which their old stocke yet stores,
Which now we call the Welsh, or the Cornubian Shores.
What Countrey lets ye see those soyles within her Seat,
But shee in little hath, what it can shew in great?
As first without her selfe at Sea to make her strong,
(Yet how soe'r expos'd, doth still to her belong)
And fence her furthest poynt, from that rough Neptunes rage,
The Isle of Walney lyes, whose longitude doth swage
His fury when his waves, on Furnesse seeme to warre,
Whose crooked back is arm'd with many a rugged scarre
Against his boystrous shocks, which this defensive Isle
Of Walney still assayle, that shee doth scorne the while,
Which to assist her hath the Pyle of Fouldra set,
And Fulney at her backe, a pretty Insulet,
Which all their forces bend, their Furnesse safe to keepe:
But to his inner earth, divert we from the deepe,
Where those two mightie Meres, out-stretcht in length do wander,
The lesser Thurstan nam'd, the famouser Wynander,
So bounded with her Rocks, as Nature would descry,
By her how those great Seas Mediterranean lye.
To Sea-ward then shee hath her sundry Sands agen,
As that of Dudden first, then Levin, lastly Ken,
Of three bright Naiades nam'd, as Dudden on the West,
That Cumberland cuts off from this Shire, doth invest
Those Sands with her proud Style, when Levin from the Fells,
Besides her naturall source, with the abundance swells,
Which those two mighty Meres, upon her either side
Contrribute by recourse, that out of very pride,
Shee leaves her ancient name, and Fosse her selfe doth call,

Till comming to the Sands, even almost at her fall,
On them her ancient Style shee liberally bestowes.
Upon the East from these, cleere Ken her beautie showes,
From Kendale comming in, which shee doth please to grace,
First with her famous Type, then lastly in her race,
Her name upon those Sands doth liberally bequeath,
Whereas the Muse awhile may sit her downe to breath,
And after walke along tow'rds Yorkshire on her way,
On which shee strongly hopes to get a noble day.

THE EIGHT AND TWENTIETH SONG

THE ARGUMENT

Invention hence her Compasse steeres,
Towards Yorke the most renown'd of Shires,
Makes the three Ridings in their Stories,
Each severally to shew their glories.
Ouse for her most-lov'd Cities sake,
Doth her Dukes Title undertake;
His Floods then Humber welcomes in,
And showes how first he did begin.

The Muse from Blackstonedge, no whit dismaid at all,
With sight of the large Shire, on which shee was to fall,
(Whose Forrests, Hils, & Floods, then long for her arive
From Lancashire, that lookt her Beauties to contrive)
Doth set her selfe to sing, of that above the rest
A Kingdome that doth seeme, a Province at the least,
To them that thinke themselves no simple Shires to be;
But that wherein the world her greatnesse most may see,
And that which doth this Shire before the rest preferre,
Is of so many Floods, and great, that rise from her,
Except some silly few out of her Verge that flow,
So neere to other Shires, that it is hard to know,
If that their Springs be hers, or others them divide,
And those are onely found upon her Setting side.
Else be it noted well, remarkeable to all,
That those from her that flow, in her together fall.
Nor can small praise beseeme so beautious Brooks as these,
For from all other Nymphs these be the Nayades,
In Amphitrites Bower, that princely places hold,
To whom the Orkes of Sea dare not to be so bold,
As rudely once to touch, and wheresoere they come,
The Tritons with their Trumps proclaime them publique roome.
Now whiles the Muse prepares these Floods along to lead,

The wide West-riding first, desires that shee may plead
The right that her belongs, which of the Muse she winnes,
When with the course of Don, thus she her Tract begins.
Thou first of all my Floods, whose Banks doe bound my South,
And offrest up thy Streame to mightie Humbers mouth,
Of Ewe, and climing Elme, that crown'd with many a spray,
From thy cleare Fountaine first through many a Mead dost play,
Till Rother, whence the name of Rotheram first begun,
At that her christened Towne doth loose her in my Don,
Which proud of her recourse, tow'rds Doncaster doth drive,
Her greatst and chiefest towne, the name that doth derive
From Don's neere bordering Banks, when holding on her race,
Shee dancing in and out, indenteth Hatfield Chase,
Whose bravery hourely adds, new honors to her Banke:
When Sherwood sends her in slow Iddle, that made ranke
With her profuse excesse, shee largely it bestowes
On Marshland, whose swolne wombe with such abundance flowes,
As that her batning brest, her Fatlings sooner feeds,
And with more lavish waste, then oft the Grasier needs:
Whose soyle, as some report that be her Borderers note,
With th'water under earth undoubtedly doth flote:
For when the waters rise, it risen doth remaine
High whilst the Floods are high, and when they fall againe,
It falleth: but at last, when as my lively Don,
Along by Marshlands side, her lusty course hath runne,
The little wandring Went, wonne by the lowd report
Of the magnifique State, and height of Humbers Court,
Drawes on to meet with Don, at her approch to Aire:
Now speake I of a Flood, who thinks there's none should dare
(Once) to compare with her, supposd by her discent,
The darling daughter borne of loftie Penigent,
Who from her fathers foot, by Skipton downe doth scud,
And leading thence to Leeds, that delicatest Flood,
Takes Caldor comming in by Wakefield, by whose force,
As from a lusty Flood, much strengthened in her course;
But Caldor as shee comes, and greater still doth wax,
And travelling along by Heading-Halifax,
Which Horton once was cald, but of a Virgins haire,
(A Martyr that was made, for Chastity, that there
was by her Lover slaine) being fastned to a tree:
The people that would needs it should a Relique be,
It Halifax since nam'd, which in the Northerne tongue,
Is Holy haire: but thence as Caldor comes along,
It chanc'd shee in her Course on Kirkbey cast her eye,
Where merry Robbin Hood, that honest Thiefe doth lye,
Beholding fitly too before how Wakefield stood,
Shee doth not onely thinke of lustie Robin Hood,
But of his merry man, the Pindar of the Towne

Of Wakefield, George a Greene, whose fames so farre are blowne,
For their so valiant fight, that every free mans Song,
Can tell you of the same, quoth she be talk'd on long,
For yee were merry Lads, and those were merry dayes;
When Aire to Caldor calls, and bids her come her wayes,
Who likewise to her helpe, brings Hebden, a small Rill:
Thus Aire holds on her course tow'rds Humber, till she fill
Her fall with all the wealth that Don can her affoord.
Quoth the West-riding thus, with Rivers am I stor'd.
Next guide I on my Wharfe, the great'st in her degree,
And that I well may call the worthiest of the three,
Who her full fountaine takes from my wast Westerne wild,
(Whence all but Mountaineers, by Nature are exild)
On Langstrethdale, and lights at th'entrance of her race,
When keeping on her course, along through Barden Chase,
Shee watreth Wharfdales breast, which proudly beares her name;
For by that time shees growne a flood of wondrous fame,
When Washbrooke with her wealth her Mistris doth supply;
Thus Wharfe in her brave course imbracing Wetherby,
Small Cock, a sullen Brooke comes to her succour then,
Whose Banks receav'd the blood of many thousand men,
On sad Palme-Sunday slaine, that Towton-Field we call,
Whose Channell quite was chok'd with those that there did fall,
That Wharfe discolored was with gore, that then was shed,
The bloodiest field betwixt the White Rose, and the Red,
Of welneere fifteene fought in England first and last:
But whilst the goodly Wharfe doth thus tow'rds Humber haste,
From Wharnside Hill not farre, outflowes the nimble Nyde,
Through Nydersdale along, as neatly she doth glide
Tow'rds Knarsburg on her way, a pretty little Rill,
Call'd Kebeck, stowes her streame, her Mistris Banks to fill,
To intertaine the Whafe where that brave Forrest stands,
Entitled by the Towne, who with upreared hands
Makes signes to her of joy, and doth with Garlands crowne
The River passing by; but Wharfe that hasteth downe
To meet her Mistris Ouse, her speedy course doth hie;
Dent, Rother, Rivell, Gret, so on my Set have I,
Which from their fountaines there all out of me do flow,
Yet from my bounty I on Lancashire bestow,
Because my rising soyle doth shute them to the West:
But for my Mountaines I, will with the Isle contest,
All other of the North in largenesse shall exceed,
That ages long before it finally decreed,
That Ingleborow Hill, Pendle, and Penigent,
Should named be the high'st betwixt our Tweed and Trent.
My Hills, brave Whelpston then, thou Wharnside, and thou Cam,
Since I West-Riding still your onely mother am;
All that Report can give, and justly is my due,

I as your naturall Dam, share equally with you;
And let me see a Hill that to the North doth stand,
The proudest of them all, that dare but lift a hand
O'r Penigent to peere; not Skiddo, that proud Mount,
Although of him so much, Rude Cumberland account,
Nor Cheviot, of whose height Northumberland doth boast
Albania to survey; nor those from Coast to Coast
That welneere runne in length, that rew of Mountaines tall,
By th'name of th'English Alpes, that our most learned call;
As soone shall those, or these remove out of their place,
As by their lofty lookes, my Penigent out-face:
Yee thus behold my Hills: my Forrests, Dales, and Chases
Upon my spacious breast note too how Nature places,
Farre up into my West, first Langstrethdale doth lye,
And on the Banke of Wharfe, my pleasant Bardon by,
With Wharfdale hard by her, as taking hand in hand:
Then lower tow'rds the Sea brave Knarsborough doth stand,
As higher to my North, my Niddersdale by Nyde,
And Bishopsdale above upon my Setting side,
Marshland, and Hatfield Chase, my Easterne part doe bound,
And Barnsdale there doth butt on Dons wel-watred ground:
And to my great disgrace, if any shall object
That I no wonder have that's worthy of respect
In all my spacious Tract, let them (so wise) survey
My Ribbles rising Banks, their worst, and let them say;
At Giggleswick where I a Fountaine can you show,
That eight times in a day is sayd to ebbe and flow,
Who sometime was a Nymph, and in the Mountaines hye
Of Craven, whose blew heads for Caps put on the Skye,
Amongst th'Oread's there, and Sylvans made abode,
(It was e'r humane foot upon those Hills had trod)
Of all the Mountaine kind and since she was most faire,
It was a Satyrs chance to see her silver haire
Flow loosely at her backe, as up a Cliffe she clame,
Her Beauties noting well, her Features, and her Frame,
And after her he goes; which when she did espie,
Before him like the winde, the nimble Nymph doth flie,
They hurry downe the Rocks, o'r Hill and Dale they drive;
To take her he doth straine, t'outstrip him shee doth strive,
Like one his kind that knew, and greatly fear'd his Rape,
And to the Topick gods by praying to escape,
They turn'd her to a Spring, which as she then did pant,
When wearied with her course, her breath grew wondrous scant:
Even as the fearefull Nymph, then thicke and short did blow,
Now made by them a Spring, so doth shee ebbe and flow.
And neere the Streame of Nyde, another Spring have I,
As well as that, which may a wonders place supply,
Which of the forme it beares, men Dropping well doe call,

Because out of a Rock, it still in drops doth fall,
Neere to the foot whereof it makes a little Pon,
Which in as little space converteth Wood to Stone,
Chevin, and Kilnsey Crags, were they not here in me,
In any other place, right well might Wonders be,
For their Gygantick height, that Mountaines doe transcend?
But such are frequent here, and thus she makes an end.
When Your thus having heard the Genius of this Tract,
Her well-deserved praise so happily to act,
This River in her selfe that was extreamely loth,
The other to deferre, since that shee was to both
Indifferent, straitly wills West-riding there to cease;
And having made a signe to all the watry prease
For silence; which at once, when her commaund had wonne,
The proud North-Riding thus for her great selfe begunne.
My soveraigne Flood, quoth shee, in nature thou art bound
T'acknowledge me of three to be the worthiest ground:
For note of all those Floods, the wild West-Riding sends,
Ther's scarcely any one thy greatnesse that attends,
Till thou hast passed Yorke, and drawest neere thy fall;
And when thou hast no need of their supplies at all,
Then come they flattring in, and will thy followers be;
So as you oftentimes these wretched worldlings see,
That whilst a man is poore, although some hopes depend
Upon his future age, yet ther's not one will lend
A farthing to releeve his sad distressed state,
Not knowing what may yet befall him; but when Fate
Doth poure upon his head his long expected good,
Then shall you see those Slaves, aloofe before that stood,
And would have let him starve, like Spaniels to him crouch,
And with their glavering lips, his very feet to touch:
So doe they by thee Your; whereas the Floods in me,
That spring and have their Course, (even) give thy life to thee:
For till that thou and Swale, into one Banke doe take,
Meeting at Borough-Bridge, thy greatnesse there to make:
Till then the name of Ouse thou art not knowne to owe,
A tearme in former times the Ancients did bestow
On many a full-bankt Flood; but for my greater grace,
These Floods of which I speake, I now intend to trace
From their first springing Founts, beginning with the Your,
From Morvils mightie foot which rising, with the power
That Bant from Sea-mere brings, her somewhat more doth fill,
Neere Bishops-dale at hand, when Couer a cleere Rill,
Next commeth into Your, whereas that lustie Chace
For her lov'd Couers sake, doth lovingly embrace
Your as shee yeelds along, amongst the Parks and Groves,
In Middlehams amorous eye, as wandringly shee roves,
At Rippon meets with Skell, which makes to her amaine,

Whom when she hath receav'd into her Nymphish traine,
(Neere to that towne so fam'd, for Colts there to be bought,
For goodnesse farre and neere, by Horsemen that are sought)
Fore-right upon her way shee with a merryer gale,
To Borough Bridge makes on, to meet her sister Swale,
(A wondrous holy Flood (which name she ever hath)
For when the Saxons first receav'd the Christian Faith,
Paulinus of old Yorke, the zealous Bishop then,
In Swales abundant streame Christned ten thousand men,
With women and their babes, a number more beside,
Upon one happy day, whereof shee boasts with pride)
Which springs not farre from whence Your hath her silver head;
And in her winding Banks along my bosome led,
As shee goes swooping by, to Swaledale whence shee springs,
That lovely name shee leaves, which foorth a Forrest brings,
The Vallies Style that beares, a braver Sylvan Mayd,
Scarce any Shire can show; when to my Rivers ayd,
Come Barney, Arske, and Marske, their soveraigne Swale to guide,
From Applegarths wide waste, and from New Forrest side.
Whose Fountaines by the Fawnes, and Satyrs, many a yeere,
With youthfull Greens were crownd, yet could not stay then there,
But they will serve the Swale, which in her wandring course,
A Nymph nam'd Holgat hath, and Risdale, all whose force,
Small though (God wot) it be, yet from their Southerne shore,
With that salute the Swale, as others did before,
At Richmond and arive, which much doth grace the Flood,
For that her Precinct long amongst the Shires hath stood:
But Yorkshire wills the same her glory to resigne.
When passing thence the Swale, this mineon Flood of mine
Next takes into her traine, cleere Wiske, a wanton Gyrle,
As though her watry path were pav'd with Orient Pearle,
So wondrous sweet she seemes, in many a winding Gyre,
As though shee Gambolds made, or as she did desire,
Her Labyrinth-like turnes, and mad Meandred trace,
With marvell should amaze, and comming doth imbrace
North-Alerton, by whom her honour is increast,
Whose Liberties include a County at the least,
To grace the wandring Wiske, then well upon her way,
Which by her count'nance thinks to carry all the sway;
When having her receav'd, Swale bonny Codbeck brings,
And Willowbeck with her, two pretty Rivellings,
And Bedall bids along, then almost at the Ouze,
Who with these Rills enrich'd begins her selfe to rouse.
When that great Forrest-Nymph faire Gautresse on her way,
Shee sees to stand prepar'd, with Garlands fresh and gay
To decke up Ouze, before her selfe to Yorke she show,
So out of my full wombe the Fosse doth likewise flow,
That meeting thee at Yorke, under the Cities side,

Her glories with thy selfe doth equally divide,
The East part watring still, as thou dost wash the West,
By whose Imbraces Yorke aboundantly is blest.
So many Rivers I continually maintaine,
As all those lesser Floods that into Darwin straine,
Their Fountaines find in me, the Ryedale naming Rye,
Fosse, Rycall, Hodbeck, Dow, with Semen, and them by
Cleere Costwy, which her selfe from Blackmore in doth bring,
And playing as shee slides through shady Pickering,
To Darwent homage doth; and Darwent that divides
The East-riding and me, upon her either sides,
Although that to us both, she most indifferent bee,
And seemeth to affect her equally with me,
From my Division yet her Fountaine doth derive,
And from my Blackmore here her Course doth first contrive.
Let my Demensions then be seriously pursude,
And let great Britaine see in my brave Latitude,
How in the high'st degree, by nature I am grac'd;
For tow'rds the Craven Hills, upon my West are plac'd
New-Forrest, Applegarth, and Swaledale, Dryades all,
And lower towards the Ouze, if with my Floods ye fall,
The goodly Gautresse keeps chiefe of my Sylvan kind,
There stony Stanmore view, bleake with the Sleet and Wind,
Upon this Easterne side, so Ryedale darke and deepe,
Amongst whose Groves of yore, some say that Elves did keepe;
Then Pickering, whom the Fawnes beyond them all adore,
By whom not farre away lyes large-spred Blackimore,
The Cleeveland North from these, a State that doth maintaine,
Leaning her lustie side to the great Germane Maine,
Which if she were not heere confined thus in me,
A Shire even of her selfe might well be said to be.
Nor lesse hath Pickering Leigh, her libertie then this,
North-Alerton a Shire so likewise reckoned is;
And Richmond of the rest, the greatest in estate,
A Countie justly call'd, that them accommodate;
So I North-Riding am, for spaciousnesse renown'd,
Our mother Yorkshires eld'st, who worthily is crown'd
The Queene of all the Shires, on this side Trent, for we
The Ridings severall parts of her vaste greatnesse be,
In us, so we againe have severall seats, whose bounds
Doe measure from their sides so many miles of grounds,
That they are called Shires; like to some mightie King,
May Yorkshire be compar'd, (the lik'st of any thing)
Who hath Kings that attend, and to his State retaine,
And yet so great, that they have under them againe
Great Princes, that to them be subject, so have we
Shires subject unto us, yet wee her subjects be;
Although these be ynough sufficiently to show,

That I the other two for bravery quite out-goe:
Yet looke yee up along into my Setting side,
Where Teis first from my bounds, rich Dunelme doth divide,
And you shall see those Rills, that with their watry prease,
Their most beloved Teis so plenteously increase,
The cleere yet lesser Lune, the Bauder, and the Gret,
All out of me doe flow; then turne ye from the Set,
And looke but tow'rds the Rise, upon the German Maine,
Those Rarities, and see, that I in me containe;
My Scarborough, which looks as though in heaven it stood,
To those that lye below, from th' Bay of Robin Hood,
Even to the fall of Teis; let me but see the man,
That in one Tract can show the wonders that I can,
Like Whitbies selfe I thinke, ther's none can shew but I,
O'r whose attractive earth there may no Wild-geese flie,
But presently they fall from off their wings to ground:
If this no wonder be, wher's there a wonder found,
And stones like Serpents there, yet may yee more behold,
That in their naturall Gyres are up together rold.
The Rocks by Mouligrave too, my glories forth to set,
Out of their cranied Cleeves, can give you perfect Jet,
And upon Huntclipnab, you every where may find,
(As though nice Nature lov'd to vary in this kind)
Stones of a Spherick forme of sundry Mickles fram'd,
That well they Globes of stone, or bullets might be nam'd
For any Ordnance fit: which broke with Hammers blowes,
Doe headlesse Snakes of stone, within their Rounds enclose.
Marke Gisboroughs gay Scite, where Nature seemes so nice,
As in the same shee makes a second Paradice,
Whose Soyle imbroydered is, with so rare sundry Flowers,
Her large Okes so long greene, as Summer there her Bowers,
Had set up all the yeare, her ayre for health refin'd,
Her earth with Allome veines most richly intermin'd.
In other places these might Rarities be thought,
So common but in me, that I esteeme as nought.
Then could I reckon up my Ricall, making on
By Rydale, towards her dear-lov'd Darwent, who's not gone
Farre from her pearly Springs, but under-ground she goes;
As up towards Craven Hills, I many have of those,
Amongst the cranied Cleeves, that through the caverns creepe,
And dimbles hid from day, into the earth so deepe,
That oftentimes their sight, the senses doth appall,
Which for their horrid course, the people Helbecks call,
Which may for ought I see, be with my Wonders set,
And with much marvell seene: that I am not in debt
To none that neigboureth me; nor ought can they me lend.
When Darwent bad her stay, and there her speech to end,
For that East-Riding cald, her proper cause to plead:

For Darwent a true Nymph, a most impartiall Mayd,
And like to both ally'd, doth will the last should have
That priviledge, which time to both the former gave,
And wills th'East-Riding then, in her owne cause to speake,
Who mildly thus begins; Although I be but weake,
To those two former parts, yet what I seeme to want
In largenesse, for that I am in my Compasse scant,
Yet for my Scite I know, that I them both excell;
For marke me how I lye, yea note me very well,
How in the East I raigne, (of which my name I take)
And my broad side doe beare up to the German Lake,
Which bravely I survey; then turne ye and behold
Upon my pleasant breast, that large and spacious Ould
Of Yorke that takes the name, that with delighted eyes,
When he beholds the Sunne out of the Seas to rise,
With pleasure feeds his Flocks, for which he scarse gives place
To Cotswold, and for what becomes a Pastorall grace,
Doth goe beyond him quite; then note upon my South,
How all along the Shore, to mighty Humbers mouth,
Rich Holdernesse I have, excelling for her graine,
By whose much plentie I, not onely doe maintaine
My selfe in good estate, but Shires farre off that lye,
Up Humber that to Hull, come every day to buy,
To me beholding are; besides, the neighbouring Townes,
Upon the Verge whereof, to part her, and the Downes,
Hull downe to Humber hasts, and takes into her Banke
Some lesse but lively Rills, with waters waxing ranke,
Shee Beverley salutes, whose beauties so delight
The fayre-enamoured Flood, as ravisht with the sight,
That shee could ever stay, that gorgeous Phane to view,
But that the Brooks, and Bournes, so hotly her pursue,
To Kingston and convey, whom Hull doth newly name,
Of Humber-bordring Hull, who hath not heard the fame:
And for great Humbers selfe, I challenge him for mine:
For whereas Fowlwy first, and Shelfleet doe combine,
By meeting in their course, so courteously to twin,
Gainst whom on th'other side, the goodly Trent comes in,
From that especiall place, great Humber hath his raigne,
Beyond which hee's mine owne: so I my Course maintaine,
From Kilnseys pyle-like poynt, along the Easterne shore,
And laugh at Neptunes rage, when lowdl'est he doth rore,
Till Flamborough jutt foorth into the German Sea.
And as th'East-Riding more yet ready was to say,
Ouse in her owne behalfe doth interrupt her speech,
And of th'Imperious land doth liberty beseech,
Since she had passed Yorke, and in her wandring race,
By that faire Cities scite, received had such grace,
Shee might for it declame, but more to honor Yorke,

Shee who supposd the same to bee her onely worke,
Still to renowne those Dukes, who strongly did pretend
A title to the Crowne, as those who did descend
From them that had the right, doth this Oration make,
And to uphold their claime, thus to the Floods she spake.
They very idly erre, who thinke that blood then spilt,
In that long-lasting warre, proceeded from the guilt,
Of the proud Yorkists part; for let them understand,
That Richard Duke of Yorke, whose brave and martiall hand
The Title undertooke, by tyranny and might,
Sought not t'attaine the Crowne, but from succesfull right,
Which still upheld his claime, by which his valiant sonne,
Great Edward Earle of March, the Garland after wonne:
For Richard Duke of Yorke, at Wakefield Battell slaine,
Who first that title broach'd, in the sixt Henries raigne,
From Edmond a fift sonne of Edward did descend,
That justly he thereby no title could pretend,
Before them com'n from Gaunt, well knowne of all to be,
The fourth to Edward borne, and therefore a degree
Before him to the Crowne; but that which did preferre
His title, was the match with Dame Anne Mortimer,
Of Roger Earle of March the daughter, that his claime,
From Clarence the third sonne of great King Edward came,
Which Anne deriv'd alone, the right before all other,
Of the delapsed Crowne, from Philip her faire mother,
Daughter and onely heire of Clarence, and the Bride
To Edmond Earle of March; this Anne her daughter tide
In wedlocke to the Earle of Cambridge, whence the right
Of Richard as I said, which fell at Wakefield fight,
Descended to his sonne, brave Edward after King,
(Henry the sixt depos'd) thus did the Yorkists bring
Their title from a straine, before the line of Gaunt,
Whose issue they by Armes did worthily supplant.
By this the Ouze perceav'd great Humber to looke grim;
(For evermore shee hath a speciall eye to him)
As though he much disdain'd each one should thus be heard,
And he their onely King, untill the last defer'd,
At which hee seem'd to frowne; wherefore the Ouze off breaks,
And to his confluent Floods, thus mighty Humber speaks.
Let Trent her tribute pay, which from their severall founts,
For thirtie Floods of name, to me her King that counts,
Be much of me belov'd, brave River; and from me,
Receive those glorious Rites that Fame can give to thee.
And thou Marsh-drowning Don, and all those that repaire
With thee, that bringst to me thy easie ambling Aire,
Embodying in one Banke: and Wharfe, which by thy fall
Dost much augment my Ouze, let me embrace you all,
My brave West-Riding Brooks, your King you need not scorne,

Proud Nyades neither yee, North-Riders that are borne;
My yellow-sanded Your, and thou my sister Swale,
That dauncing come to Ouze, through many a daintie Dale,
Doe greatly me inrich, cleare Darwent driving downe
From Cleeveland; and thou Hull, that highly dost renowne
Th'East-Riding by thy rise, doe homage to your King,
And let the Sea-Nymphs thus of mighty Humber sing;
That full an hundred Floods my watry Court maintaine,
Which either of themselves, or in their greaters traine,
Their Tribute pay to me; and for my princely name,
From Humber King of Hunns, as anciently it came;
So still I sticke to him: for from that Easterne King
Once in me drown'd, as I my Pedigree doe bring:
So his great name receives no prejudice thereby;
For as he was a King, so know ye all that I
Am King of all the Floods, that North of Trent doe flow;
Then let the idle world no more such cost bestow,
Nor of the muddy Nyle, so great a Wonder make,
Though with her bellowing fall, shee violently take
The neighbouring people deafe; nor Ganges so much praise,
That where he narrowest is, eight miles in broadnesse layes
His bosome, nor so much hereafter shall be spoke
Of that (but lately found) Guyanian Orenoque,
Whose Cateract a noyse so horrible doth keepe,
That it even Neptune frights; what Flood comes to the Deepe,
Then Humber that is heard more horribly to rore?
For when my Higre comes, I make my either shore
Even tremble with the sound, that I afarre doe send.
No sooner of this speech had Humber made an end,
But the applauding. Floods sent foorth so shrill a shout,
That they were eas'ly heard all Holdernesse about,
Above the Beachy Brack, amongst the Marshes rude,
When the East-Riding her Oration to conclude,
Goes on; My Sisters boast that they have little Shires
Their subjects, I can shew the like of mine for theirs;
My Howdon hath as large a Circuit, and as free,
On Ouse, and Humbers banks, and as much graceth me,
My Latitude compar'd with those that me oppugne:
Not Richmond nor her like, that doth to them belong,
Doth grace them more then this doth me, upon my coast,
And for their wondrous things, whereof so much they boast,
Upon my Easterne side, which jutts upon the Sea,
Amongst the white-scalp'd Cleeves, this wonder see they may,
The Mullet, and the Awke, (my Fowlers there doe finde)
Of all great Britain brood, Birds of the strangest kind,
That building in the Rocks, being taken with the hand,
And cast beyond the Cliffe, that poynteth to the land,
Fall instantly to ground, as though it were a stone,

But put out to the Sea, they instantly are gone,
And flye a league or two before they doe returne,
As onely by that ayre, they on their wings were borne.
Then my Prophetick Spring at Veipsey, I may show,
That some yeares is dry'd up, some yeares againe doth flow;
But when it breaketh out with an immoderate birth,
It tells the following yeare of a penurious dearth.
Here ended shee her speech, the Ridings all made friends,
And from my tyred hand, my labored Canto ends.

THE NINE AND TWENTIETH SONG

THE ARGUMENT

The Muse the Bishopricke assayes,
And to her fall sings downe the Teis,
Then takes shee to the dainty Wer,
And with all braveries fitted her.
Tyne tells the Victories by us got,
In foughten Fields against the Scot.
Then through Northumberland shee goes,
The Floods and Mountaines doth dispose;
And with their glories doth proceed,
Not staying till shee come to Tweed.

The Muse this largest Shire of England having sung,
Yet seeing more then this did to her taske belong,
Looks still into the North, the Bishopricke and viewes,
Which with an eager eye, whilst wistly she pursues,
Teis as a bordering Flood, (who thought her selfe divine)
Confining in her Course that Countie Palatine,
And Yorke the greatest Shire doth instantly begin,
To rouze her selfe; quoth shee, Doth every Rillet win
Applause for their small worth's, and I that am a Queene,
With those poore Brooks compar'd, shall I alone be seene
Thus silently to passe, and not be heard to sing,
When as two Countries are contending for my Spring:
For Cumberland, to which the Cumri gave the name,
Accounts it to be hers, Northumberland the same,
Will needsly hers should bee, for that my Spring doth rise,
So equally twixt both, that he were very wise,
Could tell which of these two, me for her owne may claime.
But as in all these Tracts, there's scarce a Flood of fame,
But shee some Vally hath, which her brave name doth beare:
My Teisdale, nam'd of me, so likewise have I heare,
At my first setting foorth, through which I nimbly slide;

Then Yorkshire which doth lye upon my Setting side,
Me Lune and Bauder lends, as in the Song before
Th'industrious Muse hath shew'd; my Dunelmenian shore,
Sends Huyd to helpe my course, with some few other Becks,
Which time (as it should seeme) so utterly neglects,
That they are namelesse yet; then doe I bid adiew,
To Barnards battelled Towers, and seriously pursue
My course to Neptunes Court, but as forthright I runne,
The Skern, a dainty Nymph, saluting Darlington,
Comes in to give me ayd, and being prowd and ranke,
Shee chanc'd to looke aside, and spieth neere her Banke,
Three blacke and horrid pits, which for their boyling heat,
(That from their lothsome brimms, doe breath a sulpherous sweat)
Hell-kettles rightly cald, that with the very sight,
This Water-Nymph, my Skern is put in such affright,
That with unusuall speed, she on her Course doth hast,
And rashly runnes her selfe into my widened waste.
In pompe I thus approch great Amphetrites state.
But whilst Teis undertooke her Story to relate,
Wer waxeth almost wood, that she so long should stand
Upon those loftie tearmes, as though both sea and land
Were tyde to heare her talke: quoth Wer, what wouldst thou say,
Vaine-glorious bragging Brooke, hadst thou so cleere a way
T'advance thee as I have, hadst thou such meanes and might,
How wouldst thou then exult? O then to what a height
Wouldst thou put up thy price? hadst thou but such a Trine
Of Rillets as I have, which naturally combine,
Their Springs thee to beget, as these of mine doe me,
In their consenting sounds, that doe so well agree?
As Kellop comming in from Kellop-Law her Syre,
A Mountaine much in fame, small Wellop doth require,
With her to walke along, which Burdop with her brings.
Thus from the full conflux of these three severall Springs
My greatnesse is begot, as Nature meant to show
My future strength and state; then forward doe I flow
Through my delicious Dale, with every pleasure rife,
And Wyresdale still may stand, with Teisdale for her life:
Comparing of their Scites, then casting on my Course,
So satiate with th'excesse of my first naturall source,
As petty Bournes and Becks, I scorne but once to call,
Wascrop a wearish Gyrle, of name the first of all,
That I vouchsafe for mine, untill that I arive
At Aukland, where with force me forward still to drive,
Cleere Gauntlesse gives her selfe, when I begin to gad,
And whirling in and out, as I were waxed mad,
I change my posture oft, to many a Snakie Gyre,
To my first fountaine now, as seeming to retyre:
Then suddenly againe I turne my watry trayle,

Now I endent the earth, and then I it engrayle
With many a turne and trace, thus wandring up and downe,
Brave Durham I behold, that stately seated Towne,
That Dunholme hight of yore (even) from a Desart wonne,
Whose first foundation Zeale, and Piety begun,
By them who thither first Saint Cutberts body brought,
To save it from the Danes, by fire and sword that sought
Subversion of those things, that good and holy were,
With which beloved place, I seeme so pleased here,
As that I clip it close, and sweetly hug it in
My cleare and amorous armes, as jealous time should win
Me further off from it, as our divorce to be.
Hence like a lustie Flood most absolutely free,
None mixing then with me, as I doe mix with none,
But scorning a Colleague, nor neere me any one,
To Neptunes Court I come; for note along the Strond,
From Hartlepoole (even) to the poynt of Sunderland,
As farre as Wardenlaws can possibly survey;
There's not a Flood of note hath entrance to the sea.
Here ended shee her Speech, when as the goodly Tyne,
(Northumberland that parts from this Shire Palatine)
Which patiently had heard, looke as before the Wer
Had taken up the Teis, so Tyne now takes up her,
For her so tedious talke, Good Lord (quoth she) had I
No other thing wherein my labor to imply,
But to set out my selfe, how much (well) could I say,
In mine owne proper praise, in this kind every way
As skilfull as the best; I could if I did please,
Of my two Fountaines tell, which of their sundry wayes,
The South and North are nam'd, entitled both of Tyne,
As how the prosperous Springs of these two Floods of mine
Are distant thirty miles, how that the South-Tyne nam'd,
From Stanmore takes her Spring, for Mines of Brasse that's fam'd,
How that nam'd of the North, is out of Wheel-fell sprung,
Amongst these English Alpes, which as they runne along,
England, and Scotland here impartially divide.
How South-Tyne setting out from Cumberland is plide,
With Hartley which her hasts, and Tippall that doth strive,
By her more sturdy Streame, the Tyne along to drive;
How th'Allans, th'East, and West, their bounties to her bring,
Two faire and full-brim'd Floods, how also from her Spring,
My other North-nam'd Tyne, through Tyndale maketh in,
Which Shele her Hand-mayd hath, and as she hasts to twin
With th'other from the South, her sister, how cleere Rhead,
With Perop comes prepar'd, and Cherlop, me to lead,
Through Ridsdale on my way, as farre as Exham, then
Dowell me Homage doth, with blood of Englishmen,
Whose Streame was deeply dy'd in that most cruell warre

Of Lancaster and Yorke. Now having gone so farre,
Their strengths me their deare Tyne, doe wondrously enrich,
As how cleere Darwent drawes downe to Newcastle, which
The honour hath alone to entertaine me there,
As of those mighty ships, that in my mouth I beare,
Fraught with my country Coale, of this Newcastle nam'd,
For which both farre and neere, that place no lesse is fam'd,
Then India for her Mynes; should I at large declare
My glories, in which Time commands me to bee spare,
And I but slightly touch, which stood I to report,
As freely as I might, yee both would fall too short
Of me; but know that Tyne hath greater things in hand:
For, to tricke up our selves, whilst trifling thus we stand,
Bewitch'd with our owne praise, at all we never note,
How the Albanian Floods now lately set afloat,
With th'honour to them done, take heart, and lowdly crie
Defiance to us all, on this side Tweed that lye;
And hearke the high-brow'd Hills alowd begin to ring,
With sound of things that Forth prepared is to sing:
When once the Muse arives on the Albanian shore;
And therefore to make up our forces here before
The on-set they begin, the Battels wee have got,
Both on our earth and theirs, against the valiant Scot,
I undertake to tell; then Muses I intreat
Your ayd, whilst I these Fights in order shall repeat.
When mighty Malcolme here had with a violent hand,
(As he had oft before) destroy'd Northumberland,
In Rufus troubled Raigne, the warlike Mowbray then,
This Earledome that possest, with halfe the power of men,
For conquest which that King from Scotland hither drew,
At Anwick in the field their Armies overthrew;
Where Malcolme and his sonne, brave Edward both were found,
Slaine on that bloody field: So on the English ground,
When David King of Scots, and Henry his sterne sonne,
Entitled by those times, the Earle of Huntingdon,
Had forradg'd all the North, beyond the River Teis,
In Stephens troubled raigne, in as tumultuous dayes
As England ever knew, the Archbishop of Yorke,
Stout Thurstan, and with him joynd in that warlike work,
Ralfe, (both for wit and Armes) of Durham Bishop then
Renownd, that called were the valiant Clergy men,
With th'Earle of Aubemarle, Especk, and Peverell, Knights,
And of the Lacies two, oft try'd in bloody fights,
Twixt Alverton and Yorke, the doubtfull battell got,
On David and his sonne, whilst of th'invading Scot,
Ten thousand strew'd the earth, and whilst they lay to bleed,
Ours followed them that fled, beyond our sister Tweed.
And when Fitz-Empresse next in Normandy, and here,

And his rebellious sonnes in high combustions were,
William the Scottish King, taking advantage then,
And entring with an Host of eighty thousand men,
As farre as Kendall came, where Captaines then of ours,
Which ayd in Yorkshire raisd, with the Northumbrian powers,
His forces overthrew, and him a prisoner led.
So Longshanks, Scolands scourge, him to that Country sped,
Provoked by the Scots, that England did invade,
And on the Borders here such spoyle and havock made,
That all the land lay waste betwixt the Tweed and me.
This most coragious King, from them his owne to free,
Before proud Berwick set his puisant army downe,
And tooke it by strong siege, since when that warlike towne,
As Cautionary long the English after held.
But tell me all you Floods, when was there such a Field
By any Nation yet, as by the English wonne,
Upon the Scottish power, as that of Halidon,
Seaven Earles, nine hundred Horse, and of Foot-souldiers more,
Neere twenty thousand slaine, so that the Scottish gore
Ranne downe the Hill in streames (even) in Albania's sight.
By our third Edwards prowesse, that most renowned Knight,
As famous was that Fight of his against the Scot,
As that against the French, which he at Cressy got.
And when that conquering King did afterward advance
His Title, and had past his warlike powers to France,
And David King of Scots heere entred to invade,
To which the King of France did that false Lord perswade,
Against his given Faith, from France to draw his Bands,
To keepe his owne at home, or to fill both his hands
With warre in both the Realmes: was ever such a losse,
To Scotland yet befell, as that at Nevills Crosse,
Where fifteene thousand Scots their soules at once forsooke,
Where stout John Copland then, King David prisoner tooke,
I'th head of all his troups, that bravely there was seene.
When English Philip, that brave Amazonian Queene,
Encouraging her men, from troupe to troupe did ride,
And where our Cleargy had their ancient Valour tride:
Thus often comming in, they have gone out too short.
And next to this the fight of Nesbit I report,
When Hebborn that stout Scot, and his had all their hire,
Which in t'our Marches came, and with invasive fire,
Our Villages laid waste, for which defeat of ours,
When doughty Douglasse came with the Albanian powers.
At Holmdon doe but see, the blow our Hotspurre gave
To that bold daring Scot, before him how he drave
His Armie, and with shot of our brave English Bowes,
Did wound them on the backs, whose brests were hurt with blows,
Ten thousand put to sword, with many a Lord and Knight,

Some prisoners, wounded some, some others slaine outright,
And entring Scotland then, all Tividale o'r-ran.
Or who a braver field then th'Earle of Surrey wan,
Where their King James the fourth himselfe so bravely bore,
That since that age wherein he liv'd, nor those before,
Yet never such a King in such a Battell saw,
Amongst his fighting friends, where whilst he breath could draw,
Hee bravely fought on foot, where Flodden Hill was strew'd
With bodies of his men, welneere to mammocks hew'd,
That on the Mountaines side, they covered neere a mile,
Where those two valiant Earles of Lenox and Arguyle,
Were with their Soveraigne slaine, Abbots, and Bishops there,
Which had put Armor on, in hope away to beare
The Victory with them, before the English fell.
But now of other Fields, it fits the Muse to tell,
As when the Noble Duke of Norfolke made a Road
To Scotland, and therein his hostile fire bestow'd
On welneere thirtie Townes, and staying there so long,
Till victuall waxed weake, the Winter waxing strong,
Returning over Tweed, his Booties home to bring,
Which to the very heart did vex the Scottish King,
The fortune of the Duke extreamely that did grutch,
Remaining there so long, and doing there so much,
Thinking to spoyle and waste, in England as before,
The English men had done on the Albanian shore,
And gathering up his force, before the English fled
To Scotlands utmost bounds, thence into England sped,
When that brave Bastard sonne of Dacres, and his friend,
John Musgrave, which had charge the Marches to attend,
With Wharton, a proud Knight, with scarce foure hundred Horse,
Encountring on the Plaine with all the Scottish force,
Thence from the Field with them, so many prisoners brought,
Which in that furious fight were by the English caught,
That there was scarce a Page or Lackey but had store,
Earles, Barrons, Knights, Esquires, two hundred there and more,
Of ordinary men, seven hundred made to yeeld,
There scarcely hath been heard, of such a foughten field,
That James the fifth to thinke, that but so very few,
His universall power so strangely should subdue,
So tooke the same to heart, that it abridg'd his life.
Such foyles by th'English given, amongst the Scots were rife.
These on the English earth, the English men did gaine;
But when their breach of faith did many times constraine
Our Nation to invade, and carry conquests in
To Scotland; then behold, what our successe hath bin,
Even in the latter end of our eight Henries dayes,
Who Seymor sent by Land, and Dudley sent by Seas,
With his full forces then, O Forth, then didst thou beare,

That Navy on thy Streame, whose Bulke was fraught with feare,
When Edenbrough and Leeth, into the ayre were blowne
With Powders sulphurous smoke, & twenty townes were throwne
Upon the trampled earth, and into ashes trod;
As int' Albania when we made a second Road,
In our sixt Edwards dayes, when those two Martiall men,
Which conquered there before, were thither sent agen:
But for their high desarts, with greater Titles grac'd,
The first created Duke of Somerset, the last
The Earle of Warwicke made, at Muscleborough Field,
Where many a doughty Scot that did disdaine to yeeld,
Was on the earth layd dead, where as for five miles space
In length, and foure in bredth, the English in the chase,
With carkeises of Scots, strew'd all their naturall ground,
The number of the slaine were fourteene thousand found,
And fifteene hundred more ta'n Prisoners by our men.
So th'Earle of Sussex next to Scotland sent agen,
To punish them by warre, which on the Borders here,
Not onely rob'd and spoyl'd, but that assistants were
To those two puisant Earles, Northumberland, who rose
With Westmerland his Peere, suggested by the foes
To great Eliza's raigne, and peacefull government;
Wherefore that puisant Queene him to Albania sent,
Who fiftie Rock-reard Pyles and Castles having cast
Farre lower then their Scites, and with strong fires defac'd
Three hundred townes, their wealth, with him worth carrying brought
To England over Tweed, when now the floods besought
The Tyne to hold her tongue, when presently began
A rumour which each where through all the Country ran,
Of this proud Rivers speech, the Hills and Floods among,
And Lowes, a Forrest-Nymph, the same so lowdly sung,
That it through Tindale straight, and quite through Ridsdale ran,
And sounded shriller there, then when it first began,
That those high Alpine Hills, as in a row they stand,
Receiv'd the sounds, which thus went on from hand to hand.
The high-rear'd Red-Squire first, to Aumond Hill it told,
When Aumond great therewith, nor for his life could hold,
To Kembelspeth againe, the businesse but relate,
To Black-Brea he againe, a Mountaine holding state
With any of them all, to Cocklaw he it gave;
And Cocklaw it againe, to Cheviot, who did rave
With the report thereof, hee from his mighty stand,
Resounded it againe through all Northumberland,
That White-Squire lastly caught, and it to Berwick sent,
That brave and warlike Towne, from thence incontinent,
The sound from out the South, into Albania came,
And many a lustie Flood, did with her praise inflame,
Affrighting much the Forth, who from her trance awooke,

And to her native strength her presently betooke,
Against the Muse should come to the Albanian Coast.
But Pictswall all this while, as though he had been lost,
Not mention'd by the Muse, began to fret and fume,
That every petty Brooke thus proudly should presume
To talke; and he whom first the Romans did invent,
And of their greatnesse yet, the longst-liv'd monument,
Should this be over-trod; wherefore his wrong to wreake,
In their proud presence thus, doth aged Pictswall speake.
Me thinks that Offa's ditch in Cambria should not dare
To thinke himselfe my match, who with such cost and care
The Romans did erect, and for my safeguard set
Their Legions, from my spoyle the proling Pict to let,
That often In-roads made, our earth from them to win,
By Adrian beaten back, so he to keepe them in,
To Sea from East to West, begun me first a wall
Of eightie myles in length, twixt Tyne and Edens fall:
Long making mee they were, and long did me maintaine.
Nor yet that Trench which tracts the Westerne Wiltshire Plaine,
Of Woden, Wansdyke cal'd, should paralell with me,
Comparing our descents, which shall appeare to be
Mere upstarts, basely borne; for when I was in hand,
The Saxon had not then set foot upon this land,
Till my declining age, and after many a yeare,
Of whose poore petty Kings, those the small labors were.
That on Newmarket-Heath, made up as though but now,
Who for the Devils worke the vulgar dare avow,
Tradition telling none, who truly it began,
Where many a reverent Booke can tell you of my Man,
And when I first decayd, Severus going on,
What Adrian built of turfe, he builded new of stone,
And after many a time, the Britans me repayr'd,
To keepe me still in plight, nor cost they ever spar'd.
Townes stood upon my length, where Garrisons were laid,
Their limits to defend; and for my greater ayd,
With turrets I was built where Sentinels were plac'd,
To watch upon the Pict; so me my Makers grac'd,
With hollow Pipes of Brasse, along me still that went,
By which they in one Fort still to another sent,
By speaking in the same, to tell them what to doe,
And so from Sea to Sea could I be whispered through:
Upon my thicknesse, three march'd eas'ly breast to breast,
Twelve foot was I in height, such glory I possest.
Old Pictswall with much pride thus finishing his plea,
Had in his utmost course attain'd the Easterne Sea,
Yet there was Hill nor Flood once heard to clap a hand;
For the Northumbrian Nymphs had come to understand,
That Tyne exulting late o'r Scotland in her Song,

(Which over all that Realme report had loudly rung)
The Calidonian Forth so highly had displeas'd,
And many an other Flood, (which could not be appeas'd)
That they had vow'd revenge, and Proclamation made,
That in a learned warre the foe they would invade,
And like stout Floods stand free from this supputed shame,
Or conquered give themselves up to the English name:
Which these Northumbrian Nymphs, with doubt & terror strook,
Which knew they from the foe, for nothing were to looke,
But what by skill they got, and with much care should keepe,
And therefore they consult by meeting in the Deepe,
To be delivered from the ancient enemies rage,
That they would all upon a solemne Pilgrimage
Unto the Holy-Isle, the vertue of which place,
They knew could very much availe them in this case:
For many a blessed Saint in former ages there,
Secluded from the world, to Abstinence and Prayer,
Had given up themselves, which in the German Maine,
And from the shore not farre, did in it selfe conteine
Sufficient things for food, which from those holy men,
That to devotion liv'd, and sanctimony then,
It Holy-Isle was call'd, for which they all prepare,
As I shall tell you how, and what their number are.
With those the farthest off, the first I will begin,
As Pont a pearlesse Brook, brings Blyth which putteth in
With her, then Wansbeck next in wading to the Maine,
Neere Morpet meets with Font, which followeth in her traine;
Next them the little Lyne alone doth goe along,
When Cocket commeth downe, and with her such a throng,
As that they seeme to threat the Ocean; for with her
Comes Ridley, Ridland next, with Usway, which preferre
Their Fountaines to her Flood, who for her greater fame,
Hath at her fall an Isle, call'd Cocket, of her name,
As that great Neptune should take notice of her state;
Then Alne by Anwicke comes, and with as proud a gate,
As Cocket came before, for whom at her faire fall,
(In bravery as to show, that she surpast them all)
The famous Isle of Ferne, and Staples aptly stand,
And at her comming foorth, doe kisse her Christall hand.
Whilst these resolv'd upon their Pilgrimage, proceed,
Till for the love shee beares to her deare Mistris Tweed,
Of Bramish leaves the name, by which shee hath her birth;
And though shee keepe her course upon the English earth,
Yet Bowbent, a bright Nymph, from Scotland comming in,
To goe with her to Tweed, the wanton Flood doth winne.
Though at this headstrong Stream, proud Flodden from his height,
Doth daily seeme to fret, yet takes he much delight
Her lovelinesse to view, as on to Tweed she straines,

Where whilst this Mountaine much for her sweet sake sustaines,
This Canto we conclude, and fresh about must cast,
Of all the English Tracts, to consummate the last.

THE THIRTIETH SONG

THE ARGUMENT

Of Westmerland the Muse now sings,
And fetching Eden from her Springs,
Sets her along, and Kendall then
Surveying, beareth backe agen;
And climing Skidows loftie Hill,
By many a River, many a Rill,
To Cumberland, where in her way,
Shee Copland calls, and doth display
Her Beauties, backe to Eden goes,
Whose Floods, and Fall shee aptly showes.

Yet cheerely on my Muse, no whit at all dismay'd,
But look aloft tow'rds heaven, to him whose powerfull ayd;
Hath led thee on thus long, & through so sundry soiles,
Steep Mountains, Forrests rough, deepe Rivers, that thy toyles
Most sweet refreshings seeme, and still thee comfort sent,
Against the Bestiall Rout, and Boorish rabblement
Of those rude vulgar sots, whose braines are onely Slime,
Borne to the doting world, in this last yron Time,
So stony, and so dull, that Orpheus which (men say)
By the inticing Straines of his melodious Lay,
Drew Rocks and aged Trees, to whether he would please;
He might as well have moov'd the Universe as these;
But leave this Frie of Hell in their owne filth defilde,
And seriously pursue the sterne Westmerian Wilde,
First ceazing in our Song, the South part of the Shire,
Where Westmerland to West, by wide Wynander Mere,
The Eboracean fields her to the Rising bound,
Where Can first creeping forth, her feet hath scarcely found,
But gives that Dale her name, where Kendale towne doth stand,
For making of our Cloth scarce match'd in all the land.
Then keeping on her course, though having in her traine,
But Sput, a little Brooke, then Winster doth retaine,
Tow'rds the Vergivian Sea, by her two mighty Falls,
(Which the brave Roman tongue, her Catadupæ calls)
This eager River seemes outragiously to rore,
And counterfetting Nyle, to deafe the neighboring shore,
To which she by the sound apparantly doth show,

The season foule or faire, as then the wind doth blow:
For when they to the North, the noyse doe easliest heare,
They constantly affirme the weather will be cleere;
And when they to the South, againe they boldly say,
It will be clouds or raine the next approaching day.
To the Hibernick Gulfe, when soone the River hasts,
And to those queachy Sands, from whence her selfe she casts,
She likewise leaves her name as every place where she,
In her cleare course doth come, by her should honored be.
But backe into the North from hence our course doth lye,
As from this fall of Can, still keeping in our eye,
The source of long liv'd Lun, I long-liv'd doe her call;
For of the British Floods, scarce one amongst them all,
Such state as to her selfe, the Destinies assigne,
By christning in her Course a Countie Palatine,
For Luncaster so nam'd, the Fort upon the Lun,
And Lancashire the name from Lancaster begun:
Yet though shee be a Flood, such glory that doth gaine,
In that the British Crowne doth to her state pertaine,
Yet Westmerland alone, not onely boasts her birth,
But for her greater good the kind Westmerian earth,
Cleere Burbeck her bequeaths, and Barrow to attend
Her grace, till shee her name to Lancaster doe lend.
With all the speed we can, to Cumberland we hye,
(Still longing to salute the utmost Albany)
By Eden, issuing out of Husseat-Morvill Hill,
And pointing to the North, as then a little Rill,
There simply takes her leave of her sweet sister Swale,
Borne to the selfe same Sire, but with a stronger gale,
Tow'rds Humber hyes her course, but Eden making on,
Through Malerstrang hard by, a Forrest woe begone
In love with Edens eyes, of the cleere Naiades kind,
Whom thus the Wood-Nymph greets: What passage shalt thou find,
My most beloved Brook, in making to thy Bay,
That wandring art to wend through many a crooked way,
Farre under hanging Hills, through many a cragged strait,
And few the watry kind, upon thee to await,
Opposed in thy course with many a rugged Cliffe,
Besides the Northern winds against thy streame so stiffe,
As by maine strength they meant to stop thee in thy course,
And send thee easly back to Morvill to thy source.
O my bright lovely Brooke, whose name doth beare the sound
Of Gods first Garden-plot, th'imparadized ground,
Wherein he placed Man, from whence by sinne he fell.
O little blessed Brooke, how doth my bosome swell,
With love I beare to thee, the day cannot suffice
For Malerstang to gaze upon thy beautious eyes.
This sayd, the Forrest rubd her rugged front the while,

Cleere Eden looking back, regreets her with a smile,
And simply takes her leave, to get into the Maine;
When Below a bright Nymph, from Stanmore downe doth straine
To Eden, as along to Appleby shee makes,
Which passing, to her traine, next Troutbeck in shee takes,
And Levenant, then these, a somewhat lesser Rill,
When Glenkwin greets her well, and happily to fill,
Her more abundant Banks, from Ulls, a mightie Mere
On Cumberlands confines, comes Eymot neat and cleere,
And Loder doth allure, with whom she haps to meet,
Which at her comming in, doth thus her Mistris greet.
Quoth shee, thus for my selfe I say, that where I swell
Up from my Fountaine first, there is a Tyding-well,
That daily ebbs and flowes, (as Writers doe report)
The old Euripus doth, or in the selfe same sort,
The Venedocian Fount, or the Demetian Spring,
Or that which the cold Peake doth with her wonders bring,
Why should not Loder then, her Mistris Eden please,
With this, as other Floods delighted are with these.
When Eden, though shee seem'd to make unusuall haste,
About cleere Loders neck, yet lovingly doth cast
Her oft infolding Armes, as Westmerland shee leaves,
Where Cumberland againe as kindly her receives.
Yet up her watry hands, to Winfield Forrest holds
In her rough wooddy armes, which amorously infolds
Cleere Eden comming by, with all her watry store,
In her darke shades, and seemes her parting to deplore.
But Southward sallying hence, to those Sea-bordring sands,
Where Dudden driving downe to the Lancastrian lands,
This Cumberland cuts out, and strongly doth confine,
This meeting there with that, both meerly Maratine,
Where many a daintie Rill out of her native Dale,
To the Virgivian makes, with many a pleasant gale;
As Eske her farth'st, so first, a coy bred Cumbrian Lasse,
Who commeth to her Road, renowned Ravenglasse,
By Devock driven along, (which from a large-brim'd Lake,
To hye her to the Sea, with greater haste doth make)
Meets Nyte, a nimble Brooke, their Rendevous that keepe
In Ravenglasse, when soone into the blewish Deepe
Comes Irt, of all the rest, though small, the richest Girle,
Her costly bosome strew'd with precious Orient Pearle,
Bred in her shining Shels, which to the deaw doth yawne,
Which deaw they sucking in, conceave that lusty Spawne,
Of which when they grow great, and to their fulnesse swell,
They cast, which those at hand there gathering, dearly sell.
This cleare pearle-paved Irt, Bleng to her harbor brings,
From Copland comming downe, a Forrest-Nymph, which sings
Her owne praise, and those Floods, their Fountaines that derive

From her, which to extoll, the Forrest thus doth strive.
Yee Northerne Dryades all adorn'd with Mountaines steepe,
Upon whose hoary heads cold Winter long doth keepe,
Where often rising Hils, deepe Dales and many make,
Where many a pleasant Spring, and many a large-spread Lake,
Their cleere beginnings keepe, and doe their names bestow
Upon those humble Vales, through which they eas'ly flow;
Whereas the Mountaine Nymphs, and those that doe frequent
The Fountaines, Fields, and Groves, with wondrous meriment,
By Moone-shine many a night, doe give each other chase,
At Hood-winke, Barley-breake, at Tick, or Prison-base,
With tricks, and antique toyes, that one another mocke,
That skip from Crag to Crag, and leape from Rocke to Rocke.
Then Copland, of this Tract a corner, I would know,
What place can there be found in Britan, that doth show
A Surface more austere, more sterne from every way,
That who doth it behold, he cannot chuse but say,
Th'aspect of these grim Hills, these darke and mistie Dales,
From clouds scarce ever cleer'd, with the strongest Northern gales,
Tell in their mighty Roots, some Minerall there doth lye,
The Islands generall want, whose plenty might supply:
Wherefore as some suppose of Copper Mynes in me,
I Copper-land was cald, but some will have't to be
From the old Britans brought, for Cop they use to call
The tops of many Hils, which I am stor'd withall.
Then Eskdale mine Ally, and Niterdale so nam'd,
Of Floods from you that flow, as Borowdale most fam'd,
With Wasdale walled in, with Hills on every side,
Hows'ever ye extend within your wasts so wide,
For th'surface of a soyle, a Copland, Copland cry,
Till to your shouts the Hills with Ecchoes all reply.
Which Copland scarce had spoke, but quickly every hill,
Upon her Verge that stands, the neigbouring Vallies fill;
Helvillon from his height, it through the Mountaines threw,
From whom as soone againe, the sound Dunbalrase drew,
From whose stone-trophied head, it on to Wendrosse went,
Which tow'rds the Sea againe, resounded it to Dent,
That Brodwater therewith within her Banks astound,
In sayling to the Sea, told it in Egremound,
Whose Buildings, walks, and streets, with Ecchoes loud and long,
Did mightily commend old Copland for her Song.
Whence soone the Muse proceeds, to find out fresher Springs,
Where Darwent her cleere Fount from Borowdale that brings,
Doth quickly cast her selfe into an ample Lake,
And with Thurls mighty Mere, betweene them two doe make
An Island, which the name from Darwent doth derive,
Within whose secret breast nice Nature doth contrive,
That mighty Copper Myne, which not without its Vaines,

Of Gold and Silver found, it happily obtaines
Of Royaltie the name, the richest of them all
That Britan bringeth forth, which Royall she doth call.
Of Borowdale her Dam, of her owne named Isle,
As of her Royall Mynes, this River proud the while,
Keepes on her Course to Sea, and in her way doth win
Cleere Coker her compeere, which at her comming in,
Gives Coker-mouth the name, by standing at her fall,
Into faire Darwents Banks, when Darwent therewithall,
Runnes on her watry Race, and for her greater fame,
Of Neptune doth obtaine a Haven of her name,
When of the Cambrian Hills, proud Skiddo that doth show
The high'st, respecting whom, the other be but low,
Perceiving with the Floods, and Forrests, how it far'd,
And all their severall tales substantially had heard,
And of the Mountaine kind, as of all other he,
Most like Pernassus selfe that is suppos'd to be,
Having a double head, as hath that sacred Mount,
Which those nine sacred Nymphs held in so hie account,
Bethinketh of himselfe what he might justly say,
When to them all he thus his beauties doth display.
The rough Hibernian sea, I proudly overlooke,
Amongst the scattered Rocks, and there is not a nooke,
But from my glorious height into its depth I pry,
Great Hills farre under me, but as my Pages lye;
And when my Helme of Clouds upon my head I take,
At very sight thereof, immediatly I make
Th'Inhabitants about, tempestuous stormes to feare,
And for faire weather looke, when as my top is cleere;
Great Fournesse mighty Fells, I on my South survay:
So likewise on the North, Albania makes me way,
Her Countries to behold, when Scurfell from the skie,
That Anadale doth crowne, with a most amorous eye,
Salutes me every day, or at my pride lookes grim,
Oft threatning me with Clouds, as I oft threatning him:
So likewise to the East, that rew of Mountaines tall,
Which we our English Alpes may very aptly call,
That Scotland here with us, and England doe divide,
As those, whence we them name upon the other side,
Doe Italy, and France, these Mountaines heere of ours,
That looke farre off like clouds, shap't with embattelled towers,
Much envy my estate, and somewhat higher be,
By lifting up their heads, to stare and gaze at me.
Cleere Darwent dancing on, I looke at from above,
As some enamoured Youth, being deeply struck in love,
His Mistris doth behold, and every beauty notes;
Who as shee to her fall, through Fells and Vallies flotes,
Oft lifts her limber selfe above her Banks to view,

How my brave by-clift top, doth still her Course pursue.
O all yee Topick Gods, that doe inhabite here,
To whom the Romans did, those ancient Altars reare,
Oft found upon those Hills, now sunke into the Soyles,
Which they for Trophies left of their victorious spoyles,
Ye Genii of these Floods, these Mountaines, and these Dales,
That with poore Shepheards Pipes, & harmlesse Heardsmans tales
Have often pleased been, still guard me day and night,
And hold me Skidow still, the place of your delight.
This Speech by Skidow spoke, the Muse makes forth againe,
Tow'rds where the in-borne Floods, cleere Eden intertaine,
To Cumberland com'n in, from the Westmerian wasts,
Where as the readyest way to Carlill, as shee casts,
Shee with two Wood-Nymphs meets, the first is great and wilde,
And Westward Forrest hight; the other but a childe,
Compared with her Phere, and Inglewood is cald,
Both in their pleasant Scites, most happily instald.
What Sylvan is there seene, and be she nere so coy,
Whose pleasures to the full, these Nymphs doe not enjoy,
And like Dianas selfe, so truly living chast?
For seldome any Tract, doth crosse their waylesse waste,
With many a lustie leape, the shagged Satyrs show
Them pastime every day, both from the Meres below,
And Hils on every side, that neatly hemme them in;
The blushing morne to breake, but hardly doth begin,
But that the ramping Goats, swift Deere, and harmelesse Sheepe,
Which there their owners know, but no man hath to keepe,
The Dales doe over-spread, by them like Motley made;
But Westward of the two, by her more widened Slade,
Of more abundance boasts, as of those mighty Mynes,
Which in her Verge she hath: but that whereby she shines,
Is her two daintie Floods, which from two Hils doe flow,
Which in her selfe she hath, whose Banks doe bound her so
Upon the North and South, as that she seemes to be
Much pleased with their course, and takes delight to see
How Elne upon the South, in sallying to the Sea
Confines her: on the North how Wampull on her way,
Her purlews wondrous large, yet limitteth againe,
Both falling from her earth into the Irish Maine.
No lesse is Westward proud of Waver, nor doth win
Lesse praise by her cleere Spring, which in her course doth twin
With Wiz, a neater Nymph scarce of the watry kind;
And though shee be but small, so pleasing Wavers mind,
That they entirely mix'd, the Irish Seas imbrace,
But earnestly proceed in our intended Race.
At Eden now arriv'd, whom we have left too long,
Which being com'n at length, the Cumbrian hils among,
As shee for Carlill coasts, the Floods from every where,

Prepare each in their course, to entertaine her there,
From Skidow her tall Sire, first Cauda cleerely brings
In Eden all her wealth; so Petterell from her Springs,
(Not farre from Skidows foot, whence dainty Cauda creeps)
Along to overtake her Soveraigne Eden sweeps,
To meet that great concourse, which seriously attend
That dainty Cumbrian Queene; when Gilsland downe doth send
Her Riverets to receive Queene Eden in her course;
As Irthing comming in from her most plenteous source,
Through many a cruell Crag, though she be forc'd to crawle,
Yet working forth her way to grace her selfe with all,
First Pultrosse is her Page, then Gelt shee gets her guide,
Which springeth on her South, on her Septentrion side,
Shee crooked Cambeck calls, to wait on her along,
And Eden overtakes amongst the watry throng.
To Carlill being come, cleere Bruscath beareth in,
To greet her with the rest, when Eden as to win
Her grace in Carlils sight, the Court of all her state,
And Cumberlands chiefe towne, loe thus shee doth dilate.
What giveth more delight, (brave Citie) to thy Seat,
Then my sweet lovely selfe? a River so compleat,
With all that Nature can a dainty Flood endow,
That all the Northerne Nymphs me worthily allow,
Of all their Nyades kind the neatest, and so farre
Transcending, that oft times they in their amorous warre,
Have offered by my course, and Beauties to decide
The mastery, with her most vaunting in her pride,
That mighty Roman Fort, which of the Picts we call,
But by them neere those times was stil'd Severus wall,
Of that great Emperour nam'd, which first that worke began,
Betwixt the Irish Sea, and German Ocean,
Doth cut me in his course neere Carlill, and doth end
At Boulnesse, where my selfe I on the Ocean spend.
And for my Country here, (of which I am the chiefe
Of all her watry kind) know that shee lent reliefe,
To those old Britains once, when from the Saxons they,
For succour hither fled, as farre out of their way,
Amongst her mighty Wylds, and Mountains freed from feare,
And from the British race, residing long time here,
Which in their Genuine tongue, themselves did Kimbri name,
Of Kimbri-land, the name of Cumberland first came;
And in her praise bee't spoke, this soyle whose best is mine,
That Fountaine bringeth forth, from which the Southern Tyne.
(So nam'd for that of North, another hath that stile)
This to the Easterne Sea, that makes forth many a mile,
Her first beginning takes, and Vent, and Alne doth lend,
To wait upon her foorth; but further to transcend
To these great things of note, which many Countries call

Their wonders, there is not a Tract amongst them all,
Can shew the like to mine, at the lesse Sakeld, neere
To Edens Bank, the like is scarcely any where,
Stones seventie seven stand, in manner of a Ring,
Each full ten foot in height, but yet the strangest thing,
Their equall distance is, the circle that compose,
Within which other stones lye flat, which doe inclose
The bones of men long dead, (as there the people say;)
So neere to Loders Spring, from thence not farre away,
Be others nine foot high, a myle in length that runne,
The victories for which these Trophies were begun,
From darke oblivion thou, O Time shouldst have protected;
For mighty were their minds, them thus that first erected:
And neere to this againe, there is a piece of ground,
A little rising Bank, which of the Table round,
Men in remembrance keepe, and Arthurs Table name.
But whilst these more and more, with glory her inflame,
Supposing of her selfe in these her wonders great,
All her attending Floods, faire Eden doe entreat,
To lead them downe to Sea, when Leuen comes along,
And by her double Spring, being mightie them among,
There overtaketh Eske, from Scotland that doth hye,
Faire Eden to behold, who meeting by and by,
Downe from these Westerne Sands into the Sea doe fall,
Where I this Canto end, as also therewithall
My England doe conclude, for which I undertooke,
This strange Herculean toyle, to this my thirtieth Booke.

FINIS.

Michael Drayton – A Short Biography by Cyril Brett

Michael Drayton was born in 1563, at Hartshill, near Atherstone, in Warwickshire.

He became a page to Sir Henry Goodere, at Polesworth Hall: his own words give the best picture of his early years here. His education would seem to have been good, but ordinary; and it is very doubtful if he ever went to a university. Besides the authors mentioned in the Epistle to Henry Reynolds, he was certainly familiar with Ovid and Horace, and possibly with Catullus: while there seems no reason to doubt that he read Greek, though it is quite true that his references to Greek authors do not prove any first-hand acquaintance. He understood French, and read Rabelais and the French sonneteers, and he seems to have been acquainted with Italian. His knowledge of English literature was wide, and his judgement good: but his chief bent lay towards the history, legendary and otherwise, of his native country, and his vast stores of learning on this subject bore fruit in the Poly-Olbion.

While still at Polesworth, Drayton fell in love with his patron's younger daughter, Anne; and, though she married, in 1596, Sir Henry Raynsford of Clifford, Drayton continued his devotion to her for many years, and also became an intimate friend of her husband's, writing a sincere elegy on his death.

About February, 1591, Drayton paid a visit to London, and published his first work, the Harmony of the Church, a series of paraphrases from the Old Testament, in fourteen-syllabled verse of no particular vigour or grace. This book was immediately suppressed by order of Archbishop Whitgift, possibly because it was supposed to savour of Puritanism. The author, however, published another edition in 1610; indeed, he seems to have had a fondness for this style of work; for in 1604 he published a dull poem, Moyses in a Map of his Miracles, re-issued in 1630 as Moses his Birth and Miracles. Accompanying this piece, in 1630, were two other 'Divine poems': Noah's Floud, and David and Goliath. Noah's Floud is, in part, one of Drayton's happiest attempts at the catalogue style of bestiary; and Mr. Elton finds in it some foreshadowing of the manner of Paradise Lost. But, as a whole, Drayton's attempts in this direction deserve the oblivion into which they, in common with the similar productions of other authors, have fallen. In the dedication and preface to the Harmony of the Church are some of the few traces of Euphuism shown in Drayton's work; passages in the Heroical Epistles also occur to the mind He was always averse to affectation, literary or otherwise, and in Elegy VIII deliberately condemns Lyly's fantastic style.

Probably before Drayton went up to London, Sir Henry Goodere saw that he would stand in need of a patron more powerful than the master of Polesworth, and introduced him to the Earl and Countess of Bedford. Those who believe Drayton to have been a Pope in petty spite, identify the 'Idea' of his earlier poems with Lucy, Countess of Bedford; though they are forced to acknowledge as self-evident that the 'Idea' of his later work is Anne, Lady Raynsford. They then proceed to say that Drayton, after consistently honouring the Countess in his verse for twelve years, abruptly transferred his allegiance, not forgetting to heap foul abuse on his former patroness, out of pique at some temporary withdrawal of favour. Not only is this directly contrary to all we know and can infer of Drayton's character, but Mr. Elton has decisively disproved it by a summary of bibliographical and other evidence. Into the question it is here unnecessary to enter, and it has been mentioned only because it alone, of the many Drayton-controversies, has cast any slur on the poet's reputation.

In 1593, Drayton published Idea, the Shepherds Garland, in nine Eclogues; in 1606 he added a tenth, the best of all, to the new edition, and rearranged the order, so that the new eclogue became the ninth. In these Pastorals, while following the Shepherds Calendar in many ways, he already displays something of the sturdy independence which characterized him through life. He abandons Spenser's quasi-rustic dialect, and, while keeping to most of the pastoral conventions, such as the singing-match and threnody, he contrives to introduce something of a more natural and homely strain. He keeps the political allusions, notably in the Eclogue containing the song in praise of Beta, who is, of course, Queen Elizabeth. But an over-bold remark in the last line of that song was struck out in 1606; and the new eclogue has no political reference. He is not ashamed to allude directly to Spenser; and indeed his direct debts are limited to a few scattered phrases, as in the Ballad of Dowsabel. Almost to the end of his literary career, Drayton mentions Spenser with reverence and praise.

It is in the songs interspersed in the Eclogues that Drayton's best work at this time is to be found: already his metrical versatility is discernible; for though he doubtless remembered the many varieties of metre employed by Spenser in the Calendar, his verses already bear a stamp of their own. The long but impetuous lines, such as 'Trim up her golden tresses with Apollo's sacred tree', afford a striking contrast to the archaic romance-metre, derived from Sir Thopas and its fellows, which appears in Dowsabel, and it again to the melancholy, murmuring cadences of the lament for Elphin. It must, however, be confessed that certain of the songs in the 1593 edition were full of recondite conceits and laboured antitheses, and were rightly struck out, to be replaced by lovelier poems, in the edition of 1606. The song to Beta was printed in Englands Helicon, 1600; here, for the first time, appeared the song of Dead Love, and for the only time, Rowlands Madrigal. In these songs, Drayton offends least in grammar, always a weak point with him; in the body of the Eclogues, in the earlier Sonnets, in the Odes, occur the most extraordinary and perplexing inversions. Quite the most striking feature of the Eclogues, especially in their later form, is their bold attempt at greater realism, at a breaking-away from the conventional images and scenery.

Having paid his tribute to one poetic fashion, Drayton in 1594 fell in with the prevailing craze for sonneteering, and published Ideas Mirrour, a series of fifty-one 'amours' or sonnets, with two prefatory poems, one by Drayton and one by an unknown, signing himself Gorbo il fidele. The title of these poems Drayton possibly borrowed from the French sonneteer, de Pontoux: in their style much recollection of Sidney, Constable, and Daniel is traceable. They are ostensibly addressed to his mistress, and some of them are genuine in feeling; but many are merely imitative exercises in conceit; some, apparently, trials in metre. These amours were again printed, with the title of 'sonnets', in 1599, 1600, 1602, 1603, 1605, 1608, 1610, 1613, 1619, and 1631, during the poet's lifetime. It is needless here to discuss whether Drayton were the 'rival poet' to Shakespeare, whether these sonnets were really addressed to a man, or merely to the ideal Platonic beauty; for those who are interested in these points, I subjoin references to the sonnets which touch upon them. From the prentice-work evident in many of the Amours, it would seem that certain of them are among Drayton's earliest poems; but others show a craftsman not meanly advanced in his art. Nevertheless, with few exceptions, this first 'bundle of sonnets' consists rather of trials of skill, bubbles of the mind; most of his sonnets which strike the reader as touched or penetrated with genuine passion belong to the editions from 1599 onwards; implying that his love for Anne Goodere, if at all represented in these poems, grew with his years, for the 'love-parting' is first found in the edition of 1619. But for us the question should not be, are these sonnets genuine representations of the personal feeling of the poet? but rather, how far do they arouse or echo in us as individuals the universal passion? There are at least some of Drayton's sonnets which possess a direct, instant, and universal appeal, by reason of their simple force and straightforward ring; and not in virtue of any subtle charm of sound and rhythm, or overmastering splendour of diction or thought. Ornament vanishes, and soberness and simplicity increase, as we proceed in the editions of the sonnets. Drayton's chief attempt in the jewelled or ornamental style appeared in 1595, with the title of Endimion and Phoebe, and was, in a sense, an imitation of Marlowe's Hero and Leander. Hero and Leander is, as Swinburne says, a shrine of Parian marble, illumined from within by a clear flame of passion; while Endimion and Phoebe is rather a curiously wrought tapestry, such as that in Mortimer's Tower, woven in splendid and harmonious colours, wherein, however, the figures attain no clearness or subtlety of outline, and move in semi-conventional scenery. It is, none the less, graceful and impressive, and of a like musical fluency with other poems of its class, such as Venus and Adonis, or Salmacis and Hermaphrodius. Parts of it were re-set and spoilt in a 1606 publication of Drayton's, called The Man in the Moone.

In 1593 and 1594 Drayton also published his earliest pieces on the mediaeval theme of the 'Falls of the Illustrious'; they were Peirs Gavesson and Matilda the faire and chaste daughter of the Lord Robert Fitzwater. Here Drayton followed in the track of Boccaccio, Lydgate, and the Mirrour for Magistrates, walking in the way which Chaucer had derided in his Monkes Tale: and with only too great fidelity does Drayton adapt himself to the dullnesses of his model: fine rhetoric is not altogether wanting, and there is, of course, the consciousness that these subjects deal with the history of his beloved country, but neither these, nor Robert, Duke of Normandy (1596), nor Great Cromwell, Earl of Essex (1607 and 1609), nor the Miseries of Margaret (1627) can escape the charge of tediousness. England's Heroical Epistles were first published in 1597, and other editions, of 1598, 1599, and 1602, contain new epistles. These are Drayton's first attempt to strike out a new and original vein of English poetry: they are a series of letters, modelled on Ovid's Heroides, addressed by various pairs of lovers, famous in English history, to each other, and arranged in chronological order, from Henry II and Rosamond to Lady Jane Grey and Lord Guilford Dudley. They are, in a sense, the most important of Drayton's writings, and they have certainly been the most popular, up to the early nineteenth century. In these poems Drayton foreshadowed, and probably inspired, the smooth style of Fairfax, Waller, and Dryden. The metre, the grammar, and the thought, are all perfectly easy to follow, even though he employs many of the Ovidian 'turns' and 'clenches'. A certain attempt at realization of the different characters is observable, but the poems are fine rhetorical exercises rather than realizations of the dramatic and passionate possibilities of their themes. In 1596, Drayton, as we have seen, published the Mortimeriados, a kind of epic, with Mortimer as its hero, of the wars between King Edward II and the Barons. It was written in the seven-line stanza of Chaucer's Troilus and Cressida and Spenser's Hymns. On its republication in 1603, with the title of the Barons' Wars, the metre was changed to ottava rima, and Drayton showed, in an excellent preface, that he fully appreciated the principles and the subtleties of the metrical art. While possessing many fine passages, the Barons' Wars is somewhat dull, lacking much of the poetry of the older version; and does not escape from Drayton's own criticism of Daniel's Chronicle Poems: 'too much historian in verse, ... His rhymes were smooth, his metres well did close, But yet his manner better fitted prose'. The description of Mortimer's Tower in the sixth book recalls the ornate style of Endimion and Phoebe, while the fifth book, describing the miseries of King Edward, is the most moving and dramatic. But there is a general lifelessness and lack of movement for which these purple passages barely atone. The cause of the production of so many chronicle poems about this time has been supposed to be the desire of showing the horrors of civil war, at a time when the queen was growing old, and no successor had, as it seemed, been accepted. Also they were a kind of parallel to the Chronicle Play; and Drayton, in any case even if we grant him to have been influenced by the example of Daniel, never needed much incentive to treat a national theme.

About this time, we find Drayton writing for the stage. It seems unnecessary here to discuss whether the writing of plays is evidence of Drayton's poverty, or his versatility; but the fact remains that he had a hand in the production of about twenty. Of these, the only one which certainly survives is The first part of the true and honorable historie, of the life of Sir John Oldcastle, the good Lord Cobham, &c. It is practically impossible to distinguish Drayton's share in this curious play, and it does not, therefore, materially assist the elucidation of the question whether he had any dramatic feeling or skill. It can be safely affirmed that the dramatic instinct was nor uppermost in his mind; he was a Seneca rather than a Euripides: but to deny him all dramatic idea, as does Dr. Whitaker, is too severe. There is decided, if slender, dramatic skill and feeling in certain of the Nymphals. Drayton's persons are usually, it must be said, rather figures in a tableau, or series of tableaux; but in the second and seventh Nymphals, and occasionally in the tenth, there is real dramatic movement. Closely connected with this question is the consideration of humour, which is wrongly denied to Drayton. Humour is observable first, perhaps, in the Owle (1604); then in the Ode to his Rival (1619); and later in the Nymphidia, Shepheards Sirena, and Muses Elyzium. The second Nymphal shows us the quiet laughter, the humorous twinkle, with which Drayton writes at times. The subject is an [Greek: agôn] or contest between two shepherds for the affections of a nymph called Lirope: Lalus is a vale-bred swain, of refined and elegant manners, skilled, nevertheless, in all manly sports and exercises; Cleon, no less a master in physical prowess, was nurtured by a hind in the mountains; the contrast between their manners is admirably sustained: Cleon is rough, inclined to be rude and scoffing, totally without tact, even where his mistress is concerned. Lalus remembers her upbringing and her tastes; he makes no unnecessary or ostentatious display of wealth; his gifts are simple and charming, while Cleon's are so grotesquely unsuited to a swain, that it is tempting to suppose that Drayton was quietly satirizing Marlowe's Passionate Shepherd. Lirope listens gravely to the swains in turn, and makes demure but provoking answers, raising each to the height of hope, and then casting them both down into the depths of despair; finally she refuses both, yet without altogether killing hope. Her first answer is a good specimen of her banter and of Drayton's humour.

On the accession of James I, Drayton hastened to greet the King with a somewhat laboured song To the Maiestie of King James; but this poem was apparently considered to be premature: he cried Vivat Rex, without having said, Mortua est eheu Regina, and accordingly he suffered the penalty of his 'forward pen', and was severely neglected by King and Court. Throughout James's reign a darker and more satirical mood possesses Drayton, intruding at times even into his strenuous recreation-ground, the Poly-Olbion, and manifesting itself more directly in his satires, the Owle (1604), the Moon-Calfe (1627), the Man in the Moone (1606), and his verse-letters and elegies; while his disappointment with the times, the country, and the King, flashes out occasionally even in the Odes, and is heard in his last publication, the Muses Elizium (1630). To counterbalance the disappointment in his hopes from the King, Drayton found a new and life-long friend in Walter Aston, of Tixall, in Staffordshire; this gentleman was created Knight of the Bath by James, and made Drayton one of his esquires. By Aston's 'continual bounty' the poet was able to devote himself almost entirely to more congenial literary work; for, while Meres speaks of the Poly-Olbion in 1598, and we may easily see that Drayton had the idea of that work at least as early as 1594, yet he cannot have been able to give much time to it till now. Nevertheless, the 'declining and corrupt times' worked on Drayton's mind and grieved and darkened his soul, for we must remember that he was perfectly prosperous then and was not therefore incited to satire by bodily want or distress.

In 1604 he published the Owle, a mild satire, under the form of a moral fable of government, reminding the reader a little of the Parlement of Foules. The Man in the Moone (1606) is partly a recension of Endimion and Phoebe, but is a heterogeneous mass of weakly satire, of no particular merit. The Moon-Calfe (1627) is Drayton's most savage and misanthropic excursion into the region of Satire; in which, though occasionally nobly ironic, he is more usually coarse and blustering, in the style of Marston. In 1605 Drayton brought out his first 'collected poems', from which the Eclogues and the Owle are omitted; and in 1606 he published his Poemes Lyrick and Pastorall, Odes, Eglogs, The Man in the Moone. Of these the Eglogs are a recension of the Shepherd's Garland of 1593: we have already spoken of The Man in the Moone. The Odes are by far the most important and striking feature of the book. In the preface, Drayton professes to be following Pindar, Anacreon, and Horace, though, as he modestly implies, at a great distance. Under the title of Odes he includes a variety of subjects, and a variety of metres; ranging from an Ode to his Harp or to his Criticks, to a Ballad of Agincourt, or a poem on the Rose compared with his Mistress. In the edition of 1619 appeared several more Odes, including some of the best; while many of the others underwent careful revision, notably the Ballad. 'Sing wee the Rose,' perhaps because of its unintelligibility, and the Ode to his friend John Savage, perhaps because too closely imitated from Horace, were omitted. Drayton was not the first to use the term Ode for a lyrical poem, in English: Soothern in 1584, and Daniel in 1592 had preceded him; but he was the first to give the name popularity in England, and to lift the kind as Ronsard had lifted it in France; and till the time of Cowper no other English poet showed mastery of the short, staccato measure of the Anacreontic as distinct from the Pindaric Ode. In the Odes Drayton shows to the fullest extent his metrical versatility: he touches the Skeltonic metre, the long ten-syllabled line of the Sacrifice to Apollo; and ascends from the smooth and melodious rhythms of the New Year through the inspiring harp-tones of the Virginian Voyage to the clangour and swing of the Ballad of Agincourt. His grammar is possibly more distorted here than anywhere, but, as Mr. Elton says, 'these are the obstacles of any poet who uses measures of four or six syllables.' His tone throughout is rather that of the harp, as played, perhaps, in Polesworth Hall, than that of any other instrument; but in 1619 Drayton has taken to him the lute of Carew and his compeers. In 1619 the style is lighter, the fancy gayer, more exquisite, more recondite. Most of his few metaphysical conceits are to be found in these later Odes, as in the Heart, the Valentine, and the Crier. In the comparison of the two editions the nobler, if more strained, tone of the earlier is obvious; it is still Elizabethan, in its nobility of ideal and purpose, in its enthusiasm, in its belief and confidence in England and her men; and this even though we catch a glimpse of the Jacobean woe in the Ode to John Savage: the 1619 Odes are of a different world; their spirit is lighter, more insouciant in appearance, though perhaps studiedly so; the rhythms are more fantastic, with less of strength and firmness, though with more of grace and superficial beauty; even the very textual alterations, while usually increasing the grace and the music of the lines, remind the reader that something of the old spontaneity and freshness is gone.

In 1607 and 1609, Drayton published two editions of the last and weakest of his mediaeval poems—the Legend of Great Cromwell; and for the next few years he produced nothing new, only attending to the publication of certain reprints and new editions. During this time, however, he was working steadily at the Poly-Olbion, helped by the patronage of Aston and of Prince Henry. In 1612-13, Drayton burst upon an indifferent world with the first part of the great poem, containing eighteen songs; the title-page will give the best idea of the contents and plan of the book: 'Poly-Olbion or a Chorographicall Description of the Tracts, Riuers, Mountaines, Forests, and other Parts of this renowned Isle of Great Britaine, With intermixture of the most Remarquable Stories, Antiquities, Wonders, Rarityes, Pleasures, and Commodities of the same: Digested in a Poem by Michael Drayton, Esq. With a Table added, for direction to those occurrences of Story and Antiquities, whereunto the Course of the Volume easily leades not.' &c. On this work Drayton had been engaged for nearly the whole of his poetical career. The learning and research displayed in the poem are extraordinary, almost equalling the erudition of Selden in his Annotations to each Song. The first part was, for various reasons, a drug in the market, and Drayton found great difficulty in securing a publisher for the second part. But during the years from 1613 to 1622, he became acquainted with Drummond of Hawthornden through a common friend, Sir William Alexander of Menstry, afterwards Earl of Stirling. In 1618, Drayton starts a correspondence; and towards the end of the year mentions that he is corresponding also with Andro Hart, bookseller, of Edinburgh. The subject of his letter was probably the publication of the Second Part; which Drayton alludes to in a letter of 1619 thus: 'I have done twelve books more, that is from the eighteenth book, which was Kent, if you note it; all the East part and North to the river Tweed; but it lies by me; for the booksellers and I are in terms; they are a company of base knaves, whom I both scorn and kick at.' Finally, in 1622, Drayton got Marriott, Grismand, and Dewe, of London, to take the work, and it was published with a dedication to Prince Charles, who, after his brother's death, had given Drayton patronage. Drayton's preface to the Second Part is well worth quoting:

'To any that will read it. When I first undertook this Poem, or, as some very skilful in this kind have pleased to term it, this Herculean labour, I was by some virtuous friends persuaded, that I should receive much comfort and encouragement therein; and for these reasons; First, that it was a new, clear, way, never before gone by any; then, that it contained all the Delicacies, Delights, and Rarities of this renowned Isle, interwoven with the Histories of the Britons, Saxons, Normans, and the later English: And further that there is scarcely any of the Nobility or Gentry of this land, but that he is in some way or other by his Blood interested therein. But it hath fallen out otherwise; for instead of that comfort, which my noble friends (from the freedom of their spirits) proposed as my due, I have met with barbarous ignorance, and base detraction; such a cloud hath the Devil drawn over the world's judgment, whose opinion is in few years fallen so far below all ballatry, that the lethargy is incurable: nay, some of the Stationers, that had the selling of the First Part of this Poem, because it went not so fast away in the sale, as some of their beastly and abominable trash, (a shame both to our language and nation) have either despitefully left out, or at least carelessly neglected the Epistles to the Readers, and so have cozened the buyers with unperfected books; which these that have undertaken the Second Part, have been forced to amend in the First, for the small number that are yet remaining in their hands. And some of our outlandish, unnatural, English, (I know not how otherwise to express them) stick not to say that there is nothing in this Island worth studying for, and take a great pride to be ignorant in any thing thereof; for these, since they delight in their folly, I wish it may be hereditary from them to their posterity, that their children may be begg'd for fools to the fifth generation, until it may be beyond the memory of man to know that there was ever other of their families: neither can this deter me from going on with Scotland, if means and time do not hinder me, to perform as much as I have promised in my First Song:

Till through the sleepy main, to Thuly I have gone,
And seen the Frozen Isles, the cold Deucalidon,
Amongst whose iron Rocks, grim Saturn yet remains
Bound in those gloomy caves with adamantine chains.

And as for those cattle whereof I spake before, Odi profanum vulgus, et arceo, of which I account them, be they never so great, and so I leave them. To my friends, and the lovers of my labours, I wish all happiness.
Michael Drayton.'

The Poly-Olbion as a whole is easy and pleasant to read; and though in some parts it savours too much of a mere catalogue, yet it has many things truly poetical. The best books are perhaps the XIII, XIV and XV, where he is on his own ground, and therefore naturally at his best. It is interesting to notice how much attention and space he devotes to Wales. He describes not only the 'wonders' but also the fauna and flora of each district; and of the two it would seem that the flowers interested him more. Though he was a keen observer of country sights and sounds (a fact sufficiently attested by the Nymphidia and the Nymphals), it is evident that his interest in most things except flowers was rather momentary or conventional than continuous and heart-felt; but of the flowers he loves to talk, whether he weaves us a garland for the Thame's wedding, or gives us the contents of a maund of simples; and his love, if somewhat homely and unimaginative, is apparent enough. But the main inspiration, as it is the main theme, of the Poly-Olbion is the glory and might and wealth, past, present, and future, of England, her possessions and her folk. Through all this glory, however, we catch the tone of Elizabethan sorrow over the 'Ruines of Time'; grief that all these mighty men and their works will perish and be forgotten, unless the poet makes them live for ever on the lips of men. Drayton's own voluminousness has defeated his purpose, and sunk his poem by its own bulk. Though it is difficult to agree with Mr. Bullen, and say that the only thing better than a stroll in the Poly-Olbion is one in a Sussex lane, it is still harder to agree with Canon Beeching, that 'there are few beauties on the road', the beauties are many, though of a quietly rural type, and the road, if long and winding, is of good surface, while its cranks constitute much of its charm. It is doubtless, from the outside, an appalling poem in these days of epitomes and monographs, but it certainly deserves to be rescued from oblivion and read.

In 1618 Drayton contributed two Elegies to Henry FitzGeoffrey's Satyrs and Epigrames. These were on the Lady Penelope Clifton, and on 'the death of the three sonnes of the Lord Sheffield, drowned neere where Trent falleth into Humber'. Neither is remarkable save for far-fetched conceits; they were reprinted in 1610, and again, with many others, in the volume of 1627. In 1619 Drayton issued a folio collected edition of his works, and reprinted it in 1620. In 1627 followed a folio of wholly fresh matter, including the Battaile of Agincourt; the Miseries of Queene Margarite, Nimphidia, Quest of Cinthia, Shepheards Sirena, Moone-Calfe, and Elegies upon sundry occasions. The Battaile of Agincourt is a somewhat otiose expansion, with purple patches, of the Ballad; it is, nevertheless, Drayton's best lengthy piece on a historical theme. Of the Miseries of Queene Margarite and of the Moone-Calfe we have already spoken. The most notable piece in the book is the Nimphidia. This poem of the Court of Fairy has 'invention, grace, and humour', as Canon Beeching has said. It would be interesting to know exactly when it was composed and committed to paper, for it is thought that the three fairy poems in Herrick's Hesperides were written about 1626. In any case, Drayton's poem touches very little, and chiefly in the beginning, on the subject of any one of Herrick's three pieces. The style, execution, and impression left on the reader are quite different; even as they are totally unlike those of the Midsummer Night's Dream. Herrick's pieces are extraordinary combinations of the idea of 'King of Shadows', with a reality fantastically sober: the poems are steeped in moonlight. In Drayton all is clear day, or the most unromantic of nights; though everything is charming, there is no attempt at idealization, little of the higher faculty of imagination; but great realism, and much play of fancy. Herrick's verses were written by Cobweb and Moth together, Drayton's by Puck. Granting, however, the initial deficiency in subtlety of charm, the whole poem is inimitably graceful and piquant. The gay humour, the demure horror of the witchcraft, the terrible seriousness of the battle, wonderfully realize the mock-heroic gigantesque; and while there is not the minute accuracy of Gulliver in Lilliput, Drayton did not write for a sceptical or too-prying audience; quite half his readers believed more or less in fairies. In the metre of the poem Drayton again echoes that of the older romances, as he did in Dowsabel. In the Quest of Cinthia, while ostensibly we come to the real world of mortals, we are really in a non-existent land of pastoral convention, in the most pseudo-Arcadian atmosphere in which Drayton ever worked. The metre and the language are, however, charmingly managed. The Shepheards Sirena is a poem, apparently, 'where more is meant than meets the ear,' as so often in pastoral poetry; it is difficult to see exactly what is meant; but the Jacobean strain of doubt and fear is there, and the poem would seem to have been written some time earlier than 1627. The Elegies comprise a great variety of styles and themes; some are really threnodies, some verse-letters, some laments over the evil times, and one a summary of Drayton's literary opinions. He employs the couplet in his Elegies with a masterly hand, often with a deliberately rugged effect, as in his broader Marstonic satire addressed to William Browne; while the line of greater smoothness but equal strength is to be seen in the letters to Sandys and Jeffreys. He is fantastic and conceited in most of the threnodies; but, as is natural, that on his old friend, Sir Henry Raynsford, is least artificial and fullest of true feeling. The epistle to Henery Reynolds. Of Poets and Poesie shows Drayton as a sane and sagacious critic, ready to see the good, but keen to discern the weakness also; perhaps the clearest evidence of his critical skill is the way in which nearly all of his judgements on his contemporaries coincide with the received modern opinions.

In his later years Drayton enjoyed the patronage of the third Earl and Countess of Dorset; and in 1630 he published his last volume, the Muses Elizium, of which he dedicated the pastoral part to the Earl, and the three divine poems at the end to the Countess. The Muses Elizium proper consists of Ten Pastorals or Nymphals, prefaced by a Description of Elizium. The three divine poems have been mentioned before, and were Noah's Floud, Moses his Birth and Miracles, and David and Goliah. The Nymphals are the crown and summary of much of the best in Drayton's work. Here he departed from the conventional type of pastoral, even more than in the Shepherd's Garland; but to say that he sang of English rustic life would hardly be true: the sixth Nymphal, allowing for a few pardonable exaggerations by the competitors, is almost all English, if we except the names; so is the tenth with the same exception; the first and fourth might take place anywhere, but are not likely in any country; the second is more conventional; the fifth is almost, but not quite, English; the third, seventh, and ninth are avowedly classical in theme; while the eighth is a more delicate and subtle fairy poem than the Nymphidia. The fourth and tenth Nymphals are also touched with the sadder, almost satiric vein; the former inveighing against the English imitation of foreigners and love of extravagance in dress; while the tenth complains of the improvident and wasteful felling of trees in the English forests. This last Nymphal, though designedly an epilogue, is probably rather a warning than a despairing lament, even though we conceive the old satyr to be Drayton himself. As a whole the Nymphals show Drayton at his happiest and lightest in style and metre; at his moments of greatest serenity and even gaiety; an atmosphere of sunshine seems to envelope them all, though the sun sink behind a cloud in the last. His music now is that of a rippling stream, whereas in his earlier days he spoke weightier and more sonorous words, with a mouth of gold.

To estimate the poetical faculty of Drayton is a somewhat perplexing task; for, while rarely subtle, or rising to empyrean heights, he wrote in such varied styles, on such various themes, that the task, at first, seems that of criticizing many poets, not one. But through all his work runs the same eminently English spirit, the same honesty and clearness of idea, the same stolidity of purpose, and not infrequently of execution also; the same enthusiasm characterizes all his earlier, and much of his later work; the enthusiasm especially characteristic of Elizabethan England, and shown by Drayton in his passion for England and the English, in his triumphant joy in their splendid past, and his certainty of their future glory. As a poet, he lacked imagination and fine fury; he supplied their place by the airiest and clearest of fancies, by the strenuous labour of a great brain illumined by the steady flame of love for his country and for his lady. Mr. Courthope has said that he lacked loftiness and resolution of artistic purpose; without these, we ask, how could a man, not lavishly dowered with poetry in his soul, have achieved so much of it? It was his very fixity and loftiness of purpose, his English stubbornness and doggedness of resolution that enabled him to surmount so many obstacles of style and metre, of subject and thought. His two purposes, of glorifying his mistress and his friends, and of sounding England's glories past and future, while insisting on the dangers of a present decadence, never flagged or failed. All his poetry up to 1627 has this object directly or secondarily; and much after this date. Of the more abstract and universal aspects of his art he had not much conception; but he caught eagerly at the fashionable belief in the eternizing power of poetry; and had it not been that, where his patriotism was uppermost, he was deficient in humour and sense of proportion, he would have succeeded better: as it is, his more directly patriotic pieces are usually the dullest or longest of his works. He requires, like all other poets, the impulse of an absolutely personal and individual feeling, a moment of more intimate sympathy, to rouse him to his heights of song. Thus the Ballad of Agincourt is on the very theme of all patriotic themes that most attracted him; Virginian and other Voyages lay very close to his heart; and in certain sonnets to his lady lies his only imperishable work. Of sheer melody and power of song he had little, apart from his themes: he could not have sat down and written a few lark's or nightingale's notes about nothing as some of his contemporaries were able to do: he required the stimulus of a subject, and if he were really moved thereby he beat the music out. Only in one or two of the later Odes, and in the volumes of 1627 and 1630, does his music ever seem to flow from him naturally. Akin to this quality of broad and extensive workmanship, to this faculty of taking a subject and when writing, with all thought concentrated on it, rather than on the method of writing about it, is his strange lack of what are usually called 'quotations'. For this is not only due to the fact that he is little known; there are, besides, so few detached remarks or aphorisms that are separately quotable; so few examples of that curiosa felicitas of diction: lines like these,

Thy Bowe, halfe broke, is peec'd with old desire;
Her Bowe is beauty with ten thousand strings....

are rare enough. Drayton, in fact, comes as near controverting the statement Poeta nascitur, non fit, as any one in English literature: by diligent toil and earnest desire he won a place for himself in the second rank of English poets: through love he once set foot in the circle of the mightiest. Sincere he was always, simple often, sensuous rarely. His great industry, his careful study, and his great receptivity are shown in the unusual spectacle of a man who has sung well in the language of his youth, suddenly learning, in his age, the tongue spoken by the younger generation, and reproducing it with individuality and sureness of touch. It is in rhetoric, splendid or rugged, in argument, in plain statement or description, in the outline sketch of a picture, that Drayton excels; magic of atmosphere and colouring are rarely present. Stolidity is, perhaps, his besetting sin; yet it is the sign of a slow, not a dull, intellect; an intellect, like his heart, which never let slip what it had once taken to itself.

As a man Drayton would seem to have been an excellent type of the sturdy, clear-headed, but yet romantic and enthusiastic Englishman; gifted with much natural ability, sedulously increased by study; quietly humorous, self-restrained; and if temporarily soured by disappointment and the disjointed times, yet emerging at last into a greater serenity, a more unadulterated gaiety than had ever before characterized him. It is possible, but from his clear and sane balance of mind improbable, that many of his light later poems are due to deliberate self-blinding and self-deception, a walking in enchanted lands of the mind.

Of Drayton's three known portraits the earliest shows him at the age of thirty-six, and is now in the National Portrait Gallery. A look of quiet, speculative melancholy seems to pervade it; there is, as yet, no moroseness, no evidence of severe conflict with the world, no shadow of stress or of doubt. The second and best-known portrait shows us Drayton at the age of fifty, and was engraved by Hole, as a frontispiece to the poems of 1619. Here a notable change has come over the face; the mouth is hardened, and depressed at the corners through disappointment and disillusionment; the eyes are full of a pathos increased by the puzzled and perturbed uplift of the brows. Yet a stubbornness and tenacity of purpose invests the features and reminds us that Drayton is of the old and sound Elizabethan stock, 'on evil days though fallen.' Let it be remembered, that he was in 1613, when the portrait was taken, in more or less prosperous circumstances; it was the sad degeneracy, the meanness and feebleness of the generation around him, that chiefly depressed and embittered him. The final portrait, now in the Dulwich Gallery, represents the poet as a man of sixty-five; and is quite in keeping with the sunnier and calmer tone of his later poetry. It is the face of one who has not emerged unscathed from the world's conflict, but has attained to a certain calm, a measure of tranquillity, a portion of content, who has learnt the lesson that there is a soul of goodness in things evil. The Hole portrait shows him with long hair, small 'goatee' beard, and aquiline nose drawn up at the nostrils: while the National portrait shows a type of nose and beard intermediate between the Hole and the Dulwich pictures: the general contour of the face, though the forehead is broad enough, is long and oval. Drayton seems to have been tall and thin, and to have been very susceptible of cold, and therefore to have hated Winter and the North. He is said to have shared in the supper which caused Shakespeare's death; but his own verses breathe the spirit of Milton's sonnet to Cyriack Skinner, rather than that of a devotee of Bacchus.

He died in 1631, probably December 23, and was buried under the North wall of Westminster Abbey. Meres's opinion of his character during his early life is as follows: 'As Aulus Persius Flaccus is reported among al writers to be of an honest life and vpright conuersation: so Michael Drayton, quem toties honoris et amoris causa nomino, among schollers, souldiours, Poets, and all sorts of people is helde for a man of uertuous disposition, honest conversation, and well gouerned cariage; which is almost miraculous among good wits in these declining and corrupt times, when there is nothing but rogery in villanous man, and when cheating and craftines is counted the cleanest wit, and soundest wisedome.' Fuller also, in a similar strain, says, 'He was a pious poet, his conscience having the command of his fancy, very temperate in his life, slow of speech, and inoffensive in company.'

A Chronology of Michael Drayton's Life and Works

1563	Drayton born at Hartshill, Warwickshire.
c. 1572	Drayton a page in the house of Sir Henry Goodere, at Polesworth.
c. 1574	Anne Goodere born
February, 1591	Drayton in London. Harmony of Church.
1593	Idea, the Shepherd's Garland. Legend of Peirs Gaveston.
1594	Ideas Mirrour. Matilda. Lucy Harrington becomes Countess of Bedford.
1595	Sir Henry Goodere the elder dies. Endimion and Phoebe, dedicated to Lucy Bedford.
1595-6	Anne Goodere married to Sir Henry Raynsford.
1596	Mortimeriados. Legends of Robert, Matilda, and Gaveston.
1597	England's Heroical Epistles.
1598	Drayton already at work on the Poly-Olbion.
1599	Epistles and Idea sonnets, new edition. (Date of Drayton portrait in National Portrait Gallery.)
1600	Sir John Oldcastle.
1602	New edition of Epistles and Idea.
1603	Drayton made an Esquire of the Bath, to Sir Walter Aston. To the Maiestie of King James. Barons' Wars.
1604	The Owle. A Pean Triumphall. Moyses in a Map of his Miracles.
1605	First collected edition of Poems. Another edition of Idea and Epistles.
1606	Poemes Lyrick and Pastorall. Odes. Eglogs. The Man in the Moone.
1607	Legend of Great Cromwell.
1608	Reprint of Collected Poems.
1609	Another edition of Cromwell.
1610	Reprint of Collected Poems.
1613	Reprint of Collected Poems. First Part of Poly-Olbion.
1618	Two Elegies in FitzGeoffrey's Satyrs and Epigrames.
1619	Collected Folio edition of Poems.
1620	Second edition of Elegies, and reprint of 1619 Poems.
1622	Poly-Olbion complete.
1627	Battle of Agincourt, Nymphidia, &c.
1630	Muses Elizium. Noah's Floud. Moses his Birth and Miracles. David and Goliah.
1631	Second edition of 1627 folio. Drayton dies December 23rd.
1636	Posthumous poem appeared in Annalia Dubrensia.
1637	Poems.

Michael Drayton – A Concise Bibliography

The Major Works

The Harmony of the Church (1591)
Idea, The Shepherd's Garland (1593)
Idea's Mirror (1594)

Peirs Gaveston (1593 or 1594)
Matilda (1594)
Endimion and Phoebe: Idea's Latmus (1595)
The Tragical Legend of Robert, Duke of Normandy (1596)
Mortimeriados (1596)
England's Heroicall Epistles (1597)
The First Part of the Life of Sir John Oldcastle (1600)
The Barons' Wars in the Reign of Edward II (1603)
The Owl (1604)
The Man in the Moon (1606)
The Legend of Thomas Cromwell, Earl of Essex (1607)
Poly-Olbion (1612 & 1622)
Idea (1619)
Pastorals: Containing Eclogues (1619)
Odes (1619)
The Battle of Agincourt (published 1627)
The Quest of Cynthia (published 1627)
Elegies Upon Sundry Occasions (1627)
Nymphidia, the Court of Fairy (1627)
The Shepherd's Sirena (1627)
Muses' Elysium (1630)
Moses' Birth and Miracles (1630)

www.ingramcontent.com/pod-product-compliance
Lightning Source LLC
Chambersburg PA
CBHW061949070426
42450CB00007BA/1101